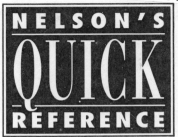

NELSON'S QUICK REFERENCE™

INTRODUCTION TO CHURCH HISTORY

HOWARD F. VOS

Publishers Since 1798

THOMAS NELSON PUBLISHERS
Nashville • Atlanta • London • Vancouver

Published in Nashville, Tennessee, by Thomas Nelson Publishers, Inc.

Revised and enlarged edition of *An Introduction to Church History* (Moody, 1984).

Unless otherwise noted, Scripture quotations are from the *New King James Version of the Bible*, © 1979, 1980, 1982, Thomas Nelson, Inc., Publishers.

Library of Congress Cataloging-in-Publication Data

Vos, Howard Frederic, 1925–
    Nelson's quick-reference introduction to church history / by Howard F. Vos.—4th ed.
        p.   cm.—(Nelson's Quick reference)
    Includes bibliographical references and index.
    ISBN 0-7852-8240-8 (pbk.)
    1. Church history. I. Title. II. Series.
BR145.2.V67   1994
270–dc20   93–41928
                                                                CIP

Printed in the United States of America

1 2 3 4 5 6 7 8 9 – 00 99 98 97 96 95 94

Contents

About the Author

HOWARD F. VOS is the Professor of History and Archaeology at The King's College, Briarcliff Manor, New York. He holds the Th.D. from Dallas Theological Seminary and the Ph.D. from Northwestern University and has authored 23 books.

PART I

♦

The Church in the Apostolic Age

ONE
The Beginnings

THE Passover season was ended. The crowds that had gathered for the occasion dispersed, and Jerusalem returned to normal. Some were puzzled, however, by the unusual circumstances surrounding the crucifixion of a certain Jesus of Nazareth, who appeared to be a revolutionist—for He had talked about setting up a kingdom of His own. A rumor had spread concerning His resurrection[1] from the dead, but certainly that was impossible, they thought. Had not the soldiers who guarded His tomb reported the theft of His body by His followers? That was sufficient explanation for most. Another Galilean rabble-rouser had come to a grisly end.

Pentecost

One hundred twenty of His followers who had gathered in an upper room in Jerusalem knew otherwise. Having seen and talked with the risen Lord, they awaited at His command the coming of the Holy Spirit (Acts

1:4, 5). On the day of Pentecost (fifty days after the crucifixion and ten days after the ascension), they were rewarded. A sound as of a rushing wind filled the house. On each of the group lighted what appeared to be a tongue of flame. Immediately they were filled with the Spirit and began to speak in other tongues.

Rapidly word of this phenomenon spread among Jews gathered for the feast of Pentecost, and a crowd came running to investigate. Upon arrival each heard the message of truth in his own language. Some marveled. Others accused the disciples of being intoxicated. But that was a foolish assertion; drunkenness would only produce gibberish, not intelligible conversation in another language. Besides, it was early in the day—too early for such a large group to be drunk.

At that point Peter, who had been the leader of Jesus' disciples, arose and addressed the throng. He argued that this remarkable phenomenon was a result of the Holy Spirit's ministry among them. Then he preached Christ: His death, resurrection, and ascension and the present necessity of receiving Him by faith as Savior and being baptized in His name. The Holy Spirit so wrought that three thousand believed on that memorable day.

Thus the church was born.[2] And wonderful was the experience of believers during succeeding days. They held to the true doctrine, were faithful in prayer, partook frequently of the Lord's Supper, enjoyed each other's fellowship, were in one accord, and lived joyous lives. Those who met them were strangely moved and awed; many believed *daily* (Acts 2:42-47). Soon the number of believers swelled to about five thousand men; there were probably women and children in addition (Acts 4:4).

Persecution and Growth

But believers were not merely to enjoy a state of ecstasy. They became painfully aware of that when the Temple priests launched a persecution against them (Acts 4). Accepting the Lord was serious business; it involved suffering for His sake. Were they any better than He? The world hated Him; it would hate His followers also (John 15:18-19). Persecution came with increasing frequency and intensity. First there was warning, then beating, then murder. Stephen was the first Christian martyr (Acts 7:54-60).

But persecution did not have the desired effect. Members of the Jerusalem church were scattered all over Judea and Samaria, preaching as they went. Philip ministered in Samaria and witnessed a wonderful spiritual awakening there. Christ's commission to preach in Jerusalem, Judea, Samaria, and the uttermost part of the earth (Acts 1:8) was being fulfilled.

Paul's Conversion

At this point a certain Saul of Tarsus, a devout Pharisee who had been present at the stoning of Stephen, became a prominent persecutor of Christians. To stamp out the hated sect, he even determined to move against believers at Damascus. On the way north he was stopped dead in his tracks by the Lord he opposed (Acts 9). This vision of Christ and its accompanying conversion brought Saul an inner peace that he had failed to gain by conformity to Jewish law and a misdirected zeal in serving God. Saul traveled on to Damascus, where he was filled with the Holy Spirit and received water baptism.

After that he spent three years in Arabia and

subsequently returned to Damascus to preach his new-found faith. Under persecution he fled from Damascus and returned to Jerusalem. There he was stymied by the suspicion of believers until Barnabas persuaded the apostles that Saul's conversion was genuine. After a most useful time with Peter and James and a Jerusalem ministry that led to a plot on his life, Saul returned to Tarsus. For the next several years he preached in the region around his home and in Syria (Acts 9:20-31; Gal. 1:16-21). Meanwhile, the Palestinian church continued to grow, and Peter introduced the gospel to the Gentiles of Cornelius' household in Caesarea (Acts 10). The church in Syria expanded rapidly too, and believers were first called Christians at Antioch of Syria (Acts 11:26).

Paul's Missions

Ultimately, church growth at Antioch required more workers. Barnabas went to Tarsus to persuade Saul—later called Paul—to join in the ministry in the Syrian metropolis. Soon the Lord revealed to the church that He wanted the pair to engage in foreign missionary activity. Barnabas and Paul departed, with the blessing of the whole church, to minister to Jews and Gentiles in the regions beyond. They traveled and preached in Cyprus and Asia Minor (modern Turkey) and returned to Antioch. When they arrived, a question of the relationship of Jew and Gentile in the church and to the law arose. Jewish Christians believed that Gentile believers had to submit to the law as well as place their faith in Christ. The issue was referred to the mother church at Jerusalem; Paul and Barnabas and others were sent there to present the case.

The decision of the great Council of Jerusalem (A.D. 49 or 50) is significant: "For it seemed good to the Holy Spirit, and to us, to lay upon you no greater burden than these necessary things: that you abstain from things offered to idols, from blood, from things strangled, and from sexual immorality. If you keep yourselves from these, you will do well" (Acts 15:28-29). Under the guidance of the Holy Spirit, the council decided that the law, which had been an impossible burden for Jews, should not be required of Gentiles.

On Paul's second missionary journey he was accompanied by Silas. The two again visited churches in Asia Minor and then, responding to the call of the man from Macedonia (Acts 16:9), they crossed over into Greece, where they established churches at Philippi, Thessalonica, Berea, and Corinth. Paul remained at Corinth for about eighteen months of successful evangelistic work. During this journey he also preached his famous sermon on Mars Hill in Athens (Acts 17). Thus the evangelization of Europe had begun.

On his third journey Paul again called on the believers in central Asia Minor. Traveling westward he stopped for much of three years at Ephesus (Acts 20:31), where he carried the gospel banner to victory over the forces of Diana. After revisiting the churches in Greece, he returned to Jerusalem, where he was apprehended by the leaders of the Jews and imprisoned. At length, appealing to Caesar, he was taken to Rome for trial. There he was imprisoned for two years (apparently under a sort of house arrest, Acts 28:30), and there he enjoyed a fairly successful ministry to the many who had access to him.

Apparently Paul was released from his first Roman imprisonment and went on a fourth missionary journey. In support of such a view, he had anticipated gaining his freedom (Phil. 1:25, Philem. 22) and even expected to go to Spain (Rom. 15:24, 28) at a future time. Moreover, there is some indication in the church fathers that he did indeed get there. On that fourth journey he seems also to have gone to Crete, where he established Titus in a leadership position, in addition to visiting some churches already founded.[3]

Missions of Other Apostles

The other apostles were also active during the first century. Several apparently evangelized areas not already mentioned. Tradition teaches that Bartholomew preached in Armenia; Andrew in the southern steppes of Russia and the Ukraine; Thomas in Persia and India; Matthew in Ethiopia; James the Younger in Egypt; Jude in Assyria and Persia; and Mark (not one of the apostles but closely related to them) in Alexandria. If the Babylon from which Peter wrote (1 Peter 5:13) was Babylon on the Euphrates instead of a symbolic representation of Rome, then Babylonia was also evangelized during the first century. Indications are that Peter ministered in Rome near the end of his life and was martyred there. Evidently, he also preached in several of the provinces of Asia Minor (1 Peter 1:1).

If there is any truth in these traditions concerning the apostles and other early church leaders, the gospel penetrated the more important inhabited areas of Europe, Asia, and Africa by the end of the first century.[4] In general support of this contention, Justin Martyr, one of the most outstanding leaders in the church about A.D. 150, observed:

> There is no people, Greek or barbarian, or of any other race, by whatever appellation or manners they be distinguished, however ignorant of arts or agricul-

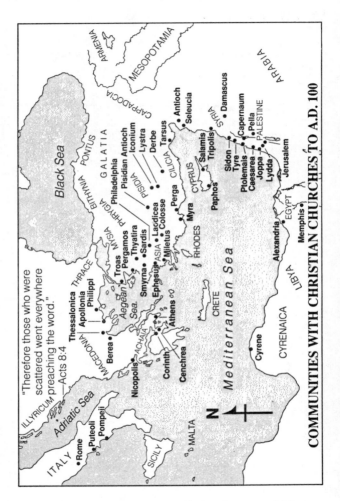

Communities with Christian Churches to A.D. 100

ture, whether they dwell in tents or wander about in covered wagons, among whom prayers and thanksgivings are not offered in the name of the crucified Jesus to the Father and Creator of all things.[5]

Although admittedly this reference must have been primarily to lands within the Roman Empire, it does show a widespread dissemination of the gospel. In a real sense, then, the pattern of evangelism laid out in Acts 1:8 was realized: "But you shall receive power when the Holy Spirit has come upon you; and you shall be witnesses to Me in Jerusalem, and in all Judea and Samaria, and even to the end of the earth."

PART II

♦

The Church in Its Early Development

TWO

Strengthening Believers
The Apostolic Fathers

AS THE apostles passed from the scene, others arose in the church to take their places. These leaders, generally elders or bishops, are called Fathers ("Fathers in God") because of the esteem in which they were held by church members or because of their historical relationship to later church developments. In fact, *Father* has come to apply to church leaders during an extended period beginning about A.D. 95.

The Fathers frequently are divided into four groups:

- the Apostolic or Post-Apostolic Fathers (c. 95-150);
- the Apologists (c. 140-200);
- the Polemicists (c. 180-225);
- and the Scientific Theologians (c. 225-460)

Sometimes they are classified as the Apostolic Fathers (second century); the Ante-Nicene Fathers (second and third centuries); the Nicene Fathers (fourth century); and the Post-Nicene Fathers (fifth century; sometimes to Gregory the Great in the West, 590; or John of Damascus in the East, c. 675).

The Apostolic Fathers are characterized by edification as they sought to build up or strengthen believers in the faith, the Apologists by defense against attacks on Christianity, the Polemicists by attacks against heresy within the church, and the Scientific Theologians by a scientific study of theology in an effort to apply to theological investigation philosophical modes of thought then current.

The Apostolic Fathers

Purpose: *to exhort and edify the church*

Writers or Writings

Clement	Papias
Shepherd of Hermas	Barnabas
Ignatius	*Didache*
Polycarp	

Clement

While the apostle John was writing Revelation on the Isle of Patmos or at Ephesus, Clement[1] served as leading elder, or bishop, in the church at Rome. In this capacity he assumed responsibility for answering an appeal (as did Paul a half century earlier; cf. 1 Cor. 7:1

ff.) from the church at Corinth for advice on how to restore harmony to a divided church. He sent a letter (c. 95 or 96) urging a demonstration of Christian graces in daily relationships and obedience to the elders and deacons against whom some were rebelling. He made frequent reference to both Old and New Testament Scripture and especially to Paul's epistles. Because this is the earliest extrabiblical Christian writing, it has attained a place of prominence among the writings of the Apostolic Fathers. Near the end of the second century this work (1 Clement) attained almost canonical status in some churches.

The Shepherd of Hermas

About a half century later another Roman, Hermas, wrote a work known as the *Shepherd of Hermas*. Actually, the *Shepherd* appears to be a composite work written in stages between about 90 and 150. Hermas himself was a slave (possibly Jewish) freed by his mistress Rhoda in Rome. Subsequently he married and became quite well to do. During a persecution he lost his property and suffered denunciation at the hands of his own children. Later he and his family did penance.

The work in its present form consists of five *Visions*, twelve *Mandates*, and ten *Similitudes*, all of which purport to be revelations. The revelator in Visions 1-4 was a woman representing the church, and in Vision 5 through Similitude 10 was the angel of repentance in the guise of a shepherd—hence the name of the work. The *Visions* focus especially on the last days and mention the imminence of the great tribulation several times. The *Mandates* and *Similitudes* provide teaching on Christian behavior and principles respectively and served as a textbook for catechetical instruction in the second and third centuries. Partly because of its claim to be divinely inspired, many regarded the *Shepherd* as Scripture during the early Christian centuries.

The central theme of the work concerns the possibility of a second repentance for sins. The issue is this: Already in the church there was a tendency to associate repentance and forgiveness of sin with baptism. Therefore, Christians often postponed baptism in order to care for as many sins as possible. What was to be done with postbaptismal sins was problematic. This work presents the possibility of a second repentance and forgiveness of sins committed after baptism. Through the *Shepherd* it is possible to pull aside the curtain and find backstage the dogma of penance and a rudimentary penitential system already operative in the church.

The book of *Second Clement* was probably written about the same time as the *Shepherd* and was not, therefore, the work of Clement of Rome. It is not really an epistle but a homily, probably delivered in Corinth or Rome, and is the oldest complete Christian sermon known. Its message emphasizes virtuous living, mercy to others, the need for repentance, and the Christian life as a warfare.

Ignatius

Ignatius, bishop of Antioch, was a Syrian Apostolic Father and the most famous of the group. About 110, he was apprehended by Roman authorities because of his Christian profession and sent to Rome for judgment and expected martyrdom in the arena. Along the way he wrote letters to various churches. These seven letters were designed to promote unity in the churches addressed. Unity was to be accomplished on the one hand by rooting out heresies that denied the full divine-human personality of Christ, and on the other hand by the subjection of leaders in local congregations to a ruling bishop.

Thus Ignatius gave impetus to the power of bishops, but only over local congregations. He did not elevate the position of the bishop of Rome over that of other bishops, but he seems to have been the first to speak of a *Catholic* (universal) church. It is not clear whether his emphasis on the ruling bishop was a view held commonly in the church in his day or whether it was largely his own position. He held that the church could not baptize, celebrate the Eucharist, or perform a marriage without the bishop.

Polycarp

In Asia Minor (modern Turkey) two Fathers were active: Polycarp and Papias. Polycarp, bishop of Smyrna (modern Izmir), is particularly interesting to modern Christians because he was a disciple of the apostle John. Though he wrote several pieces, only his letter to the Philippians remains. As one would expect from a disciple of John, Polycarp emphasized in his letter faith in Christ and the necessary outworking of that faith in daily living. Unlike those of his friend Ignatius, his concerns do not involve church organization and discipline. In his letter he quoted from thirteen New Testament books and knew of a collection of Paul's letters.

Martyred for his faith in Smyrna (probably in 155 or 156), Polycarp claimed to have served Christ for eighty-six years. A staunch defender of orthodoxy, he devoted much of his energy to combatting heretics. The *Martyrdom of Polycarp*, written by his church within a year after his death, is the first Christian account of martyrdom.

Papias

Papias, bishop of Hierapolis in Phrygia, wrote about 125. His *Interpretations of the Sayings (Oracles) of the Lord* is now lost, but parts of it survive in the writings of Irenaeus and Eusebius. These fragments deal with the life and teachings of Christ and attempt to preserve information obtained from those who had known Christ. They are especially interesting for their historical references, such as the statement that Mark got the information for his gospel from Peter. His comments on the apostolic age of the church should not be quickly dismissed because he too was a "hearer of John" the apostle. He penned one of the earliest statements on a literal material millennium when the earth will be miraculously fruitful.

Barnabas

Works assigned to the period of the Apostolic Fathers also originated in North Africa. *Barnabas* is generally considered to have been written in Alexandria—probably somewhere between A.D. 70 and 130. Like much of the other literature of Alexandria, this epistle is quite allegorical in nature, engaging in gross typology and numerology. The basic problem of the epistle concerns the necessity of a Christian's keeping the law. It holds that such was not necessary; the work of Christ was sufficient. It becomes so anti-Judaic as almost to deny a historical connection between Judaism and Christianity.

Didache

The *Didache*, or *Teachings of the Twelve*, is also believed to have originated in Alexandria (though some think it came from Syria), probably during the first decades of the second century. A church manual, divided into four parts, the *Didache* treats Christian ethics (chaps. 1-6), liturgical matters (baptism, fasting, the Eucharist, chaps. 7-10), the ministry and church government (chaps. 11-15), and the Second Coming and end of the world (chap. 16). Baptism was to be performed by immersion if possible, otherwise by threefold affusion. Believers should live a life of preparedness in view of the return of Christ.

The Apostolic Fathers must be evaluated in accordance with their apparent purpose: to exhort and edify the church. Sometimes they are criticized by evangelicals because they do not seem to grasp the New Testament concept of salvation by faith or because they seem to neglect certain doctrines. It should be remembered, however, that if one's purpose is to exhort to a higher plane of Christian living, he may make rather obscure allusions to the means by which an individual becomes a Christian. Moreover, informal utterances of pious faith are not designed to provide completeness of theological treatment and should not be judged by the same criteria as a systematic theology.

> *The Apostolic Fathers must be evaluated in accordance with their apparent purpose: to exhort and edify the church.*

Admittedly however, the Apostolic Fathers do in some instances assign a rather significant place to baptism as a medium of forgiveness of sin. Martyrdom and celibacy are also thought to have special sin-atoning power. On the whole the Apostolic Fathers picture a church still throbbing with missionary zeal, a church in which individual responsibility is still everywhere recognized, and a church in which hierarchal organization is at a minimum.

The Apostolic Fathers should be used with caution, however. Although they exhibit more than individual opinions and provide something of a cross section of doctrinal beliefs and conduct in the churches, the sampling is minimal. And since the laity was not vocal, we know only what the clergy thought about what was going on in a few churches. What they thought may not have approximated true conditions. And of course there is no way of knowing whether these churches or churchmen were typical or extreme examples of the period.

THREE

Defense of the Faith
The Apologists

THE approach and purpose of the Apologists were entirely different from those of the Apostolic Fathers. The Apologists sought to win legal recognition for Christianity and to defend it against various charges leveled by the pagan populace. In constructing this defense[2] the Apologists wrote in a more philosophical vein than the Apostolic Fathers. A generation of Christians from a higher social class and with more extensive education had arisen. As the Apologists wrote their defenses they had at hand two literary forms already in use in the Roman world: the legal speech *(apologia)* delivered before judicial authorities and subsequently published, and the literary dialogue.

The Apologists

Purpose: *to defend the faith*

Leaders
Justin Martyr
Tatian
Tertullian

In seeking to win a favorable position for Christianity, the Apologists tried on the one hand to demonstrate the superiority of the Hebrew-Christian tradition over paganism, and on the other to defend Christianity against a variety of charges. They viewed this superiority as both temporal and spiritual. To support a temporal or chronological superiority, Justin Martyr claimed that Moses wrote the Pentateuch long before the Trojan War (c. 1250 B.C.), thus antedating Greek history, to say nothing of Roman. And he and other Apologists made much of fulfillment of prophecy in an attempt to show that Christianity was not something new, but merely a continuation or culmination of the ancient Hebrew faith. As to the spiritual superiority of Christianity over paganism, the Apologists claimed that noble pagans had obtained their high ideals from God or Moses.

> *... the Apologists tried on the one hand to demonstrate the superiority of the Hebrew-Christian tradition over paganism, and on the other to defend Christianity against a variety of charges.*

Among the charges against which Apologists defended Christianity were atheism, cannibalism, immorality, and antisocial action. The first charge arose because Christians refused to worship the emperor or the Greco-Roman gods; the second, because of a misunderstanding of the celebration of the Lord's Supper; the third, because religious services generally had to be conducted in secret or after dark and because Christians displayed great love for each other; and the last, because Christians found it necessary to retire from much of public life, as most aspects of human existence were in some way connected with worship of the gods. For instance, one who held public office had to participate in and even lead the populace in sacrifices to the ruler or the goddess Roma, the personification of the state. Normally those who attended an athletic festival or a drama found themselves acquiescing in a sacrifice to a god before the event began.

In their effort to win recognition from the state for their faith, the Apologists generally took a philosophical approach. It was only natural that they should do so, because on the one hand they were trying to reason out the case for Christianity with their opponents, and because on the other hand they often wrote to men who were themselves greatly interested in philosophy. (Note, for instance, that the emperor Marcus Aurelius was a Stoic philosopher, and apologies were addressed to him.)

Because of their philosophical orientation, the Apologists have been accused of undue surrender to the world view of heathenism. Even their teachings about Jesus Christ appear in the form of the Logos doctrine. To the philosophers the Logos was an impersonal controlling and developing principle of the universe. But John in chapter one of his gospel had also used *Logos* to describe Christ, without any sacrifice of His deity or the value of His atoning work.

The Apologists on most points seem to have upheld the New Testament concept of Jesus Christ, though it must be admitted that such writers as Justin sometimes described Christ as being of inferior rank to the Father.

The very fact that the Apologists placed such great stress on the Logos demonstrates that their theology was Christ-centered. Moreover, although the practice may involve dangers, it is neither wrong nor undesirable to make one's message intelligible to one's age.

Justin Martyr

Probably the most dramatic and therefore the best known of the Apologists was Justin Martyr. Certainly he was a great literary defender of the faith. Born about A.D. 100 in a small town in Samaria (but apparently a Gentile), Justin early became well acquainted with the various philosophical systems. But his great knowledge of these philosophies also led him to a realization of their inadequacies. At this point of disillusionment and searching (c. 132), an old Christian came into Justin Martyr's life and showed him the way of faith in Christ. Thereafter, the converted philosopher became a Christian philosopher, presenting the Christian message in philosophical terms.

Justin wrote apologies to the emperor Antoninus Pius and his adopted son, Marcus Aurelius, and a dialogue with Trypho the Jew. In the apologies, he sought to defend Christianity against the charges of atheism and immorality, to demonstrate that Christians were loyal citizens (Christ's kingdom was not of this world; so the empire had no reason to fear insurrection), and to prove that the truth was taught by Christianity alone. In his dialogue with Trypho, Justin tried to show that Jesus was the Messiah. During his second stay in Rome, Justin engaged in a public debate with a philosopher by the name of Crescens. Shortly thereafter (c. 163), Justin was martyred by Marcus Aurelius, perhaps at the instigation of several philosophers close to the emperor.

The later chapters of his first apology are especially interesting because of his comments on baptismal and Eucharistic (that is, concerning the Lord's Supper) belief and practice. In fact, he was one of the foremost interpreters of the Christian faith between the late first and early third centuries. And though he is commonly presented as a Christian philosopher, his focus was Christ, and his final authority the Scripture, the Word of God. In fact, he was not afraid to sit in judgment on philosophy.

Tatian

One of Justin's converts in Rome was Tatian (a native of Assyria), a writer skilled in argumentation. His *Address to the Greeks* was largely a tirade against paganism; it ridiculed almost every pagan practice. In the latter part, he argued that since Christianity was superior to Greek religion and thought, it deserved to be tolerated. After Justin's martyrdom, Tatian went to Syria, where he founded a group later called the Encratites—known for their extreme ascetic practices. Tatian is probably best known for his *Diatessaron*, the earliest harmony of the gospels, composed about A.D. 150-60.

Tertullian

Another writer of note sometimes classified among the Apologists was Tertullian. Born in Carthage, North Africa, about 160, he may have become a lawyer and was won to Christianity late in the century. An important church father, he wrote a long list of apologetic and theological works in Latin and Greek. His *Apologeticus* (c. 197), addressed to the Roman governor of Carthage, refuted the common charges leveled against Christians, demonstrated the loyalty of Christians to the empire, and showed that persecution of Christians was foolish anyway, because they multiplied whenever persecuted. About 200, Tertullian became enmeshed in the error of Montanism (for a discussion see chap. 7). These three (Justin, Tatian and Tertullian) were the more important of the Apologists, but fragmentary or fairly complete writings of at least a half dozen others do exist.

FOUR

Attacks Against Error
The Polemicists

AS THE Christian movement grew older, errors arose within its ranks—errors that called forth defenders of the faith and that by reaction led to the development of Christian doctrine and the formulation of a New Testament canon (see chap. 8). It is significant that in refuting error the Polemicists appealed extensively to New Testament books as the source of true doctrine. Thus they gave impetus to the later official pronouncements on the contents of the New Testament canon. The work of the Polemicists also gave rise to the concept of an orthodox catholic church opposed to heresy. Since chapter 7 seeks to define those errors, attention here focuses only on some chief attackers of them.

The Polemicists

Purpose: to attack error

Leaders
Irenaeus
Hippolytus
Tertullian
Cyprian

Irenaeus

Although most of the Apologists lived in the East, most of the Polemicists lived in the West. Earliest of the group was Irenaeus, who wrote *Against Heresies* about 185, at Lyons, France, where he was bishop. Primarily aimed at the philosophical error of Gnosticism,[3] this work may be characterized as follows:

Book I—a historical sketch of Gnostic sects presented in conjunction with a statement of Christian faith;

Book II—a philosophical critique of Gnosticism;

Book III—a scriptural critique of Gnosticism;

Book IV—answers to Gnosticism from the words of Christ;

Book V—a vindication of the resurrection against Gnostic arguments.

What is especially significant about the work of Irenaeus is that in answering error he stressed the episcopate, theological tradition, and the canon of Scripture of the true orthodox church. Thus he contributed to the authority of the monarchal bishop, to reverence for the traditional teaching of the church, and to the rise of an official canon of the New Testament. So Irenaeus did more than attack the errors of his day; he was also a constructive theologian. Sometimes he is called the "Father of Church Dogmatics" because he sought to formulate the principles of Christian theology and to provide an exposition of the church's beliefs. In this connection, one should study his *Proof of the Apostolic Preaching*.

Hippolytus

Covering much the same ground as Irenaeus, Hippolytus also attacked Gnosticism, as well as other errors, in his *Refutation of All Heresies* (written about 200). Although Hippolytus may have borrowed from Irenaeus, he significantly supplemented the work of the latter. Hippolytus came into conflict with the dominant party in Rome because he criticized them for disciplinary laxity and doctrinal unsoundness. In particular, he linked Callixtus, an important pastor, with Noetianism and Sabellianism—defective forms of Trinitarian teaching (see chap. 7, "Monarchianism"). Hippolytus was the most important third century theologian. In addition to his apologetic work, he is especially known for his *Apostolic Tradition*, which provides a picture of Roman church order and worship about A.D. 200. It deals with baptism, the Eucharist (the Lord's Supper), ordination, and other church practices. He also wrote a commentary on Daniel, the oldest commentary on a biblical book to survive intact. Part of his commentary on the Song of Songs also remains. Hippolytus wanted a church of the pure and opposed forgiving those guilty of serious sins after receiving baptism.

Tertullian

In Carthage lived two other Western Polemicists: Tertullian and Cyprian. Tertullian may be classified with the Apologists if one emphasizes his *Apologeticus* or as a Scientific Theologian if one focuses on his *De Anima* (concerning the origin of the soul). In fact, he is commonly regarded as the founder of Latin (Roman Catholic) theology. But he is classified here because of his intensely passionate opposition to paganism, Judaism, early forms of Unitarianism, and Gnosticism. It has been said that he did more than anyone else to overthrow Gnosticism. Like Irenaeus, he held that the true church, through episcopal and apostolic succession, possessed the message of Christ and the correct interpretation of Scripture. One of his most important theological works was *Against Praxeas* (c. 210), which was an early statement of Trinitarian doctrine. Although he eventually lapsed into the Montanist error (see chap. 7), he enjoyed considerable popularity in the ancient, medieval, and Renaissance church. Tertullian carried on his ministry during the first decades of the third century.

Cyprian

Cyprian (martyred in 258) in his polemic activity is known for his opposition to Novatianism. Novatus (Novatian) held that those who lapsed during persecution could not be pronounced forgiven by the church and restored to its fellowship; forgiveness must be left to God alone. It was not Novatus's severity of discipline but his denial that the church had the right to grant absolution that caused his excommunication. The church had become conscious of her catholicity and unity by this time, and those who would not submit to divinely appointed bishops were regarded as heretics. In line with this common attitude, Cyprian, bishop of Carthage, felt duty bound to condemn Novatus.

Sometimes leaders of the school of Alexandria are listed among the Polemicists. Clement's *Protepticus* is an apologetic missionary document written to demonstrate the superiority of Christianity to paganism. Origen wrote his *Against Celsus* to answer certain charges against Christianity. But in my opinion, these men are more properly classified among the Scientific Theologians

FIVE

Early Development of Theology
The Scientific Theologians

AS HAS been noted already, the Scientific Theologians sought to apply current modes of thought to theological investigation. Moreover, they tried to develop scientific methods of biblical interpretation and textual criticism. The classification of these writers falls roughly into three groups. (1) Those living in Alexandria (Pantaenus, Clement, Origen, and, later, Athanasius, Cyril, and others) were the most speculative in approach and usually

---

The Scientific Theologians

Purpose: *to develop scientific methods of biblical interpretation*

Theologians

Alexandrian Theologians	**Western Theologians**
Pantaenus	Jerome
Clement	Ambrose
Origen	Augustine
Athanasius	**Eastern Theologians**
Cyril	Theodore
	John Chrysostom

followed an allegorical interpretation of Scripture; (2) writers of the West (Jerome, Ambrose, Augustine) tended to emphasize the authority of the church and its tradition; and (3) those ministering in Asia Minor and Syria (Theodore of Mopsuestia, John Chrysostom, and others) took a generally literal approach to biblical study.

Alexandrian Theologians

Clement

Earliest of the leaders of the school in Alexandria for converts from paganism and children of believers was Pantaenus, who held the reins of authority until about 190. Since the writings of Pantaenus no longer exist (or have not yet been discovered), it is necessary to move to a discussion of his more famous successors. Associated with Pantaenus from c. 180, Clement (probably an Athenian) headed the school of Alexandria from 190 to 202, when he was forced by persecution to leave the city. His writings include *Address to the Greeks*, *The Tutor*, *The Miscellanies*, and the *Outlines of Scripture Interpretation*.

The first was designed to win converts from heathenism; the second, to provide new converts with simple instruction for living the Christian life; the third, to show the superiority of Christianity to pagan philosophy; and the last, to provide commentaries on various scriptural passages, partly in answer to heretical interpretations. In the writings of Clement, the influence of Greek philosophy is prominent, especially that of Plato; but the Bible also has a place of importance. He sought to synthesize Christianity and Greek philosophy and is significant in church history as being the first to present Christianity in the forms of secular literature for the Christian community.

Clement contributed to the development of purgatory and Christian mysticism. In fact, he was one of the "inventors" of purgatory,[4] with its primary goal of eventual purification of the soul. While he did not hold to universal restorationism (i.e., that all would ultimately attain salvation), he had an optimistic view of the ultimate destiny of most human beings. And though he could not be classified as a Gnostic, his views approached those of the Gnostics at times. He held that in contemplation of the Logos, human beings receive from Christ the true *gnosis* (divine knowledge), which leads to freedom from sin and to righteousness. In this Christian mysticism the Lord's sufferings and death had little significance.

Origen

Most famous of the Alexandrian writers was Origen,[5] who led the school from 202 to 232. Thereafter he moved to Caesarea in Palestine, where he continued his illustrious career for another twenty years until the Decian persecution (see chap. 6). Origen is often called the first great theologian. He brought to scientific formulation the allegorical interpretation of Scripture. The germs of this approach may be seen in Philo of Alexandria, a contemporary of Christ who had sought to find a reconciliation between Greek philosophy and Jewish thought by searching for hidden meanings in the Old Testament. Christian writers after Philo employed the allegorical method, but Origen receives credit for the full development of the approach.

Simply described, the allegorical method proceeds on the conviction that the literal meaning of Scripture conceals a deeper meaning, available only to the mature believer. The hidden meaning that he found sometimes

bore little or no relationship to the literal. This conceal-
ing of truth by God under the guise of commonly
understood words was designed to prevent pearls from
being cast before swine.

Origen's works number in the thousands (some
say six thousand, including letters and articles), involving critical, apologetic, dogmatic, and practical treatises.
His commentaries deal with almost the whole Bible.
Although they are helpful at points, their value is restricted by his allegorisms. Highly significant are his
critical or textual studies: the *Hexapla* and *Tetrapla*. The
former has several Hebrew and Greek versions arranged
in parallel columns. The latter contains the four Greek
versions of the *Hexapla*. Only fragments of these works
remain. Origen's *On First Principles* is the earliest systematic theology that has come down to us.

Evaluating Origen's Contributions

While Origen made positive contributions to the
theology of the church, he is more commonly known
for views that did not receive general acceptance. For
instance, he taught that the souls of human beings
existed as fallen spirits before their birth, which ac-
counted for man's sinful nature. Second, he held that in
His atonement Christ paid a ransom to Satan, by whom
all were enslaved in the bondage of sin. Third, he
speculated that the love of God would through a puri-
fying fire ultimately accomplish universal salvation.[6]

How far Origen went in dogmatically declaring
universal restorationism or universal salvation is not
clear, however. Sometimes his overenthusiastic followers turned his speculations or suppositions or sugges-
tions into dogmas and made the master confidently
teach something about which he may only have been

wondering out loud. Such admirers may have been responsible for giving Origen bad press and making him out to be much more heretical than he actually was. It is not always possible to disentangle the real Origen from the Origen of theological history.

Brief mention of objectionable features of Origen's work leaves an unfair impression of the man. His literary work has three essential characteristics that constantly interpenetrate: exegesis, spirituality, and speculative theology. He was a man of prayer and love for God and His word. Usually his study of Scripture served as the basis of his doctrine, and he sought the application to the Christian of the message of Christ and the internalization in the life of the believer of all that Christ taught. He was above all a biblical theologian. But this devoutness of life could not be separated from his philosophical bent and the intellectual atmosphere in which he moved.[7]

The extent of his dedication to Christ is clear in that during the persecution of the emperor Decius in 250 (see chap. 6) he stood true to the Master throughout imprisonment and prolonged torture. Fairness to the theological position of Origen also requires the comment that nearly all of his works are very fragmentary. More complete works would give him a better chance to explain himself; perhaps he has been grossly misinterpreted.

Athanasius

Many decades later the great Athanasius (c. 293-373) rose to a position of leadership in Alexandria. To him goes special credit for the triumph of the orthodox view of Christ over Arianism, "a thinly disguised paganism," at the Council of Nicea in 325 (see chap. 9). Even prior to the outbreak of the Arian controversy, he had become a recognized theologian for his production of *Contra Gentiles* and *On the Incarnation*. In 328 he became bishop of Alexandria and thereafter steadfastly defended the Nicene position on the full deity of Christ, even though his opposition succeeded in getting him exiled periodically.

Cyril

A later figure of significance in Alexandria was Cyril (376-444). Becoming patriarch of Alexandria in 412, he devoted himself to the defense of the orthodox doctrine of the person of Christ, but sometimes did so in a highhanded and pompous manner. He advanced the veneration of Mary with his effective promulgation in the church that she was *Theotokos* or the bearer of God. An outstanding theologian, he put in systematic form the classical statement of the doctrines of the Trinity and the person of Christ.

Western Theologians

Jerome

One of the greatest of the Western Fathers was Jerome (c. 345-420). Born in northeastern Italy, he spent several years in Rome, studying languages and philosophy, and was baptized at the age of nineteen. During the next twenty years he moved around a great deal—in Gaul, the East, and Italy—perfecting his knowledge of Greek and Hebrew and becoming a convert of monasticism. Settling in Bethlehem in 386, he began his influential writing ministry. By means of extensive correspondence and dramatic telling of the lives of early ascetics, he did much to promote asceticism, celibacy, and monasticism. As a writer against heresies Jerome was primarily the interpreter of accepted church dogma; he was not original. He wrote commentaries on almost all the books of the Bible, but they were unequal in value. He utilized allegorism, according to his admission, when he was unable to discover the literal meaning. Jerome ranks first among early exegetes, and his knowledge of languages was unsurpassed in the early church. He was careful about his sources of information. He knew and used extensively early versions and manuscripts of the Bible no longer extant. Operating on the principle that only the original text of Scripture is free from error, he engaged in considerable manuscript study in order to determine what, among variant readings, should be considered the original and true text.

Out of these efforts came the work for which he is best known: the Vulgate, a translation of the Bible into Latin. Jerome also tried to bring Eusebius's *Ecclesiastical History*[8] up to date by recording events for the years 325-378. He also translated and revised Eusebius' *Onomasticon*, a gazetteer of biblical places.

Ambrose

Ambrose, bishop of Milan (374-397), was another of the most illustrious Fathers of the Western church. Because his writings represent an official witness to the teachings of the Roman church in his own time and earlier centuries, they have been constantly appealed to be popes, councils, and theologians. Commentaries on Scripture constitute more than half of his writings. In these Ambrose employed the allegorico-mystical method of interpretation: he admitted a literal sense, but sought everywhere a deeper mystical meaning that he converted into practical instruction for Christian life.

Ambrose is also known for his contributions in the field of music. In a day when church services were becoming increasingly liturgical and choirs were assuming greater importance, Ambrose championed congregational singing. He introduced into the Western Church the Eastern custom of singing psalms and hymns by the people. Usually this took the form of antiphonal chant between the choir or a leader and the congregation. Ambrose himself composed a number of hymns, most of which followed a precise metrical pattern, each stanza consisting of four lines of eight syllables each.

In the lives and teachings of the Fathers we find the seed plot of almost all that arose later.

How many hymns Ambrose composed cannot now be certainly known. After a couple of hundred years, when Ambrosian singing lost out to Gregorian Chant and the more liturgical Roman Catholic service, many of Ambrose's hymns passed out of use and were lost. On the other hand, many of his disciples wrote hymns in his style, and often it is not possible to determine authorship. Some Benedictine writers credit him with twelve hymns; other sources mention six or seven; St. Augustine mentioned four specifically, though he was not trying to indicate total output.

Ambrose must have composed a substantial number of hymns during his bishopric, and they apparently made a considerable impact on all who heard them. A story is told how on one occasion Ambrose was locked in a contest with the empress Justina, who sent troops to his church to enforce her will. The forces found the bishop and his people praying and singing in the church and refusing to capitulate. At length the soldiers were said to have joined in singing the well-known chants and the empress finally gave up her attack on the bishop.[9] Whether or not the soldiers did start to sing on that occasion, congregational singing in Ambrose's church in Milan made a profound effect on visitors. St. Augustine told of how he was emotionally overcome with the singing of hymns in services there.[10] For his efforts, Ambrose is commonly called the "Father of Latin Hymnody."[11]

Ambrose also encouraged monasticism, was one of the earliest supporters of devotion to Mary in the Western church, and promoted the cult of martyrs during his bishopric. In his diligence in teaching the faith and refuting heresy, he influenced many, not the least of whom was St. Augustine, who was his most illustrious convert.

Augustine

St. Augustine, bishop of Hippo in North Africa, stands preeminent among theologians of all time. His influence upon all Christian faiths has been significant. His emphasis on a personal experience of the grace of God as necessary to salvation has caused Protestants to accept him as a forerunner of the Reformation. His emphasis on the church, her creed, and sacraments has appealed to Roman Catholics. His teaching that the Millennium was the period between Christ's first and second comings, during which time the church would conquer the world, has contributed greatly to amillennial and postmillennial theologies of past and present. Augustine's teaching that man is in all his parts perverted by sin profoundly influenced Calvinistic theology. And such an outstanding American scholar as Perry Miller made the claim in his *New England Mind* that the Puritans were even more Augustinian than Calvinistic in their theology.

Augustine molded the theology of the Middle Ages in Europe down to the thirteenth century, when a reaction to his teaching occurred in the Aristotelian emphasis of Thomas Aquinas (see chap. 13). But that reaction has been less complete than widely supposed, and Reformers appealed to some aspects of his teaching in their attack on Scholastic theology. Martin Luther quoted Augustine over one hundred times in his commentary on Romans alone. Augustine's view on the nature of man and his salvation are described further in chapter 9.

Augustine's Writings

Augustine (354-430) came from a respectable but not a rich family. His life, a journey through periods of immorality, entanglement in appealing philosophies and heresies of the day, and spiritual crisis to the achievement of moral and spiritual victory, is one of the best-known biographies of all time and occasionally has appeared on best seller lists. The account recorded in his *Confessions*, has been read by millions. *Confessions* is Augustine's moral autobiography; *Revisions* is his intellectual autobiography, which describes the changes in his thought over the years. Most important of his theological works is his *Concerning the Trinity; Concerning Christian Doctrine* is the most important of his exegetical works.

His philosophy of history, the first to be developed, is found in his *City of God*. In it he traces the development of the city of earth and the city of God through biblical and secular history and shows the destiny of the two cities: the former to eternal punishment and the latter to eternal bliss. He portrays the sovereignty of God in human affairs and the ultimate triumph of good over evil, though currently the reverse is often true.

Actually, the literary production of Augustine was so massive that it is difficult to arrive at even an approximation of what he taught on various subjects. A book that is extremely useful in distilling the thought of the master is Bourke's *The Essential Augustine*, which deals with nine major topics in his writings. In his list of the writings of the Bishop, Bourke includes ninety-seven entries.[12] Of course any bibliography on the study of St. Augustine will list thousands of works in numerous languages. Fortunately for posterity, when the barbarians invaded Hippo a year after Augustine's death (430) and the city was burned, his library was rescued.

Theologians of Asia Minor and Syria

The Three Great Cappadocians

Three of the most important leaders of the church in Asia Minor and Syria were the Three Great Cappadocians of central Asia Minor. These men are known for their contribution to the development of the doctrine of the Trinity and the defense of the orthodox theological position of the church (see chap. 9). Of these three, Basil the Great (330-97) of Caesarea in Cappadocia is known for his opposition to heresies, especially Arianism, and for the organization of Eastern monasticism. His brother, Gregory, bishop of Nyssa (332-398), was a champion of orthodoxy at the Council of Constantinople in 381 and is respected as one of the founders of the Eastern Church. Gregory of Nazianzus (329-90) became bishop of Constantinople in 381 and preached effectively in defense of the Nicene faith against Arianism there. Highly educated, in Cappadocia, Palestine, Egypt, and Athens, he wrote extensively; about 1,200-1,500 manuscripts of his works survive.

Theodore

Two other important Scientific Theologians in the Eastern Church were John Chrysostom and Theodore. Theodore (350-428) was bishop of Mopsuestia in Cilicia (Asia Minor) for thirty-six years. A brilliant exegete, he wrote commentaries on most books of the Bible, generally following grammatico-historical and realistic explanations of the text. This method of interpreting the words of Scripture according to their ordinary grammatical meaning and in the light of their historical background was the prevailing mode of interpretation in the Antiochene school of thought, from which background Theodore had come. John Calvin was later to become famous for his contributions to the grammatico-historical method of biblical interpretation (see chap. 18).

For Theodore's attacks on the allegorical interpretation of Scripture, the Origenists of Alexandria promoted his condemnation by the church. Sometimes he has been judged unjustly for such things as phraseology that was not always precise on questions of christology and an account of the Fall that sounded somewhat Pelagian (see chap. 9). As a matter of fact, he was a strong supporter of the Nicene orthodoxy of the Council of Constantinople (381) (see chap. 9). Unfortunately, only fragments of his theological works remain. Theodore reputedly was the first to attempt to place the Psalms in their historical context.

John Chrysostom

John Chrysostom (347-407), the most prominent leader of the Greek church, also was important as a representative of the grammatico-historical interpretation of Scripture in opposition to the allegorical and mystical interpretations of Alexandria. While Chrysostom did not exclude all allegorical and mystical elements from scriptural study, he confined them to cases in which he felt the inspired author suggested such a meaning. Chrysostom is also important for the reformation of Eastern theology.

At the time of the Reformation there were long discussions whether Chrysostom was Protestant or Catholic. Though he ignored confession to a priest, he did hold to the real presence in the Eucharist, to the one church, and to tradition as a valid basis of authority. Born in Antioch and for many years preacher in the cathedral there, Chrysostom became patriarch of Constantinople near the end of his life (398). Unfortunately, his criticism of the opulent life of the court, his tactlessness, asceticism, and opposition of the Patriarch of Alexandria brought him considerable trouble, and he was finally deposed from office.

Perhaps he is best known for his preaching. The name *Chrysostom* (golden-mouthed) was bestowed upon him for his eloquence. Copies of some 650 of his sermons still exist. These sermons must often have lasted for an hour or more. Theologically, they expressed the ideas of Athanasius and the Great Cappadocians. Practically, they portrayed a deep compassion for the poor and a zeal for social righteousness.

Summary and Evaluation

A study of the Fathers is very valuable for one interested in the development of church doctrine and organization. In their lives and teachings we find the seed plot of almost all that arose later. In germ form appear the dogmas of purgatory, transubstantiation, priestly mediation, baptismal regeneration, and the whole sacramental system. They defined the allegorical, mystical, and literal interpretations of Scripture. To them we look for a formulation of the hierarchal system and the importance of the church as the sphere of salvation. But through them also came the development of the canon and formulation of the great creeds of Christendom, which serve as the basis of most successive teaching concerning the Trinity, the person of Christ, and the nature of the Holy Spirit (see chaps. 7 and 9). And among them arose great defenders of the faith; they answered the persecutors of Christianity and attacked heretics who attempted to destroy the faith from within. It is to the persecutions and perversions of the faith that we now turn.

SIX

Attacks from Without
The Persecutions

THE Christian movement had hardly begun when it faced its first persecutors. This was to be expected, for Jesus Himself had warned His disciples, "If they persecuted Me, they will also persecute you" (John 15:20). Shortly after Pentecost the success of apostolic preaching so jolted members of the Sanhedrin that they threw Peter and John into prison (Acts 4). Soon thereafter they imprisoned the whole apostolic band (Acts 5). Opposition heightened, resulting in the stoning of Stephen (Acts 7). A few years later, probably A.D. 44, Herod Agrippa I slew James the brother of John (Acts 12:2) and imprisoned Peter. So persecution of the church began with the Jews.

Reasons for Persecution

Jewish Fears

Reasons for Jewish opposition to the gospel are not hard to discover. Jewish leaders feared a rapidly rising movement that would decimate their constituency. And evidently many among them, like Saul of Tarsus, honestly believed that Christianity was a perversion of true Judaism and that they were honoring God by attacking it. Moreover, some Jews might have worried about losing their privileged position in the empire if Palestine were infected with individuals who spoke about another kingdom ruled by a king other than Caesar. And a few, of the Zealots, may have opposed Christianity because it was not willing to join Jewish nationalistic moves for independence.

Roman Political Suspicions

Reasons for Roman persecution were much more complex. Christians were politically suspect because they spoke of a kingdom with Christ as its ruler. Materialistically minded Romans took statements concerning such a kingdom to imply a plan for overthrow of the government. Moreover, there was a union of religion and state in ancient Rome; so refusal to worship the goddess Roma or the divine emperor constituted treason. And no government has ever dealt lightly with treason.

Social Reasons

Christians suffered social ostracism because they came, especially in the early days, largely from the lower classes of society and because as good Christians they could not participate in much of the public life of their time. For example, as civil servants they might be required to join in ceremonies in honor of the divine Caesar. Even engaging in sporting and theatrical events was impossible, because sacrifice to a pagan deity normally occurred before a drama or an athletic festival. For example, the Olympic Games were held in honor of Zeus and the Isthmian Games at Corinth in honor of Poseidon (see 1 Cor. 9:24-27). They also condemned public games in which gladiators fought in mortal combat to entertain spectators and in which prisoners were thrown to wild beasts for entertainment of the crowds. And the fact that Christians proclaimed the equality of all people before God put them in direct opposition to the generally accepted institution of slavery. They do not seem to have launched campaigns for its abolition, however.

Economic Reasons

There were also economic reasons for the persecution of Christians. Priests, idol makers, and other vested religious interests could hardly look on disinterestedly while their incomes dwindled and their very livelihoods stood in jeopardy. Since leaders of the old religions held important positions in society, they could easily stir up mob opposition to Christianity. The success of Demetrius and the other idol makers of Ephesus in this regard is a case in point (Acts 19). Christians were also made scapegoats for great calamities such as famine, earthquakes, and pestilence—which were sometimes regarded as divine punishment meted out because people had forsaken the Greco-Roman gods.

Religious Reasons

Religiously, Christianity suffered because it was exclusivistic, not tolerant like other faiths of the empire, and declared only one way of salvation. In fact, it was aggressive in trying to win adherents from other faiths. And because Christians had to hold religious observances in secret, it was easy for all sorts of rumors to circulate about them. Some saw in their love for each other an evidence of licentiousness. Others interpreted their statements used in connection with Communion to refer to cannibalism.

Roman Imperial Persecution

Earliest Official Persecutions: 64-100

The event that sparked official persecutions, however, was the fire of Rome, beginning on July 19 of A.D. 64. That holocaust, which lasted for nine days and gutted ten of the fourteen districts of the city, brought untold suffering to a population of about one million. Some of Nero's enemies circulated a report that he had started the fire. The charge was probably untrue, but Nero diverted attention from himself by making scapegoats out of the Christian community in Rome.[13] The penalty suffered by many of the supposed incendiaries was burning at the stake at night to light the gardens near Nero's circus in the Vaticanus section of Rome. Some were crucified and others thrown to wild beasts or mad dogs. Paul suffered martyrdom at the hands of Nero; Peter is said to have suffered the same fate.

The Neronian persecution is important because it established the precedent and the manner of persecuting Christians, though it did not lead to any persecution outside Rome. In this instance, Christians were punished for arson rather than for holding any particular beliefs or being an adherent of any particular religion.

The second persecution broke out in A.D. 95, during the reign of Domitian. It was originally directed against Jews who refused to pay a tax designed to help fund construction of the magnificent new temple to Jupiter on the Capitoline Hill in Rome. Being associated with Judaism still, Christians also suffered during this persecution. Moreover, Domitian enforced emperor worship. Upon refusal to participate, Christians were charged with treason. Some were martyred, some dispossessed of property, and others banished. At this time the apostle John was exiled to the Isle of Patmos, where he received the vision of the Revelation. It is not clear that John's exile was instigated by the emperor, however; probably local opposition in the province of Asia was responsible for that.

Imperial Policy: 111-161

Specific imperial policy concerning persecution was not developed until early in the second century. Pliny the Younger, a Roman lawyer, served as governor of the provinces of Bithynia and Pontus in Asia Minor, 111-113. While there, Pliny faced a great defection from paganism and a corresponding growth of the Christian movement. He felt obligated to deal with this situation and concluded that those brought before him for trial should be asked three times if they were Christians, each time the question being accompanied with threats. If they persisted in their faith after the third repetition of the question, they were to be led out and executed.

Uncertain of the rightness of his procedure, Pliny wrote to the emperor Trajan for advice.[14] Trajan replied that Christians were not to be sought out; but if reported and convicted they were to be punished, unless they repented and worshiped the gods. Anonymous information was not to be received against them. Thus an official policy was established. Soon governors throughout the empire were following the principles Trajan had enunciated. Many believers were martyred, including the famous Ignatius, bishop of Antioch, who apparently was thrown to wild beasts in the arena in Rome about 115.

During the reign of Trajan's successor, Hadrian (117-138), the general policy of Trajan was followed; Christians were persecuted in moderation. When it became common for mobs at heathen festivals to demand the blood of Christians, Hadrian published an edict against such riots. Accusations against Christians were to be made in court.[15] Christianity made marked progress in numbers, wealth, learning, and social influence during his reign.

Antoninus Pius (139-161) seems to have favored Christians, but he felt he had to uphold the established imperial policy concerning them. So there were many martyrs, including Polycarp, bishop of Smyrna. It should be noted that frequently during his reign, and particularly in the case of Polycarp, local mobs were responsible for much of the persecution. A good observation that applies to the reign of Antoninus as well as to that of the other Roman emperors, is that the persecutions of Christians were always of limited extent and their ferocity was dependent on local conditions and the attitude of the provincial governors.

A New Approach: Marcus Aurelius, 161-180

A new approach to persecution arose during the reign of Marcus Aurelius (161-180). An intolerant Stoic, he had no sympathy with the concept of immortality. The exultation of Christian martyrs he attributed to their desire for theatrical display. Instead of waiting for accusation to be brought against Christians, as Trajan had done, Marcus Aurelius introduced a spy system designed to accumulate evidence against them. He put no check on the riots instituted against Christians. During his reign the practice of blaming the occurrence of earthquakes, famines, floods, and pestilences on Christians began. Supposedly these calamities befell the populace because they forsook the old gods and tolerated Christianity. Persecution under Marcus Aurelius was cruel and barbarous. Thousands were beheaded or thrown to wild beasts, including the famous Justin Martyr.

But even the Aurelian persecution was not an organized, empire-wide persecution for the extermination of Christianity. Neither could the efforts of Septimius Severus (193-211) and Maximinus (235-238) be considered an all-out war on Christianity. Septimius Severus directed his attack primarily against Egypt and North Africa, and even there he was largely interested in putting a stop to proselytizing. Maximinus sought to wipe out Christian leaders only in certain areas.

Persecution across the Empire: 249-305

In the middle of the third century the situation changed, however. Rome celebrated the thousandth anniversary of her founding and looked back to the days of prosperity, stability, and unquestioned authority in the Mediterranean world. How the gods had once favored her! Now the foundations of the economic, political, and social structure were crumbling. Public calamities such as earthquakes and pestilences abounded. Barbarians hovered on the frontiers. A superstitious populace was easily persuaded that the gods were angry because so many Christians had left the old faith.

The emperor Decius (249-251) was convinced that the maintenance of a state religion was necessary for political stability and return of prosperity. Therefore in the first year of his reign he gave orders that all inhabitants of the empire should come before special officers and declare their allegiance to the gods, proving it with an act of sacrifice. This amounted to a petition on the part of the entire populace for blessing on the emperor and the seriously threatened empire. Of course this edict flushed out true Christians, who refused to sacrifice.

They became enemies of the emperor, the state, and the public good and were subjected to severe persecution.

Evidence shows that the design was not to destroy Christians but to reconvert them to the state cult. First to be seized were the higher clergy, in order to render the church leaderless and reduce its effectiveness. Multitudes recanted, because a conventional Christianity had already come into existence and the church was filled with individuals possessing only a superficial belief. But hosts of others suffered martyrdom. After about a year it became evident that the Decian persecution could not succeed. It was over by April 1, 251. In July the emperor died in battle and his edicts no longer had any force.

Decius's successor, Valerian (253-260), was at first friendly to Christianity; but after a number of public calamities, he was encouraged to resort to severe punishment of Christians to stop the trouble. Many great leaders lost their lives.

From 260 to 303 Christianity enjoyed respite from persecution. Then all fury broke loose. The emperor Diocletian, persuaded by Galerius, his colleague in the East, issued a series of edicts in 303 that commanded destruction of Christian places of worship and sacred books and imprisonment of the clergy. During the following year Christians were offered the alternative of renouncing their faith and offering pagan sacrifices or suffering martyrdom. In the eastern part of the empire persecution was especially brutal. Diocletian's co-ruler in the West, Maximian, carried out the edicts with full force in Italy and Africa. But Maximian's subordinate, Constantius, who ruled Gaul, Britain, and Spain, refused to execute anyone for his religion. The persecution ended for the most part in 305, when Diocletian abdicated the throne and retired to private life.

Toleration under Constantine, from 313

During the confused time that followed, Constantius's son, Constantine, rose to leadership in the western part of the empire. In 313 he and Licinius, as joint rulers of the empire, issued an edict giving full toleration to the Christian faith. Though Licinius subsequently reneged on his commitment and stirred up persecution in the East, full toleration of Christianity came to the entire empire when Constantine became sole ruler of the Roman world in 324. Constantine made Christianity a legal religion and favored its development in many ways. He restored property confiscated during the Dioclatian persecution and rebuilt many churches destroyed then. He also supported the efforts of his mother, Queen Helena, to build such famous churches as the Church of the Nativity in Bethlehem and the Church of the Holy Sepulcher in Jerusalem. And he granted numerous favors to the clergy, including excuse from military duty, as well as exempting church property from taxation. Near the end of the fourth century Theodosius made Christianity the official religion of the empire and persecution of paganism began. In 392 he forbade heathen worship under severe penalties.

An accommodation occurred between Christianity and paganism during the latter decades of the fourth century. Though Christianity was winning a victory of sorts over paganism, paganism achieved victories of her own by infiltrating the Christian church in numerous subtle ways. As opposition to paganism increased, many took their place in the church without experiencing conversion. Thus large segments of church membership consisted merely of baptized pagans. The distinction between Christianity and paganism became increasingly blurred as the state church was established under the ultimate authority of the emperor. Under the circumstances, it seems unwise to speak of the church's conquering the Roman Empire. One might as easily argue that the empire had conquered the church.

It seems unwise to speak of the church's conquering the Roman Empire. One might as easily argue that the empire had conquered the church.

Accounts of the deaths of martyrs during the period of the Roman persecutions have been greatly dramatized. Their faith and courage were magnificent, but theirs was the easy way. Much greater suffering was endured by those who lay in their own filth in heavy irons in hot Eastern prisons, with little water or food, until they died of disease or starvation. Equally hard was the lot of those sentenced to work the fields and mines. Half naked, underfed, beaten for low production, the damp ground their bed, these believers faced a living death.

Effects of the Persecutions

The persecutions had their effects. Usually the good effects are noted. Many were won to Christ through the manner of death of the martyrs. Tertullian is often quoted: "The blood of the martyrs is the seed of the Church." It is also frequently noted that the church was more apt to be pure if believers were in danger of their lives for naming the name of Jesus; they would not lightly join for social or economic reasons. Moreover, persecution often forced Christians to flee to areas where normally they would not have gone; thus the gospel spread more widely.

Persecution also helped to settle the question of what belonged in the New Testament canon. It is obvious that believers would not give their lives for something that was not Scripture; and under the difficult conditions of persecution, they were less likely to take the trouble to copy or preserve works of insignificant value. Last, under the duress of persecution church leaders called Apologists produced reasoned defenses of Christianity that countless generations since have used in defending their own faith.

But the persecutions had their ill effects too. Christians were so busy protecting themselves that there was little opportunity to leave a literary legacy. And a great problem arose in the church over the question of the lapsed. All did not hold true to the faith. Some buckled under persecution and then later reaffirmed their faith and wished to be reinstated to the fellowship of believers. Some believers favored restoration and some did not. Many churches split over the question. Also, the very experience of martyrdom became warped as to its purpose or benefits. Many came to believe that dying for the faith had some sin-atoning merit.

SEVEN

Attacks from Within
Early Heresies

IT IS probably true that one's greatest enemies are almost always internal. External opposition or difficulty will not ultimately overpower if internal strength is adequate for the test. So it was with the early church. The persecutions for the most part only brought about the increase of Christians, but the internal errors of the second and third centuries took a great toll of the faithful.

Early Heresies: Second Century

Ebionism

One of the earliest errors was Ebionism. Appearing in fully developed form in the second century, it was in reality only a continuation and amplification of the Judaistic opposition to the apostle Paul. In his letter to the Galatians he sternly rebuked those who sought salvation through law keeping. But human nature being what it is, men and women have always been enamored with religious systems that promise salvation by means of good works; and Ebionism was such a system.

Ebionism grew up in Palestine and assumed various forms. Some groups seem to have been quite clear on the essentials of salvation but insistent on law keeping as a way of life. Most, however, appear to have denied the deity of Christ, His virgin birth (teaching that Jesus was the human son of Joseph and Mary), and the efficacy of His sufferings. These views they held in an effort to retain a true monotheism. To them Christ was unusual in His strict law observance, and He was rewarded with messiahship for His legal piety.

The Ebionites generally rejected Paul's apostleship and his writings and tended to venerate Peter as the apostle to the circumcision. They put much stress on the law in general and on circumcision and Sabbath keeping in particular. One branch taught a kind of Jewish-Christian Gnosticism. Ebionism practically disappeared by the fifth century. It had little if any lasting effect on the church.

Gnosticism

Like Ebionism, Gnosticism seems to have existed in germ form in the days of Paul and John. For instance, Colossians 2:8, 18-19 and much of 1 John well may have been aimed at this error. Gnosticism was a product of the spirit of religious fusion that characterized the first century. It borrowed elements from Judaism, Christianity, Greek philosophy, and Oriental mysticism and constructed a system of thought that sought to combine revelation with the "wisdom of this world." Spawned primarily in Egypt and Syria, it spread to Rome, Asia Minor, Mesopotamia, and Persia.

Basic Teachings

Gnostics taught that matter was evil and spirit was good. Therefore they were faced with the problem of how a good God could create an evil world. A system of emanations was their answer. That is, there emanated from God an infinite chain of beings that became increasingly evil. Finally, at the end of the line came the Demiurge, or somewhat evil God, who was identified with the Jehovah of the Old Testament, and who was thought to be the Creator of the world and man. The good God took pity on man in his plight and sent the highest emanation, Christ, to minister to man's need of salvation. Especially, Christ came as an emissary of light from the kingdom of light to dispel man's spiritual darkness. Atonement through His death was not considered necessary. Because matter was evil, the Messiah's body was thought by some to be only an appearance, by others to be merely a human body that the Messiah used from His baptism until His death on the cross.

Gnosticism derived its name from a Greek word for knowledge (*gnosis*), and emphasis in the system was put on attaining knowledge of the good God—which would ensure salvation. The system was extremely aristocratic. It taught that the true Gnostics, of whom there were few, were born with a high degree of intuitive knowledge of God. Christ's teachings would help them to overcome the material world and enable them to establish communication with God and gain entrance into the kingdom of light. Ordinary church members could attain salvation by faith and good works. But the mass of humanity did not have a chance to be saved. Of great value to the true Gnostic and the average church member in attaining an experience of God was initiation into the mysteries of marriage to Christ, baptism, and other mystical rites of the church. The path of redemption also involved a low estimate of the flesh. Some punished the body by extreme asceticism; others gave full rein to the carnal desires of the flesh, for they felt that in such a manner the flesh could best be destroyed. At death the soul would be released from its prison of matter and would return to the Pleroma—a sort of world soul.

Short Life, Lasting Effects

Gnosticism as a system was fairly short-lived, partly because of its inherent weaknesses and partly because the Polemicists (especially Irenaeus, Tertullian, and Hippolytus) were effective in dealing with it. It left lasting effects on the church, however, negatively in asceticism and division of Christians into higher and lower orders (clergy and laity) and positively in forcing the church to come to a clearer definition of her doctrine and the limits of her canon. Gnosticism also helped to advance the institutionalization of the church in at least three ways. Its claim to be the universal church led the orthodox church to assert her claim to be the catholic church; its doctrinal inroads led to the rise of bishops as defenders of the faith; its emphasis on asceticism helped to foster the growth of monasticism in the church. Some of its teachings survived in Manicheism (see below); and a Gnostic or Manichean type sect, the Mandaeans, still exists in Mesopotamia south of Baghdad.

The three great Polemicists or Anti-Gnostic Fathers noted in the last paragraph based their answer to Gnosticism on the Scripture as interpreted by the church and as handed down from the apostles. They argued that the Creator and the Supreme God were one and the same, and they vociferously defended the reality of the physical life of Jesus on earth and His death and resurrection for salvation from evil. In all these respects they contributed to the rise of an official church with an official doctrine and an orthodox creed.

Until the end of World War II students of Gnosticism were almost entirely dependent for their information on references in the opponents of Gnosticism. Then in 1945, as a camel driver was doing some digging at Nag Hammadi in Upper Egypt, he found a jar containing the remains of thirteen codexes from the fourth century A.D. These contained Coptic versions of some fifty writings, most of which were Gnostic texts. Though these were dispersed to various antiquities dealers, they are all now housed at the Coptic Museum in Cairo. Among the most famous in the collection are the *Gospel of Thomas, Wisdom of Jesus Christ, Apocryphon of John, Apocalypse of Adam,* and the *Gospel of the Egyptians.*[16]

Montanism

About the middle of the second century there arose in Phrygia (central Asia Minor) the Montanist error, so named for its leader, Montanus. Montanism reacted against institutionalism or formalism and worldliness in the church and sought to revert to the church's supposed early fervor and spiritual emphasis. Response to deadness or formalism might take a charismatic approach, and response to worldliness could be legalism or the ascetic way. Montanists took both approaches. Groups in North Africa especially tended to require a strict asceticism (involving fasting, celibacy, rigorous moral discipline, etc.), while those of Asia Minor were more charismatic. Montanus himself preached the imminent coming of the New Jerusalem or the Millennium, the preparation for which was a new outpouring of the Holy Spirit. He wanted his followers to be an elite of spiritual Christians and to prepare for the coming age of the Holy Spirit by withdrawal from the world.

As part of the emphasis on the ministry of the Holy Spirit to the church, Montanists proclaimed a new era of prophecy and the continuation of revelation, including direct ecstatic revelations from God. They encouraged martyrdom and assigned to it a sin-atoning power. Montanus himself was accused of claiming to be the promised Paraclete. Though generally orthodox, the group's emphasis on such spiritual gifts as continuance of prophetic revelation and its requirement of ascetic practices as if they were truths of revelation caused it to be condemned by a series of church synods in Asia Minor and by the bishop of Rome. The church declared that biblical revelation had come to an end and that special spiritual gifts were no longer operative. Tertullian of Carthage was Montanism's most famous convert.

> *In studying groups that have been branded heretical, one must be extremely careful ...Most ... of the information about them ... was produced by their enemies.*

Early Heresies: Third Century

During the third century three movements arose to challenge the authority and doctrinal solidarity of the church: Novatianism, Monarchianism, and Manicheism.

Novatianism

Novatian was a presbyter of Rome, and an able defender of the doctrine of the Trinity against the Monarchians. But he fell out with the hierarchy over the treatment of those who had renounced their faith in the face of Decius's persecution (A.D. 249-50) and later sought to renew their fellowship with the church. He denied the right of the church to restore the lapsed and advocated a purist concept of church membership that smacked of Montanistic legalism. The dissenting party chose him as bishop, and the result was a schism that spread over most of the Empire and lasted until the sixth century.

In the fourth century, after the Diocletian persecution, the question of restoring the lapsed rose again; and a faction opposing restoration, known as the Donatists, emerged in North Africa. Subsequently, Novatian and Donatist groups seem to have merged. While admittedly Novatian had strong convictions against restoring to fellowship those who had buckled under persecution, one wonders how much of his schismatic action derived from doctrinal conviction and how much from personal pique and personality conflict. He had expected to be elected pope (bishop of Rome) in 251, and it was only after the lenient Cornelius was elected instead that he allowed himself to be consecrated as rival bishop and head of the purist party.

Monarchianism

Monarchianism (meaning "rule of one" and probably originating in Asia Minor) was more strictly a doctrinal error. The problem bothering the Monarchians was maintenance of the unity of the Godhead in the face of Trinitarianism. Their solution was something less than orthodox. Some of them, like the later Socinians and Unitarians, taught that the Father alone possessed true personality; the Son and Holy Spirit were merely impersonal attributes of the Godhead. So the power of God came upon the man Jesus and gradually penetrated and deified His humanity. But Jesus was not to be considered God in the truest sense of the word.

Other Monarchians viewed the three persons of the Godhead as mere modes of expression or activity or ways of describing God. They were not distinct, divine persons. This modalistic type of Monarchianism also came to be known as Sabellianism and Noetianism, after two of its leading exponents. The Monarchians called forth extensive and effective definition of the Trinitarian position. Although the Polemicists dealt fatal body blows to Monarchianism, groups holding the Unitarian position have arisen repeatedly in Christendom.

Manicheism

Manicheism has been described as Gnosticism with its Christian elements reduced to a minimum and Oriental elements raised to a maximum. The system was developed by Mani in southern Babylonia about 240 and thereafter spread rapidly through Persia, India, China, Egypt, North Africa, and Italy. Its appeal was great, even claiming such leaders as St. Augustine among its adherents for a time. After a somewhat meteoric initial success, Manicheism rapidly lost ground and died out, probably in part because of the sterile rigidity that the system early attained.

Like Gnosticism, Manicheism was a dualistic system. The kingdom of darkness at one time attacked the kingdom of light, and the result was a mixed creation of light and darkness (good and evil) in which the kingdom of light was engaged in a program of gradual purification. Christ came into the world to aid the good principle in human beings to overcome the thrusts of the kingdom of darkness.

At the moment, we are less concerned with the teaching of Manicheism than with its effects. In this system there were two classes: elect and auditors. Only the former were admitted to the secret rites of baptism and communion, which were celebrated with great pomp. The elect were very ascetic and occupied themselves with religious exercises. The auditors participated in the holiness of the elect in return for supplying the elect with the necessities of life. Manicheism helped to foster the ascetic spirit in the churches and was in large measure responsible for the division of church members into clergy and laity. Moreover, it promoted the growth of the priestly function, or the belief that ministers are intermediaries between God and humanity and have extraordinary power with God.

Evaluation and a Caution

The effects of the perversions in the early church were both negative and positive. They introduced erroneous views and practices into the regular churches and hindered their growth and development. But they also forced church leaders to formulate more clearly the doctrines of the church and to establish the limits of the canon, which could furnish a source of truth for combating error.

In studying groups that have been branded heretical, one must be extremely careful. Frequently most, if not nearly all, of the information about them that is still extant was produced by their enemies. Opponents commonly sought to portray them in the worst possible light. Therefore it is necessary to ask what sort of weakness their enemies would try to magnify and to figure out ways to evaluate the sources perceptively. The same sort of caution should be exercised in dealing with all minority positions in the history of the church, whether those persecuted by the medieval Inquisition, Anabaptists harried by the great Reformers, or New England revivalists opposed by the established churches during the Great Awakening. These and many others have sometimes been terribly misrepresented by those who were trying to shore up positions under severe attack.

EIGHT

Books for a New Testament
Formation of the Canon

SOME think that the books to be included in the New Testament canon were decided on hastily, by a group of early church leaders, late on a hot summer afternoon. And it is sometimes implied that the choice of those men was no better than a comparable group of church officials would make in the twentieth century. The facts of history demonstrate, however, that the New Testament was not formed hastily, nor was it formed by the councils. It was the product of centuries of development, and its official ratification came in response to the practical needs of the churches.

Developments that Forced the Church to Establish a Canon

Need for a Scripture to spell out the message of the Apostles

Need to decide on what should be read in the churches

Need for a true canon to answer heretical ones

Need to establish authoritative truth to answer error

Need to decide which of many books claiming to be canonical were false

Need to decide which books to die for when possession resulted in martyrdom

---

The Need for a Canon

Six main developments forced the church to formulate a canon of the New Testament. First, by the end of the first century contemporary witnesses to the message of Jesus and the apostles were mostly gone. The oral traditions became corrupt and conflicting, and believers wanted a body of Scripture that would spell out the authoritative message of the apostles. Second, from the beginning of the church it was customary to read Scripture in the worship services for the edification of believers.[17] Church leaders became increasingly concerned that the readings be truly the message of God for the people. Third, such heretics as Marcion[18] were formulating canons to promote their own special viewpoints. About A.D. 140 Marcion composed a canon of a mutilated Luke and ten of Paul's epistles. He rejected the Old Testament. In self-defense the church had to decide what books belonged in the canon.

Fourth, about the same time that Marcion and the Gnostics were making great inroads into the established churches, the Montanists began to promulgate ideas of continuing revelation. As noted in the last chapter, the church in retaliation declared that revelation had ceased. Fifth, apocryphal works began to appear in increasing numbers. These gospels, acts, and epistles attempted to fill in gaps in the narrative of the life of Christ and the apostles and to round out the theological message of the church. Some of these books were obviously not on a par with the books we now recognize as canonical, but others were very close to the New Testament message. An effort needed to be made to separate the wheat from the chaff.

Last, the persecutions called for a decision on the

contents of the New Testament canon. For instance, the Diocletian persecution in 303 called for the burning of all sacred books and the punishment of those who possessed them. Preservation of Scripture in the face of such determined imperial opposition required great effort and endangered the lives of those who hid or copied it. Therefore, one wanted to be sure he was expending effort or risking his life to disseminate or protect a genuine work.

We have been talking about the need for forming a canon, but have not yet defined the term. The Greek word *kanon* (rule or standard) designated the laws that governed the behavior society expected or the state demanded of its citizens. Paul used the word in that sense in Galatians 6:16. By the middle of the second century, the terms *canon of truth* or *canon of faith* were applied to the creed of the church. The connection of the word with books of the New Testament seems to have originated with Athanasius about the middle of the fourth century. Later, in his *Festal Epistle*, written in 367, he spoke of the Scripture as "canonized" in contrast to the apocrypha. Thus the word came into church vocabulary, although the idea behind it had arisen in the earliest days of the church. Canonical Scripture, then, on the one hand provides a standard of doctrine and holy living and, on the other hand, meets the standard or tests of inspiration.

Development of the Canon

Tests of Canonicity

It is one thing to determine the need for a canon; it is quite another to decide what belongs in it. Tests of canonicity had to be employed. Early church Fathers suggested that those books were canonical that were inspired. But inspiration is rather intangible and subject to differences of opinion. So secondary tests were required. One of the most important of these was apostolicity: that is, was a book written by an apostle or someone very close to the apostles? Thus, Luke's gospel was accepted because of his close relationship with Paul; Mark's because of his close association with Peter and Paul. Of course Matthew and John were apostles. Then there was the test of internal appeal. Did a book contain moral or doctrinal elements that measured up to the standards set by the apostles in their acknowledged writings?

When Certain Books Became Accepted As Canonical

As these and other tests were applied in various ways over the centuries, the canon gradually developed. Conservatives have long held that all the New Testament books were written by about the end of the first century, in spite of liberal claims to the contrary. And archaeological evidence now quite effectively confirms the conservative position.[19] It seems that almost from the time of their composition, the four Gospels and Acts were accepted as

The New Testament was ... formed... in response to the practical needs of the churches.

divinely inspired accounts of the life of Christ and the development of the early church. Various churches to which Paul addressed his epistles accepted his word to them as coming from the mouth of God. And gradually nearby churches came to feel that letters sent to sister churches were of value for them too; so they made copies. In this way the Pauline epistles began to circulate individually and by the end of the second century as a collection. The story concerning the rest of the New Testament books is not so simple.

Testimony in the writings of the church Fathers to the existence and value of various New Testament books is extensive, beginning as early as the end of the first century with Clement of Rome. And there are other notable pieces of evidence. A full catalog of this information is quite out of the question; a few of the outstanding items are noted here. About the middle of the second century, Tatian composed the first harmony of the gospels. This wove together elements of the four gospels in such a way as to present a continuous narrative of the life of Christ. Composed about the same time, the *Gospel of Truth*, one of the Gnostic works from Nag Hammadi, refers to an authoritative group of New Testament writings, including Matthew, Luke (possibly with Acts), John, the Pauline epistles (except the Pastorals), Hebrews, 1 John, and Revelation.

Early Lists of the Canon

A decade or two later a canon was drawn up, now bearing the name Muratori, after the Italian scholar who published it (1740). The work is not quite complete in the condition it has come to us. It apparently recognizes the four Gospels, Acts, the Pauline epistles, Revelation, two (or three) epistles of John, and Jude. But it adds the Apocalypse of Peter and omits 1 and 2 Peter and Hebrews and possibly one of John's epistles.

From the time of Irenaeus (c. 175), the principal spokesman of the church's response to Gnosticism, the canon was thought to contain essentially the same books that appear in it today, though there were continuing disputes over some inclusions. The eminent Clement of Alexandria (c. 200) seemed to recognize all the New Testament books. His greater student, Origen (c. 250), divided the books into categories of universally accepted works and disputed works. In the former he put the four Gospels, the thirteen epistles of Paul, 1 Peter, 1 John, Acts and Revelation. In the latter he put Hebrews, 2 Peter, 2 and 3 John, James, Jude, and four works not now part of the New Testament. He himself seems to have accepted nearly all the books now included in the New Testament.

Hebrews was disputed because its authorship was uncertain; 2 Peter, because it differed in style and vocabulary from 1 Peter; James and Jude, because they represented themselves as servants rather than apostles of Christ; 2 and 3 John because the author called himself an elder rather than an apostle.

Eusebius, the great historian of the fourth century, also divided the New Testament books into accepted and disputed categories. In the former he listed the same ones as had Origen. He himself seemed to accept all those now included, and apparently he put them all into the fifty copies of the New Testament that Constantine ordered him to have made in 330. Later in the century the great Jerome also accepted the present twenty-seven books in his production of the Latin version of the Bible (the Vulgate).

The Official List of the Canon: The Councils of Carthage

At a local council in 393 at Hippo, where St. Augustine was bishop, the contents of the canon were probably spelled out officially as our current twenty-seven books for the first time. Though the record of that decision has not been preserved, it was repeated at the Third Council of Carthage, a provincial council, in 397, with the proviso that no other books were to be used in the churches as authoritative Scripture. When the Sixth Council of Carthage (419) reaffirmed the earlier decision on the canon, it directed that the statement be sent to the bishop of Rome and other bishops. From that time on, there was little further debate on the subject in the West. The example of the West and the influence of several great theologians in the East finally settled the matter there also. Since the fifth century there has been no serious controversy over the contents of the New Testament canon. The major debates have swirled around the validity of the Old Testament apocrypha.[20]

Thus it can readily be seen that the story of the formation of the New Testament canon was a long one, not involving any hasty decision on the part of an ecclesiastical body. Basically, three steps were included in the process: divine inspiration, gradual human recognition and acceptance of the separate works, and official ratification or adoption of those books already universally accepted in the church.

NINE

Theological Debate
The Early Creeds

JUST as the New Testament canon developed in response to a need in the church, so did the creeds. In the days before the canon was formulated and when there were few copies of any of the New Testament books in circulation, believers required some standard to keep them in the path of truth. Moreover, they needed a standard by which to test heretical opinions. So very early, possibly near the end of the first century or beginning of the second, a rule of faith came into existence.

Assuming different forms in different churches, it generally taught that Christ, the Son of God, suffered under Pontius Pilate, was crucified and died, was buried, rose again, and ascended into Heaven—for the remission of sins. This rule of faith, which has come to be called the Apostles' Creed, reached its present form about 750. In the early church, candidates for baptism often were asked if they assented to the various clauses of this standard of faith.

Other creeds were formulated too, in an effort to settle controversies that tore the church into opposing factions. Some of the controversies had to do with the nature of Christ, some with the Holy Spirit, and one with the nature of man. These doctrinal quarrels of the fourth and following centuries were handled very differently from those of the second and third centuries. When

Christianity became a legal religion early in the fourth century, the emperor Constantine regarded himself as head of the Christian religion along with the other religions of state. Therefore when difficulties arose he called a church-wide or ecumenical council to deal with the matter and to formulate a statement (creed) of settlement. Other emperors followed the same practice. Although these struggles concerning Christ, the Holy Spirit, and man sometimes were going on concurrently, for the sake of clearer presentation they are separated here.

Controversies Concerning the Nature of Christ

Since there was no clear statement describing the nature of Christ among the early church fathers, there was ample opportunity for controversy on the subject. In the early fourth century two opposing parties arose in contention over the deity of Christ and His relationship to the Father.

The Arian Controversy: Nicea

About 318 Arius, an elder of Alexandria, found great difficulty in accepting the trinitarian nature of the Godhead. He was torn doctrinally between a desire to maintain the monotheist principle of Christianity on the one hand and a wish to preserve the Logos-Christ as an independent being on the other. Hence he began to teach that Christ was different in essence from the Father—that He was created by the Father and before that He did not exist. Athanasius, archdeacon of Alexandria, rose to meet the challenge, asserting that Christ and the Father were the same in essence and that the Son was eternal. His primary concern was that if Christ were a mere creature, faith in Him could not bring salvation to humanity. To be sure, as a man He could suffer the penalty for the sin of another human being, but that substitutionary suffering could not have value for all mankind unless the quality of infinity was linked to humanity in the God-man.

The controversy raged. The fact that a synod at Alexandria deposed Arius in 321 did not end the struggle. Arius was able to win over some of the leading churchmen of the East, and matters only grew worse. Finally Constantine felt obliged to step in and restore harmony. In 325 he called an ecumenical council at Nicea, in northwest Asia Minor. Over three hundred bishops and a number of lesser dignitaries gathered for the occasion. Ultimately the Athanasian party was able to carry the day, and the emperor himself was persuaded to throw his weight behind them. The creed drawn up declared that the Son was the same in essence with the Father, the only begotten of the Father, and very God of very God.

But the troubles of the Athanasian party had only begun. In the seesawing fortunes of subsequent years, as emperors and church personnel changed, Athanasius was banished no less than five times, with the consequent periodic restoration of the Arian party. Gradually, however, the situation improved and the orthodox party came to enjoy a definite majority in the empire. In the West, however, as barbarians penetrated the Roman provinces and set up separate states during the following century, they were gradually converted to the Arian point of view. Arianism reigned in the West until the conversion of the Franks and the rise of their orthodox empire, but that is a story to be told in the next chapter.

Controversy Concerning Christ's Humanity: Constantinople I

In the process of asserting the full deity of Christ, some theologians had done so at the expense of His humanity. They taught that a complete humanity could not be sinless and that the divine nature, while assuming a human body, took the place of the higher rational principle in man. Several synodical meetings condemned the idea of the defective humanity of Christ, and in 381 the ecumenical council of Constantinople finally asserted His true and full humanity.

The Nestorian Controversy: Ephesus

Then a third issue arose. If Christ was both fully divine and fully human, how were the two natures related in one person? Nestorius, bishop of Constantinople, was one of those who saw the two natures in loose mechanical conjunction. Neither nature shared in the properties of the other; so the divine did not have a part in the sufferings of the human nature of Christ. It takes little effort to discover that this is not merely an academic question. As Cyril of Alexandria pointed out, if Nestorius were right, a sinner would be redeemed by the sufferings of a mere man, and a mere man could accomplish no redemption. Moreover, though a man might pay a penalty for himself or a limited number of others, it took the linkage of the divine with the human in the God-man to make the payment of the penalty effective for an infinite number of human beings.

The Nestorian controversy led to the calling of a third ecumenical council, at Ephesus in 431. The council met and anathematized the teachings of Nestorius before the Nestorian party arrived. When the outlawed party appeared, it set up a rival council. The emperor finally decided against the Nestorians, and Nestorius entered a monastery. The result of the council was to demonstrate that the majority of bishops were in favor of the doctrines of Cyril (who argued for a true union of the two natures), but clarification of the matter was left to a later council. Though the error called Nestorianism is correctly represented above, Nestorius argued that he himself did not hold such views. Possibly he was the victim of smear tactics and a power struggle in the early church.

Following the Council of Ephesus there was a great deal of dissatisfaction on the part of many. As has been pointed out, the Council of Ephesus was not a true meeting of minds in an effort to resolve issues. Moreover, Eutyches, abbot of a monastery near Constantinople, in an effort to demonstrate the true unity of the person of Christ, began to teach that after the incarnation of Christ the two natures fused into one so that the one nature partook of the properties of the other. Distinctions between the two natures were obliterated. His arguments heightened the controversy considerably.

Again it should be pointed out that this is not a mere academic issue. Complete confusion reigns if Eutyches was right. Two examples will make the point. Omniscience is an attribute of deity only; according to the flesh Christ grew in wisdom and stature and favor with God and men. Omnipresence is an attribute of deity only; one of the important characteristics of a human body is that it is confined to a specific locality. If Christ is already physically omnipresent, how can He come a second time from heaven?

One Person, Two Natures: Chalcedon and Constantinople

At length a new general council was called at Chalcedon in 451. Its decision was that Christ was both truly God and truly man, and that the two natures were united in one Person without confusion, change, division, or separation.

Like the other councils discussed above, the Council of Chalcedon did not bring final settlement. In Palestine, Egypt, and Syria, groups arose to perpetuate the teachings of Cyril and Eutyches. They held out strongly for one nature in Christ. Ultimately they were able to force a fifth ecumenical council, the second at Constantinople, in 553, which ratified the Chalcedonian creed but made changes that tended to favor the Eutychians.

After the second Constantinopolitan Council, another conflict arose over the person of Christ and concerned the issue of whether Christ had only one will. The supporters of this view held that if Christ had two wills, He would have sinned, because certainly the human will would have succumbed to temptation. Ultimately a council, the third at Constantinople, met in 681 to deal with this issue. The decision was to ratify the Chalcedonian Creed with the addition that Christ had two wills, the human and divine, the human will being subject to the divine.

While these great ecumenical councils did not settle for all time discussion concerning the nature of the person of Christ, they did set forth the chief elements that have characterized an orthodox Christology down through the ages: His true and full deity, His true and full humanity, and the true union of the two natures in one person, without fusion or confusion.

Controversies Concerning the Holy Spirit

Reference has already been made to Montanist and Monarchian perversions of the doctrine of the Holy Spirit. And in connection with the Council of Nicea the name Arius has surfaced. He requires further attention here, however. Not only did Arius hold that Christ was different in essence from the Father and a creature of the Father; he also taught that the Holy Spirit was different in essence. In fact he seems to have believed that the Holy Spirit was the creature of a creature, that is, of Christ. Being particularly concerned with the nature of the person of Christ, the Nicene Council did not make detailed pronouncement about the Holy Spirit. It merely affirmed, "we believe also in one Holy Spirit."

But after the Nicene Council, further attacks of the Arian sort (known as Macedonianism because espoused by Macedonius) on the deity of the Holy Spirit produced an array of orthodox literature. Thus the ground was prepared for the First Council of Constantinople in 381, which formulated a creed with phrases asserting that the Holy Spirit was to be worshiped and glorified as was the Father, that He proceeded from the Father, and that He was responsible for revelation. In succeeding decades the doctrine of His deity was further defined; and in 451 the Council of Chalcedon made the declarations of the First Council of Constantinople more explicit.

Controversy Concerning Humanity

The controversy concerning the nature of humankind was the only one that took place in the West; all the rest took place in the East. Chief protagonists in the struggle were St. Augustine, bishop of Hippo in North Africa, and Pelagius, a British or Irish monk who ultimately found his way to North Africa. These men formed their views independently, not in reaction to one another.

Pelagianism

Soon after arriving at Carthage, Pelagius clashed head on with the prevailing theological viewpoint; and the controversy spread rapidly to other provinces.

Pelagius taught that Adam's sin affected only Adam; mankind, he said, was still born on the same plane as Adam. There was, therefore, no such thing as original sin. Sins of individuals in history involved acts of the will and were due to the bad example of Adam and society since Adam's time. God's grace was especially an enlightenment of mankind's reason, enabling persons to see and do the will of God. Humans could do right without such aid; in fact, it was possible for them to lead a sinless life. Divine grace sought only to assist man, who chooses and acts in complete independence. Physical death had nothing to do with sin but was a natural feature or concomitant of the human organism.

Pelagianism was not a new teaching but merely a systematization of some of the views of the popular Catholicism of the day, and it is not exactly clear how much of the Pelagian position Pelagius himself subscribed to. Investigation has shown that he was a man of personal piety and that he wanted to rely on Christ for forgiveness of sins.

Augustinianism

Augustine, on the other hand, held to the unity of the race—that all had sinned in Adam. So men sinned because they were sinners and were so totally corrupt in their natures that they were unable to do good works that could achieve salvation. He viewed faith to believe as a gift from God. God elected some unto salvation; He simply passed by the nonelect. On occasion Augustine did, however, refer to some as predestined by God to everlasting damnation. He also spoke of the divine gift of perseverance in faith; so salvation was for him a work of God from start to finish. Unfortunately, Augustine confused justification and sanctification; so justification was for him a process rather than a single act of God as taught in Paul's great epistle to the Romans.[21]

The early creeds: from the days before the canon, ... when few copies of any New Testament books were in circulation, when believers required some standard to keep them in the path of truth.

Settlement

Pelagius experienced considerable opposition almost as soon as he arrived in North Africa. He was condemned by a Carthaginian synod in 412, by Pope Innocent I in 416, by a general council of African churches in 418, and finally by the ecumenical council at Ephesus in 431.

But this did not mean the triumph of Augustinianism. Augustine was out of step with the church of his day. He stressed too much the inner Christian life and too little the external ceremonies. He denied that the

Eucharist had any sin-atoning power apart from the faith of the partaker. Although he advocated asceticism, he denied that it had any value apart from transformation of life into Christlikeness. He opposed the predominant sacramental method of achieving salvation. Unfortunately, his own statements about the value of baptism and his confusion between justification and sanctification contributed to the weakening of his legacy. So although Pelagianism was condemned, a sort of semi-Pelagianism was to win out—a system in which grace and human works were to join in achieving salvation, within the framework of the church and the sacramental system.

The years during which the first six great ecumenical councils met (325-681) were turbulent ones. They were years during which the church was torn apart by theological controversy—controversy that produced great statements of faith. They were also years when the barbarians were chipping away at the borders of the Roman Empire, conquering the whole western portion of it. And they were years when the heirarchical church was developing its doctrine and organizational machinery. Let us now take a quick look at the rise and decline of the Roman church during the Middle Ages.

PART III

♦

The Church in the Middle Ages

TEN

Early Developments in the Middle Ages

THE Roman Catholic and Eastern Orthodox churches as they existed at the end of the Middle Ages and as they appear in the twentieth century are products of historical evolution. Though apologists for Roman Catholicism have been particularly adept at finding "biblical" precedents for new dogmas and organizational developments they have propounded, those with a less biased approach to history have not always been similarly convinced.

Ignatius

In the New Testament the office of bishop is placed alongside those of the elder and deacon—whether equatable with that of elder it is not our purpose now to discuss. With Ignatius (about 110) arose an emphasis on obedience to the bishop.[1] How many of the exhortations in his writings are genuine is debated; some are thought to be interpolations by later writers trying to bolster their points of view. In any case his heavy stress on obedience to bishops seems to be an indication that such subordination did not then exist.

Moreover, there is no hint that by *bishop* Ignatius meant anything more than an overseer or pastor of a single congregation. He nowhere exhorted presbyters (elders) to obey bishops. Furthermore, he urged congregations on some occasions to obey presbyters and on others to obey deacons. Of paramount importance is the fact that in his writings he urged obedience to bishops to help prevent churches from being doctrinally torn apart—not to facilitate their normal functions.

Irenaeus

By the end of the second century Irenaeus was asserting the unity of the church (a spiritual unity, not organic) by virtue of the headship of Christ and community of belief as handed down through a succession of elders and bishops. Thereafter a tendency arose to transform the spiritual unity into an organic unity. Irenaeus also taught that the Roman church had been established by Peter and Paul and that they had appointed successors.

Moreover, in speaking of the church at Rome, Irenaeus categorically declared, "For with this church, because of its position of leadership and authority, must needs agree every church, that is, the faithful everywhere; for in her the apostolic tradition has always been preserved by the faithful from all parts" (*Against Heresies*, III. 1). During following decades the distinction between presbyters and bishops became firmly established, and bishops with authority over the several individual churches of a large city became commonly accepted. A community of belief was also developing. Polemicists frequently appealed to a body of true doctrine handed down by apostolic succession in an effort to defeat heretics. Such was the approach of Tertullian in his *On the Prescription Against Heretics* (XX, XXI).

Cyprian

By the middle of the third century the influential Cyprian, bishop of Carthage, taught that the universal church (outside of which there was no salvation) was ruled by bishops who were the successors of the apostles. Apostolic authority, he held, was first given to Peter. So the church at Rome became predominant because Peter was believed to have founded it. Moreover, Cyprian asserted the priestly function of the clergy. Cyprian's *On the Unity of the Catholic Church* incorporates much of his thinking on the nature and government of the church.

The Rise of Rome

By the time Christianity became a tolerated religion during Constantine's day (about A.D. 325), the concepts of the priestly function of the clergy, apostolic succession, the ruling bishop, and the recognition of the Roman bishop as first among equals were established. In 325 at the Council of Nicea (Canon 6), the bishops of Alexandria, Antioch, and Rome were given authority over divisions of the empire in which they were located. Of course this did not provide a niche for Constantinople, which was to be dedicated as the new capital of the Roman Empire in a "ribbon-cutting ceremony" on May 11, 330. In an effort to rectify the situation and give a place of importance to the bishop of Constantinople, the First Council of Constantinople in 381 declared in Canon 3: "The Bishop of Constantinople shall have the primacy of honour after the Bishop of Rome, because Constantinople is new Rome."[2] Obviously this statement undercut the position of the sees of Alexandria and Antioch but left the primacy with Rome.

When the Fourth Ecumenical Council met at Chalcedon in 451, it sought to elevate the position of Constantinople, declaring in Canon 28 that New Rome was to have "equal privileges" with "the elder royal Rome." But on May 22, 452, Pope Leo I of Rome wrote to officials in the East to annul Canon 28 of Chalcedon, declaring that the decrees of the Council of Nicea should take precedence. Of course that First Ecumenical Council met before Constantinople was in the picture. It was to Leo's advantage to remove the official competition of Constantinople; the competition posed by Antioch and Alexandria was not so formidable. As a matter of fact, Rome had been claiming primacy over them all along. It remained for the Roman bishop to transform his primacy into supremacy.

> *By about A.D. 325, the concepts of the priestly function of the clergy, apostolic succession, the ruling bishop, and . . . the Roman bishop as first among equals were established.*

There were several reasons why Rome could effectively compete against the others in her struggle for supremacy. *First, she claimed Petrine foundation* (actually a double apostolic foundation—Paul and Peter). Peter was chief of the apostles and the one, according to

Rome, on whom the church was founded. And the dogma of apostolic succession, though it recognized that other bishops could trace their authority to other apostles, would grant prominence to Peter's successors. *Second, the bishop of Rome was superior in the West,* while bishops of Constantinople, Antioch, and Alexandria competed for supremacy within a relatively small area in the East. After Antioch and Alexandria fell to the Muslims in the seventh century, the only competition Rome faced came from Constantinople.

Third, after the move of the capital from Rome to Constantinople in 330, political power in the West gradually declined. With the barbarian invasions of the fifth century and the chaos that ensued, the bishop of Rome became the most powerful figure there. At times he represented the only living institution, and the church took on civil functions.

In Constantinople, on the other hand, the continuing Roman Empire maintained itself through varying fortunes until 1453. There the bishop (patriarch) found himself subservient to the emperor and therefore less capable of asserting himself. In this connection it should be pointed out that when the power of the imperial government was weak, it was sometimes advantageous to the emperor to recognize the pretensions of Rome, in which case the bishop of Rome held virtual authority over the bishop of Constantinople.

Finally, the church in the West was not constantly torn apart by doctrinal controversy as was the church in the East. And in the midst of the controversies that did arise, the church at Rome always proved to be orthodox. So Rome was in a much stronger position to develop her program and extend her influence than were churches of the East.

Advancing the Cause of the Papacy

In discussing the period of the beginnings of the Roman church (prior to the pivotal pontificate of Gregory I in 590), several important persons and developments should be mentioned. The formation of the canon and creeds has already been described, as has been the rise of errors and their effect on the development of Roman Catholic doctrine and practice. We have also noted the contributions of the church Fathers, especially those of Augustine, the great theologian, and Jerome, the translator of the Vulgate. But a few others require comment at this point.

Bishop Leo I, 440-461

The first of these is Leo I, bishop of Rome 440-461. He did much to advance the cause of the papacy. Taking advantage of disorder resulting from the Vandal conquest of the province of Africa, he managed to secure the recognition of his authority by the church there. He interfered in the affairs of the church in Gaul to the advantage of papal power, and he asserted his authority in Illyricum (Yugoslavia) and Spain. By means of his statesmanship he saved Rome from being sacked by Attila the Hun in 452 and from mass murder of the populace by Genseric (or Gaiseric) the Vandal in 455; in the process, he added much to his prestige. And he obtained from the emperor Valentinian III the declaration that bishops of Gaul and other Western provinces were to be subservient to the pope of Rome and that governors of provinces were to compel bishops to go to Rome when summoned by the pope.

Leo energetically enforced uniformity in church government and doctrine, both in the area around Rome and extensively in the western part of the Empire. This he did especially on the assertion that as successors to the apostle Peter, the bishops of Rome possessed authority over all other bishops. He was a vigorous opponent of heresy, and his sermons (96 extant) evidence a care for the spiritual needs of his congregations. The *Tome of Leo* was a statement to the bishop of Constantinople (449) on the two natures of Christ that greatly influenced the phraseology of the Council of Chalcedon in 451—a statement that constitutes the orthodox statement on Christology for all Christendom.

Bishop Gelasius, 492-496

Gelasius (bishop of Rome 492-496) instituted the claim of moral superintendence over political rulers on the part of the pope. While he recognized that there were two spheres of rule, the spiritual and the temporal, he claimed that the church must give account to God for the deeds of kings, and so the king must submit to the church in spiritual matters. This claim influenced much of medieval political doctrine. He was the first bishop of Rome to receive the title "Vicar of Christ," granted at the Roman synod of 495.

The Conversion of Clovis, 496

Of particular importance to the advance of the papacy was the conversion of Clovis, a Frankish chieftain, in 496. Soon afterward, three thousand of his followers (probably the standing army of Frankland) were baptized into the Roman church. The significance of Clovis's conversion can hardly be overestimated. It was momentous *politically* because it won for Clovis the support of the Roman Catholics in the West, where he was the only orthodox Roman Catholic prince. All the rest were Arian.[3] And it gave him an excuse to attack and defeat adjacent Arian Goths. Ultimately, he was able to conquer over half of modern France. Out of this beginning the empire of Charlemagne later emerged. Clovis's conversion was also significant *religiously* because it meant that orthodox Christianity would win out in the West. Moreover, Frankish kings would protect or aid popes on various occasions in the future and would contribute to the establishment of the institutional church as it has become known in the medieval and modern worlds.

Furthermore, his conversion was important *culturally* because the medieval church was to a large degree the carrier of culture. The Roman Catholic church helped to preserve and modify the classical heritage that has been passed on to Europe and the Americas, and to a lesser degree to the entire world. The services of the church were conducted in Latin. The educators and writers of the Middle Ages were Latin churchmen. The texts taught in the schools were in Latin and were Greco-Roman in content. Fortunately for the papacy, the conversion of Clovis was supplemented by the decision of Recared, the Visigothic king of Spain, to abandon Arianism and become a Roman Catholic in 586.[4] Henceforth orthodox Christianity maintained a foothold on the Iberian peninsula even after the Muslim conquest in 711-718.

As a direct or indirect result of the conversion of Clovis and Recared, Roman Catholicism ultimately was to become the virtually uncontested faith in most of the West and was to penetrate effectively elsewhere. All of Western Europe was to be organized into dioceses and parishes ruled over by the pope and the princes of the church. The totality of the populace was born into the

Roman Catholic church, was baptized into the church, was married by the church, lived under the ministrations of the church, and was buried by the church. Throughout the Middle Ages Western Europe never knew anything else.

And as is true of any monopolistic power, conditions grew lax within the institutional church because of lack of competition to keep the church vibrant and effective. The form of religious establishment characteristic of mother countries was passed on to colonies with the advent of the modern era. Thus all of Latin America, the Philippines, and segments of Africa became Roman Catholic.

ELEVEN

Gregory the Great and His Successors

Seventh- and Eighth-Century Developments

Gregory the Great

GREGORY I, the Great (540-604),[5] was one of the greatest leaders that the Roman church has ever had. Coming on the scene at the time of widespread political confusion with its consequent effects on the life and organization of the church, he became a stabilizing political influence and was largely responsible for the creation of the medieval papacy. Born into a noble, wealthy, and devout family, Gregory was for a while the prefect of Rome, the highest civil administrator in the city. This experience would later be invaluable to him. Gregory early turned to the monastic life as a way to glorify God, and he spent his inherited fortune to found seven monasteries. Pope Pelagius II called him back into public life, and from 579 to 586 he represented the Roman bishop at Constantinople. Elected bishop of Rome in 590, he strongly resisted the appointment but finally became reconciled to the calling. He much preferred the monastic life.

With the decline of imperial power in Italy, Gregory found himself raising an army to fight the Lombards, appointing commanders, conducting a war effort, caring for thousands of refugees, and concluding a peace arrangement with the Lombards in 592-93. After the war was over, he did much to meet the needs of the poor in Rome and elsewhere. He became the real ruler of Rome and the virtual civil ruler of Italy in the last years of the sixth century. His administrative responsibility in Italy was important in the establishment of the Papal States. Gregory's great achievement was to organize the papal government as an elaborate, smoothly functioning machine in a period when society in Italy and the West in general was falling irretrievably into decay. Significantly, he was spurred on in his work by the conviction that the end of the world was imminent.

Gregory's Importance

For many reasons Gregory was one of the most important popes in the history of Roman Catholicism. *First,* as noted above, *he transformed the bishopric of Rome into a papal system that endured through the Middle Ages.* His pontificate did much to establish the idea that the papacy was the supreme authority in the church. *Second, he introduced changes into the liturgy and sought the stand-ardization of it.* Although Gregory was not responsible for the type of chant that bears his name, he did much to promulgate its use in worship services and established schools for the training of singers.

Third, from a theological standpoint, his system served as something of a converging point for lines of thought found in the councils and in the Fathers. Though Gregory's theology was not original, he is important for his definition of dogma and his incorporation of elements of the popular piety of his day into the official teachings of the Roman Catholic church. He put tradition on an equal basis with Scripture in determining dogma.

Though he accepted the Augustinian view of original sin, he held that through baptism sin was forgiven and faith implanted so that an individual might work the works of God. For sins committed subsequently penance was required. He expanded the concept of purgatory and converted the Eucharist from a sacrament into a sacrifice for redemption, having value for the living and the dead. He officially approved the invocation of saints and martyrs and the use of relics and amulets to reduce temporal punishments. His view of Christ and the Trinity followed the decisions of the ecumenical councils.

> *Gregory I ... was largely responsible for the creation of the medieval papacy.*

Fourth, he was important for his writings. The *Moralia*, a commentary on Job, provided one of the patterns for the allegorical interpretation of Scripture common during the Middle Ages. His superstitious nature and that of the age is well displayed in his *Dialogues*, which concerns the lives and miracles of pious Fathers in Italy. And his *Pastoral Rule* was a practical work that instructed the bishop in the care of his flock and became the standard manual for the conduct of bishops. It was translated into Greek in his lifetime and into Anglo-Saxon by King Alfred the Great three hundred years later.

Gregory was a good preacher too, as evidenced by his forty sermons that have survived. They indicate a real concern for the spiritual and material needs of Christians in Rome. Gregory's writings have earned for him a place among the four great Latin doctors of the Western church: Ambrose, Augustine, Jerome, Gregory. *Fifth, Gregory promoted asceticism,* especially as he enforced the celibacy of the clergy and as he restored monastic[6] discipline. The first pope to be monk, he was a great propagator of monasticism.

Last, Gregory possessed great missionary zeal. He sent forty monks to England in 596 under the leadership of Augustine (not the famous bishop of Hippo, who died in 430). Their success was pronounced, especially in the area of Canterbury, which became the religious capital of England and the seat of the archbishop.

Gregory's Successors

During the seventh century Gregory's successors hardly maintained the high place he had earned for them. His first five successors were undistinguished and lasted for only twenty-one years. Rome suffered famine, plague, and natural disasters during their reigns. During most of the rest of the century there was a running battle between the emperors and the popes over matters of doctrine and administration. The emperor arrested Martin I (649-53), smuggled him out of Rome, subjected him to cruel treatment and condemned him to death. But later the emperor commuted Martin's sentence to banishment, and he died in the Crimea. Though the popes of the period were generally orthodox, Honorius I was anathematized by the Third Council of Constantinople in 681. The century was also a period when Roman monks in Britain were engaged in a struggle for supremacy with Irish monks who had preceded them there.

Missionary Activity in Britain and Ireland

St. Patrick

For a long time Irish missionary activity had been extensive in Britain and Ireland. St. Patrick evangelized Ireland during the fifth century; various bits of information lead to the conclusion that his ministry occurred during the first half of the century.[7] Many legends have sprung up around his name, and later biographies of him have been concocted; the legends and traditions must be stripped away.

What is clear from his autobiographical *Confession* and other meager information is that Patrick was born in Britain, probably in the southwestern part. Though of British parentage, he was not English, for his Britain was pre-Anglo-Saxon Britain. He was carried off by pirates at the age of sixteen and forced to work as a slave in Ireland. After six years there, during which time he had a conversion experience, he escaped and returned to Britain and his family.

Subsequently he had a night vision in which he received a call to evangelize Ireland. Apparently he received his training in Britain, rather than on the Continent, as many claim, and subsequently became the greatest single force in the Christianization of Ireland. Evidently Patrick was biblical and evangelical in his preaching and his ministry, and the churches he founded were independent of Rome. So it may be concluded that he was neither Irish nor Roman Catholic. As bishop of Ireland he ranged far and wide over the island, was instrumental in the conversion of thousands, established them in churches and ordained clergy to serve them.

Irish Monasticism

On the foundation that Patrick laid, Finnian of Clonard[8] built the superstructure of Irish monasticism early in the sixth century. Soon monasteries were founded all over Ireland. As they rose in number and prestige, the ecclesiastical organization that Patrick had established withered away. By the end of the sixth century the Irish church had become a church of monks; the bishop no longer had an administrative function. From the very beginning Irish monks valued literacy and emphasized missionary activity. But it is not always clear whether evangelistic impulse or self-imposed penitential exile was the motivation for their going to pagan lands (de Paor, 52).

Learned Irish monks, filled with missionary zeal, ranged far and wide across Europe during the sixth and seventh centuries. St. Columba (c. 597), who received his training at Clonard, established the famous monastery on the island of Iona, off the west coast of Scotland, and became the apostle to Scotland. He was successful in converting Brude, king of the Picts; and in 574, Aidan, the new king of the Scots, came to Iona to receive Columba's official blessing. The monastery at Iona continued for two hundred years to send missionaries to all parts of the British Isles and Europe.

St. Columbanus (c. 615) ministered on the Continent, establishing monasteries in Gaul, Switzerland, and northern Italy. Other Irish monks went north to the Shetlands, the Hebrides, the Orkneys, and Iceland; south into England and east onto the Continent—along the Rhine, into Hungary and Italy.

The Conflict Between Irish and Roman Christianity

A contest between free Irish Christianity and Roman Catholicism was inevitable. After a number of meetings between the Irish and Roman Catholics, King Oswy (Oswiu) of Northumbria (northeastern England) called a synod at Whitby in 663 to determine which group should be considered the official one. Roman Catholic spokesmen won him over, and Irish monks gradually withdrew northward. In 636 south Ireland had already submitted to the papacy, and in 697 north Ireland followed suit. Their home base within the fold of Roman Catholicism, the Irish lost much of their ability to establish new missions. But primitive British Christianity held out in the mountains of Wales and the highlands of Scotland and on offshore islands for a long time.

Five Pillars of Islam

Acceptance of the Creed:
*"There is no God but Allah,
and Mohammed is his prophet."*

Prayer five times a day toward Mecca

Pilgrimage to Mecca

Giving alms

Fasting during Ramadan

The Challenge of Islam

Meanwhile, far to the east a new and much greater threat was rising to challenge medieval Christianity. In

622 Mohammed made his famous move or flight *(Hegira)* from Mecca to Medina, and thereafter began the successful period of his preaching. Constructing a theology that utilized elements of Judaism, Christianity, and Arabian heathenism, and infusing a fanatical zeal that brooked no opposition, he produced a steam roller movement that soon flattened the Middle East, North Africa, and part of Europe. In fact, Islam[9] has gained adherents until today it can claim about one-fifth of the world's population.

Although it is not the purpose of the present study to engage in theological discussion, Islam is so important in world history and culture that at least the five pillars that characterize the lifestyle of the faithful should be noted: (1) accepting the creed, "There is no God but Allah, and Mohammed is his prophet"; (2) praying five times a day toward Mecca; (3) making a pilgrimage to Mecca at least once during one's lifetime; (4) giving alms for pious and charitable purposes; (5) fasting from sunrise to sunset throughout the sacred month of Ramadan. Often holy war *(jihad)* is listed as a sixth pillar.

Islam's Early Spread

Several factors contributed to the rapid spread of Islam.

(1) A positive, fanatical, monotheistic program that promised booty, positions of leadership, and salvation to those who would engage in world conquest was certainly a powerful incentive in obtaining followers.

(2) The Roman Empire was rapidly decaying from within while it exhausted its resources and those of the Persian Empire as well in a

grueling fight almost to the death. This continuing struggle took place during the reign of the emperor Heraclius (610-641), the very time when the Muslim movement began. Thus, a power vacuum was created at the eastern end of the Mediterranean. Neither the Persians nor the Byzantines[10] were any match for the fanatical Arabs.

(3) The Byzantines alienated many of their provincials by extracting high taxes to finance the Persian wars and excommunicating them for heretical religious views.

(4) Many Semitic people of the Byzantine provinces actually had more in common with the Semitic Arab invaders than they did with their Byzantine (Greek) overlords.

(5) The Muslims were not mere despoilers like the Huns. Often they replaced only the top bureaucrats; most of the population remained relatively undisturbed. Moreover, in the early days of the movement only non-Muslims paid taxes. Therefore, it was to the advantage of the Muslims to maintain a prosperous economy in areas they conquered.

(6) Often Islam had superior generals.

(7) The development of image worship in the Catholic church made the Christianity of the day look polytheistic to both the Muslims and many Catholics. Therefore, Islam with its strict monotheistic emphasis seemed to be superior.

Before his death in 632, Mohammed had won much of western Arabia. His successor, Abu Bakr (632-

634), rapidly conquered the rest of the peninsula and at the same time sent volunteers into Syria and Persia. Omar (634-644) began systematic conquest of the Roman provinces. In 635 he took Damascus and in 638 conquered Jerusalem. Alexandria and most of Egypt surrendered in 640, and

> *Islam today can claim about one-fifth of the world's population.*

about the same time most of the Persian Empire capitulated. Conquests continued rapidly under successive leaders. Between 685 and 705 the conquest of North Africa was completed, including the conversion of the Moors. In 711 the Muslims invaded Spain and in seven years reached the borders of France. On they went. It seemed as if all Europe were doomed. Meanwhile, the advance continued into India.

Eighth-Century Papal Successes and Problems

At this point some abler popes came to the chair of St. Peter. And their efforts coincided with the continuing rise of the Frankish Kingdom and the efforts of great missionaries.

Pope Gregory II

The pontificate of Gregory II (715-731) was a time of especially great advance. Just before his reign, Willibrord, a native of York in England, succeeded in planting the standards of the Roman church among the pagan peoples of Holland and Denmark.

Meanwhile Boniface (from Devonshire, England) became the great missionary of central Europe and is often called "the apostle to Germany." He organized the church of Bavaria and later became archbishop of Mainz. With the support of Gregory II and after the death of Charles Martel, the real ruler of the Franks, he succeeded in reforming the Frankish churches, abolishing heathen customs, improving the morals of the priests, and systematizing church organization. Boniface brought the Frankish bishops to full support of Rome. He presided at the coronation of Pepin when he became king of the Franks in 751.

Back in Rome, Gregory was having his troubles. Leo the Isaurian, emperor at the time, sought to rid himself of the pope by violence, because Gregory opposed Leo's taxation policies in Italy and his interference with the church's use of images (to be discussed later). Supported by the people of Rome and the Lombards in northern Italy, Gregory managed to die a natural death. He was also able to contain the expansionist moves of the Lombards in Italy.

The Venerable Bede

Contemporary with Gregory II lived one of England's best known sons, the Venerable Bede (c. 673-735), a monk who worked at the monasteries of Wearmouth and Jarrow in Northumbria. Though he wrote various biblical works (about forty in number), they are overshadowed by his *Ecclesiastical History of the English People.* This book provides much important detail concerning early English church history, and it earned for the author the title "Father of English history." His historical works did much to establish the practice of dating events from the Incarnation (B.C. and A.D.).[11]

Pope Gregory III

At the beginning of the rule of Gregory III (731-741), it looked as if Romanism were doomed in Western Europe. The Lombards had gotten out of hand and threatened to destroy the church in Italy. But the greater danger was posed by the Muslims, who were advancing steadily north into France. Charles Martel, not actual king of the Franks, but mayor of the palace, summoned enough force to defeat the Muslims near Tours in central France in 732. This victory threw the Moors back into Spain and made Charles the defender and leader of Western Christendom. Negotiations began during those years for an alliance between the Franks and the papacy. And the next half century was characterized by increasing cooperation between the king and the pope, the king often coming to the aid of the pope.

Pepin, King of the Franks, and the Rise of the Papal State

In fact, Pope Zacharias recognized Pepin, son of Charles Martel, as king of the Franks in 751. Then, when the Lombard king Aistulf threatened to take Rome and the properties of the church, Pope Stephen II appealed to Pepin for aid and for a safe conduct to the court of Pepin. The Frankish king responded favorably and Stephen became the first pope to cross the Alps and leave the country. On July 24, 754 he solemnly anointed Pepin and his wife and sons, confirming the legitimacy of their dynasty, and bestowed on them the title "Patricians of the Romans" as a token of their role as protectors of the Holy See. In two military campaigns (754, 756) Pepin then worsted Aistulf and forced him to give up territory which he presented in perpetuity to the

Roman church; thus the Papal State came into existence.[12] All this was a foreshadowing of the time when the pope would crown Charlemagne and create the Holy Roman Empire.

This strengthening of ties with the Franks resulted from the loosening of ties with the East. The empire was losing political power and territory and alienating the papacy with its stand on the use of images in the church. Gregory III was the last pope to seek approval of his election by the Byzantine governor at Ravenna in eastern Italy. Then, at the end of the reign of Pope Zacharias (741-752), the Lombards conquered remaining Byzantine holdings in eastern Italy and started to threaten the papacy. With the unwillingness and inability of the Byzantine government to come to the aid of the pope, and with the emperor seeking to interfere in the doctrine and practices of the Roman Church, the pope turned West—to the Frankish court—for support.

TWELVE

Church-State Alliance
The Church from 800 to 1073

The Holy Roman Empire

THE year 800 serves as a pivotal date in history. On Christmas day in Rome, Pope Leo III crowned Charlemagne "emperor of the Romans." Charlemagne seems to have interpreted this to mean that he was the leader of Western Christendom, the monarch of a new "Christian empire," rather than the inheritor of the old Roman imperial office. His son Louis the Pious and successive kings in the line made more of Roman imperial ideals. Hence there came into being the concept of a Holy Roman Empire. This empire was called Roman because it was to succeed the now defunct power of Rome in the West. It was called holy because it was to be supreme over Christendom.

This new arrangement constituted an alliance of sorts between the pope and the emperor, according to which each was to have dominion within his own sphere and each was to cooperate with the other and promote the interests of the other. But as a matter of fact, during succeeding generations popes and emperors engaged in periodic struggles to see who could dominate the other. Beyond the immediate significance, the concept of the Holy Roman Empire was to have some long-range effects on European history. For a thousand years one

European ruler or another tore up the countryside with his armies in an effort to establish himself as successor of the Caesars. Finally, Napoleon abolished the empire in 1806.

As a matter of fact, the Holy Roman Empire was virtually synonymous with Western Christendom. In this whole vast area the Roman Catholic church was supreme. Everyone born within the empire became a baptized member of the church and remained within the church throughout life. Even beyond the empire in England and Spain the Roman church was the recognized religious authority. The whole of society divided religiously into dioceses ruled by bishops continued to be the order of the day, even after the decline and breakup of the Holy Roman Empire itself. This arrangement was to continue until the Reformation in the sixteenth century, and in many places long after that, and helps to explain much of the history of modern Europe. Culturally the Holy Roman Empire involved a fusion of Gallo-Roman, Germanic, and Christian elements.

> *The Holy Roman Empire was virtually synonymous with Western Christendom, over which the Roman Catholic church was supreme.*

By inheritance and force of arms, Charlemagne won control of a vast chunk of Western Europe—it stretched from the Atlantic eastward to the Elbe and Danube rivers and from the North Sea to the Mediterranean and included much of Italy and a little of Spain.

In the process he maintained rather effective control of the pope and the Roman church. His capitularies, or laws, had to do with both church and secular affairs. Not only did he regulate the lives of the clergy, but he also directed that bishops and abbots should set up schools. This effort, along with establishment of his famous Palace School, gave rise to what is known as the Carolingian Renaissance. To help with this venture, Charlemagne turned to York in England to find the necessary scholars.

Breakdown of the Empire

Charlemagne's son Louis was not so capable as he, and his grandsons split the empire three ways in the Treaty of Verdun in 843. According to that arrangement, Charles took the area roughly encompassing that of modern France; Louis, modern Germany; and Lothair, a strip of territory in between extending from the lowlands into northern Italy.

Thereafter the process of political disintegration went forward rapidly. The territory of Lothair suffered encroachment by the other two descendants of Charlemagne. With the death of Charles III (the Fat) in 887, the Carolingian line came to an end in Germany; at the same time the Carolingian empire as any sort of unit also came to an end. After a time of confusion, Otto I was crowned king of the East Franks in 936 and introduced the Saxon line.

Carolingians continued to rule weakly in France until 987, when the line of Hugh Capet rose to the kingship. Henceforth the Holy Roman Empire was essentially a German entity, with a king elected by and checkmated by a number of powerful nobles. In reality, under feudalism it was divided into a host of small antagonistic principalities.

While political disintegration occurred internally in the empire, external attacks multiplied. During the ninth century Vikings terrorized the northwest and western parts of the empire, Muslims ravaged Sardinia and Corsica and the coasts of southern France and western Italy, and the Magyars (from Russia) raided the eastern borders of the Christian lands and settled down in the area now known as Hungary. Slavs and Bulgars also attacked in the eastern parts just prior to incursions of the Magyars.

Consequent Decline of the Papacy

The whole period from 800 to 1073 is included under this heading of Church—State Alliance. The papacy reached a high point of development when allied with Charlemagne, but it declined with the fortunes of his house and the political disintegration of Europe.

By the time of Pope John VIII (872-882), the Carolingian line was about to expire. Muslim pirates ranged all along the Italian coast and threatened Rome itself. Though the emperor tried to help John, he had little strength left. The pope himself was forced to raise a fleet and do battle with the Muslims to save the Italian coast. To keep them out of Rome, he had to agree to pay annual tribute.

During much of the period between 880 and 1000, Italy was in anarchy, and the papacy suffered accordingly. For instance, there were twelve popes between 882 and 904. Wealthy families sometimes bought their way into the papacy. Military and political forces were exerted on the choice and conduct of popes. The chair of St. Peter was occupied by some very unworthy individuals between 880 and 1060.

For example, near the end of the period Benedict IX was pope. His father paid bribes to get Benedict elected. Apparently in his late twenties at the time (rather than a boy of ten or twelve, as some traditions have alleged), he was violent and dissolute. Contemporary chroniclers accused him of all sorts of vice and crime, but we have no way of knowing whether the scandals were heightened in the telling. It is possible that some of them did not involve much more than an "immoderate taste for enjoyment."

Whether or not his enemies made him out to be much worse than the facts warranted, he was repeatedly driven from office, and he was the only pope to hold office for three separate periods. Near the end of his pontificate he was forced out of office and a new pope elected (Silvester III), but Benedict had not abdicated. Then he presumably resigned in favor of Gregory VI but later claimed not to have done so. Thus there were three popes in 1045 and 1046: Benedict IX, Silvester III, and Gregory VI.

But nothing is served by portraying the papacy at its worst. As a matter of fact, it is amazing that so many popes of the period were quite capable and that the church advanced considerably under such handicaps.

The Spread of the Church, 800-1073

Surprisingly, the boundaries of Christendom greatly increased between 800 and 1073. Before the middle of the ninth century an archbishopric was established at Hamburg, and around the same time Roman Catholicism claimed Bohemia and Moravia. Approximately a century later it was officially adopted in Poland. About 1000, Olaf I made it the faith of Norway; and shortly thereafter Norwegian missionaries won Iceland to Christianity. About the same time, Leif the Lucky evangelized Greenland, the Swedish King Olaf established Roman Catholicism as the faith of Sweden, and Canute the Great did much to Christianize Denmark. Concurrently, King Stephen I (St. Stephen) effectively established the church in Hungary.

Meanwhile Eastern Christians were evangelizing to the north of Constantinople. Cyril and Methodius were successful in Moravia and their disciples in Bulgaria during the ninth century; in the latter King Boris made it the official faith of the realm. Cyril was also culturally significant because he is credited with creating an alphabet in which Slavonic languages could be written; this was the basis of the alphabets in which almost all Slavonic languages are written to this day. During the tenth and eleventh centuries Russia was won over. Following the baptism of King Vladimir in 988 the Eastern Slavs as one body turned to Christianity—just as the Franks had at the baptism of Clovis.

From 800 to 1073, Christendom greatly expanded to include Bohemia, Morovia, Poland, Norway, Iceland, Greenland, Sweden, Denmark, Hungary, Bulgaria, and Russia.

Not only did the Roman church greatly extend her territory from 800 to 1073, she also greatly extended her power. With the political fragmentation of Europe, the pope often stood a better chance of bringing princes, particularly the lesser ones, to terms. As Christianity spread and with it the idea that salvation came only through membership in the church, the threat of excommunication was often enough to force rulers to capitulate. If it was not, the papacy could try interdict—withholding services of the church from the people of a whole area. In such cases the populace usually brought enough pressure on the king or noble to ensure a victory for the pope.

Factors Leading to Split of the Catholic and Orthodox Churches in 1054

Controversy over use of images
Controversy over procession of the Holy Spirit
Personality conflicts between Roman bishop and patriarch of Constantinople
Boundary disputes
Cultural differences
Differences in relation to political authority
Liturgical and social differences

The East—West Split in Christendom

One more development needs to be considered before going on to view the medieval papacy at his height: the split between the Eastern Orthodox and Roman Catholic churches. Several factors were responsible for the split. *First, the two churches engaged in the iconoclastic controversy: the controversy over the use of images.* Leo the Isaurian, the Byzantine emperor, issued the first decree against their use in 726—in part to meet the

Muslim charge that Christianity was polytheistic. He was supported by the patriarch of Constantinople and the higher clergy but was opposed by many of the monks and the common people. Gregory II, at Rome, denounced Leo's edict—both because the problem hardly existed in the West and because Rome held that political power had no right to interfere in the affairs of the church.

The controversy produced a definite breach between Rome and Constantinople. Gregory III was the last pope to seek confirmation of his election from Constantinople, and in 781 the popes ceased mentioning the name of the emperor in dating their documents. Their ties to the East cut, the popes henceforth turned to the Franks for aid; thus the Franco-papal alliance was an important result of the iconoclastic controversy. Not until 843 did a church council in the East finally settle the matter in favor of the use of images (but only pictures, not statues); by that time the damage to unity had been done.

Second, there was the conflict over the procession of the Holy Spirit, known as the Filioque Controversy. The East taught that the Holy Spirit proceeded from the Father alone; the West, believing that such a view did not give proper recognition to the Son, asserted that He proceeded from the Father and the Son (*Filioque* means *and the son*).

Third, the patriarch of Constantinople and the pope at Rome were unwilling to be subservient to each other.

Fourth, there was no sharp definition of the boundaries between territories to be ruled by Rome and Constantinople, and frequent struggles arose over administration of border areas.

Fifth, basic differences in cultural background and

influence between East and West hindered understanding and cooperation.

Sixth, in the East the church was subservient to the emperor; the church in the West insisted on independence from the state and demanded the church's right of moral superintendence over rulers of state.

Seventh, there were numerous liturgical differences between the two churches (e.g., whether leavened or unleavened bread was to be used in the Eucharist), as well as a host of other minor variations (e.g., whether clergy were to be bearded or clean shaven or married or single). Debates continued between the two bodies: finally, in 1054, a Roman delegation laid the bull of excommunication on the altar of St. Sophia in Constantinople. Of course the Greek patriarch retaliated. Thus the schism was complete.

THIRTEEN

The Medieval Papacy at Its Height
The Church from 1073 to 1305

Pope Gregory VII (Hildebrand)

A NEW chapter in papal history began in 1073, when Hildebrand assumed the chair of St. Peter under the name of Gregory VII. His program and philosophy were basic to the achievement of supremacy in Christendom attained by the popes of the thirteenth century. For some twenty years before he became pope, Hildebrand was a power behind the papal throne. During that time Nicholas II (1038-61), with Hildebrand's support, succeeded in reforming papal election procedure. Formerly popes were selected by the seven deacons of Rome, the aristocratic faction of the populace, and German emperors. Henceforth they were to be elected by the college of cardinals, a procedure that is still in effect. However, Hildebrand himself was acclaimed by the crowd at the funeral of Alexander II and carried to St. Peter's in chains and crowned pope. It took time to establish general acceptance of the new procedure.

As pontiff, Gregory held to the supremacy of the pope within the church and over temporal rulers. He carried on an unrelenting program to reduce all bishops, abbots, and clergy to absolute subjection to the papacy and was quite successful. He saw three particular abuses that needed correcting in order to root out moral abuses and free the church from lay control: the marriage of the clergy (or clerical concubinage), simony, and investiture by secular princes. Gregory issued a ban on clerical marriage in 1074 and thereby prevented the clergy from becoming a hereditary caste; instead they were to become loyal to the pope and the church. He had to fight hard, especially in France and Germany, to win this battle. On simony (the buying or selling of church offices) he made unrelenting warfare and was reasonably successful. The problem of lay investiture was another story.

Hildebrand's Reforms

Papal election procedure
Church administrative structure
Marriage of clergy
Buying and selling of church offices (simony)
Investiture of clerics by secular princes

The Investiture Controversy

When the bishop or abbot or other high church official was appointed, he was supposed to receive investiture with spiritual authority by his ecclesiastical superior and investiture with temporal authority by the secular lord of the area where he was to serve. For centuries the political leaders of Europe had been accustomed to appointing and/or investing with spiritual and secular authority the higher clergy of their realms. Understandably, such a practice often did not result in appointments of clerical leaders who were either spiritually sensitive or loyal to the church. The reforming efforts of Gregory VII could only touch off a fight.

His great test of strength arose over the choice of the archbishop of Milan. Gregory's opponent was Henry IV, emperor of the Holy Roman Empire; both emperor and pope had a candidate for the office. Henry was at a disadvantage because he was also engaged in an internal power struggle with some of the Saxon nobles. Gregory threatened excommunication if Henry IV did not comply; Henry answered by calling a synod of German bishops at Worms (1076), which deposed the pope. Gregory excommunicated Henry and absolved his subjects of allegiance to him. The German nobles then demanded that Henry achieve reconciliation with Gregory within a year or forfeit his throne. So Henry was forced to make his peace with Gregory in the famous meeting at Canossa. But in the ensuing years Henry won the last round; he marched on Rome and set up a pope of his own choice, and Gregory died in exile. But all was not lost; the views for which Gregory fought were ultimately to prevail.

In the days of Henry's son Henry V, the papacy ultimately won the investiture struggle. At Worms in 1122 a concordat was drawn up according to which the emperor consented to permit the church to elect bishops and abbots and invest them with spiritual power. Although elections were to be held in the presence of the king, he could not use simony or violence. Elected officials of the church were to receive the symbol of temporal authority from the king and to pledge allegiance to the temporal power.

The Crusades

The First Crusade, 1095-1099

In part, the call for a crusade must be viewed as connected with the investiture struggle. At the Council of Clermont in 1095, in the midst of the contest with Henry IV, Urban II proclaimed a Crusade. This was evidently a show of force in his struggle with the emperor. By this means Rome could direct the energies of Europe in a way that would bring her great advantages.

Although many went on the Crusades for economic reasons, or for adventure, or for other lesser reasons, the primary and official motive of the Crusades was religious. In fact Urban promised remission of sins to those who marched under the banner of the cross. The event that sparked the Crusades was the advance of the Seljuk Turks in the East and the call for help from the Byzantine emperor Alexis I. Tales of the sufferings pilgrims endured at the hands of the Turks in the Holy Land provided emotional appeal for many to engage in holy war. And, in fact, Urban's professed goal was to deliver the shrines of the Holy Land from Muslim control and return them to Christian supervision.

In response to Urban's call a great host gathered from Western Europe, especially from France, the

> *Although many went on the Crusades for economic reasons, or for adventure, or for other lesser reasons, the primary and official motive of the Crusades was religious.*

Lowlands, and Italy, and finally took Jerusalem in 1099. The Crusaders then set up the kingdom of Jerusalem and a series of Crusader states along the coast of Syria and Palestine. Estimates of the number participating in this Crusade vary greatly. About 40,000 arrived at Nicaea (northwestern Turkey) in June of 1097; of these less than 5,000 were nobles and knights. The rest were wives, sisters, relatives, friends, retainers, an assortment of pilgrims, and even prostitutes.

Bernard and the Second Crusade, 1147

The burden of arousing enthusiasm for the Second Crusade (1147) fell on the famous Bernard of Clairvaux. Europeans were concerned with meeting the Muslim threat to the northern borders of the kingdom of Jerusalem. The king of France and the emperor of the Holy Roman Empire led the Crusade, but it was completely unsuccessful, leaving Jerusalem in greater danger than before. The crusading movement ground to a standstill until 1187, when Saladin captured Jerusalem and all Christendom was again aroused.

Third through Sixth Crusades, 1189-1229

The Third Crusade (1189-1192) is known as the Crusade of the Three Kings: Richard I of England, Philip II of France, and Frederick I of Germany. Frederick drowned on the way to Palestine; Philip stayed in Palestine for only a very short time, leaving Richard to carry on the struggle alone. Although he was unsuccessful in taking Jerusalem, he recovered territory along the coast of Palestine and won permission for pilgrims to enter the Holy City for a few years.

The Fourth Crusade began in 1202 under the leadership of Pope Innocent III. He urged the capture of Egypt as a base of operations against Palestine. When the army gathered, it found itself without sufficient funds to pay for shipping. In return for financial guarantees it agreed with Venice to recapture nearby Zara from the Hungarians. For the same reason, it subsequently decided to support the deposed Byzantine emperor in his bid to regain the throne of the empire. The attack on Byzantium was more fiercely opposed than the Crusaders had expected, however. The result was a prolonged struggle there, permanent sidetracking of the Crusade, the sacking of Constantinople and destruction of the power of the Eastern empire, and establishment of a Latin kingdom in its place. Innocent was able to have some indirect influence in this Latin kingdom and over the Eastern Orthodox church.

The last Crusade of any significance was the sixth, led by Frederick II of Germany in 1228-1229. By diplomacy he acquired for ten years Jerusalem, Bethlehem, Nazareth, and a corridor connecting Acre and Jerusalem.

The End and Effects of the Crusades

The Crusades ended in failure, with Jerusalem falling to the Egyptians in 1244 and remaining in Muslim hands until 1917, when the British General Allenby captured the Holy City from the Turks. Yet it must be said that while the Crusades lasted, the Roman church enjoyed wave after wave of popular enthusiasm in support of her causes. Moreover, while the church directed the energies of Europeans in fighting an external foe, she provided a safety valve that spared her a great deal of internal stress.

The effects of the Crusades were destined to be mainly political, social, and economic rather than religious. They contributed to the commercial revolution and its accompanying rise of the middle class, the demise of feudalism, and the decline of provincialism in Western Europe. It is hard to measure fully the impact on Western Europe of the travel of hundreds of thousands of people to strange lands where they discovered new foods, new modes of dress, and new ways of doing things. All this ferment also helped to pave the way for the coming of the Renaissance. And since profits from commerce usually do not flow in one direction, rising commercial activity also stimulated a new prosperity in Muslim lands, notably Egypt. Moreover, the Fourth Crusade helped to bring about the fall of the Byzantine Empire.

The Papacy at Its Height: Innocent III

Defeated kings of France, England,
Holy Roman Empire
Called Fourth Lateran Council
Effectively controlled the church bureaucracy

Pope Innocent III

Directing the affairs of the medieval papacy at the very height of her power was Innocent III (1198-1216). As has already been noted, he had some indirect influence over the Eastern church and empire during the Fourth Crusade. In Western Europe, he forced his will on France, England, and the Holy Roman Empire. He humiliated Philip II of France, forcing him to take back his divorced wife, who had appealed to the pope. Innocent did this by laying an interdict on the whole nation of France. Shortly thereafter he humbled King John of

England in a struggle over the appointment of a new archbishop of Canterbury. Again Innocent used the method of interdict, as well as inviting Philip of France to invade England if John refused to come to terms.[13] About the same time, Innocent interfered in the affairs of Germany, dictating the imperial succession there. Again he used a threat of French troops to accomplish his aim.

Last, Innocent called the Fourth Lateran Council (1215) to settle certain doctrinal matters. It decided that annual confession to a priest was mandatory for all laypersons. And it enunciated the dogma of transubstantiation, which means that the bread and wine become the actual body and blood of Christ upon pronouncement of the priest. The priest could then perform an actual sacrifice of Christ every time the mass was said. Moreover, the council gave official sanction to the seven sacraments and provided some definition of them.

Among the decisions of the council that the church would probably rather forget was one that Jews were ordered always to wear a distinctive dress and to stay in their ghettos. The comments here do not begin to describe adequately the power of Innocent. Over 6,000 of the pope's letters exist, showing his involvement in and control over endless aspects of church and society in Western Europe.

The Inquisition

One of the strengths of the medieval papacy in maintaining her power over the populace of Western Europe was the Inquisition. In the process of development for a couple of centuries, the medieval Inquisition came to its definitive formulation under Pope Gregory

IX (1227-1241). The reason for its implementation at that time was the decision of the Holy Roman Emperor Frederick II in 1232 to issue an edict assigning the apprehension of heretics to state officials. Gregory feared that Frederick would use this effort for political ends and also did not want to surrender the management of church affairs to the state. As a matter of fact, the Fourth Lateran Council of 1215 had spelled out aspects of the Inquisition and the church was about ready to proceed on its own anyway.

The Inquisition was designed to inquire into the spread of heresy and to call before its Tribunals Roman Catholics suspected of heresy in order to secure their repentance. The program was launched merely to keep the faithful in line, not to obtain the conversion of Jews and Muslims. The great purges against those peoples in Spain were inventions of the Spanish throne after 1479. The Inquisition was deemed a necessity because of the spread of groups such as the Waldenses (discussed in chap. 15) and the Cathari or Albigensians,[14] which, if allowed to go unchecked, threatened the very life of the papacy.

Generally, the Dominicans or Franciscans were in charge of Inquisitorial activities. Trials were held in secret. There was no way of obtaining meaningful legal defense, because any lawyer representing an accused person would himself become the target of church tribunals. Confessions might be extracted by torture, and testimony against the accused might be obtained from witnesses by the same means.

Those who confessed and were reconciled were subjected to various punishments, including penances, pilgrimages, scourgings, or fines. Those who refused to recant commonly had their property confiscated, were imprisoned, or handed over to the secular authorities to be executed, usually by burning. The excesses of the Inquisition (sometimes called "an engine of iniquity"), its violation of human rights, and in some places its reign of terror, must forever remain as a blot on the history of the Roman church.

Scholasticism

It has already been noted that at the height of her power the medieval papacy defined the dogma of transubstantiation and declared the necessity of annual confession to a priest. Other dogmas and doctrines were being formulated at this time too, largely through the efforts of the Scholastics. Scholasticism is hard to define adequately, but certain generalizations may be made concerning it. It was the sum of the teachings and methods of the prominent Western philosophers most widely accepted during the Middle Ages. It constituted a harmonization of philosophy and theology[15] in one system for the purpose of rational demonstration of theological truth. The Scholastics sought certainty and better understanding of the truth and salvation by way of knowledge and reason.

The ninth to the twelfth centuries mark the formative period of Scholasticism, the thirteenth century the height, and the fourteenth and fifteenth centuries a period of decline. Anselm and Abelard are usually thought of as cofounders; Hugh of St. Victor and Peter Lombard as important representatives along the way; Thomas Aquinas as representing the movement at its height; and Duns Scotus and William of Ockam as typical writers during the decline.

The Scholastics, and especially Aquinas, are responsible for helping to formulate the sacramental system of the Roman church—a system through which one was to obtain salvation. They pegged the number of sacraments at seven, and then spelled out in greater detail the significance of baptism, the Eucharist, confirmation, penance, extreme unction, holy orders, and marriage. Also, they set forth theories of the atonement still common today, defined the way of salvation, and in general produced many of the ideas that the Council of Trent (1545-63) would draw together in a tight, coherent system and would officially establish as orthodox Roman Catholic teaching for centuries to come. Aquinas's arguments for the existence of God have been widely used in modern times.

Mysticism

Contemporary with the Scholastic movement came mysticism, which aimed at a certainty of salvation and the truth through spiritual experience. Of course mysticism has existed in various forms and in various degrees in the church from New Testament times to the present, and it is also found in other great world religions. But it surfaces especially in an era like the Middle Ages when religion has become too institutionalized and seeks a more individualistic and personal relationship with God. Sometimes mysticism led to heresy, as adherents ignored biblical norms in favor of experience, or to social passivity, as they concentrated on personal salvation to the exclusion of service to God. Many of the Roman Catholic mystics of the Middle Ages seem to have been genuine believers, however. Parenthetically, it is useful to observe that Christian mysticism differs from that of Hinduism or Taoism, denying absorption of the soul into the divine and maintaining a distinction between the Creator and the creature.

Three of the better medieval mystics—all of the twelfth century—were Richard and Hugh of St. Victor and Bernard of Clairvaux. The latter is known for several famous hymns attributed to him. His best-known hymn, "O Sacred Head, Now Wounded," owes its beloved musical text to Johann Sebastian Bach. Four of his other great hymns all derive from the single fifty-stanza poem *De Nomine Jesu* (concerning the name of Jesus). The two best known of these are "Jesus, the Very Thought of Thee," and "Jesus, Thou Joy of Loving Hearts."

One way that mystics sought to experience Christ was by walking where He walked and suffering where He suffered. Thus participating in a Crusade was a natural outgrowth of their religious orientation. It is no accident that Bernard of Clairvaux, one of the best-known mystics, was a leader of the Second Crusade. It is important to note that Jesus was not the only object of the affections of the mystics. Bernard's[16] devotion to the "Mother of God" gave impetus to the cult of the Virgin. Mysticism and Scholasticism were a good counterbalance for each other. Mysticism kept Scholasticism from being too academic, and Scholasticism helped the mystics keep their feet on the ground.

Monasticism

In a very real sense the backbone of the medieval papacy was the monastic movement. Long is the roll of great leaders of the Middle Ages who came from the monastery or were associated with it. It includes such famous names as Gregory I and VII, Richard and Hugh of St. Victor, and Bernard of Clairvaux. The monasteries were the conservatories of learning and the centers of missionary and philanthropic work. The monks were the writers, preachers, philosophers, and theologians of the age; they headed the Inquisition and persuaded multitudes to participate in the Crusades.

And it may be said that the monasteries provided something of a safety valve for the Roman church, for in them earnest Christians had a great deal more freedom from ecclesiastical machinery than they would have had outside the cloister. Without this freedom, it is possible that much of the evangelical life would have parted company with Romanism sooner than it did. It should be remembered that Luther, Erasmus, and many other critics of the papacy had monastic backgrounds.

The backbone of the medieval papacy was the monastic movement.

St. Benedict (about 500) developed the Western European form of monastic life, and other orders were, in general, offshoots of the Benedictine order. The Cluniac order came into being in 910, the Cistercian in 1098. The latter's most illustrious son was Bernard of Clairvaux. St. Francis of Assisi founded the Franciscan order in 1209, and St. Dominic founded the Dominicans in 1216. The Augustinian Hermits were formed from several Italian groups of hermits in 1256; from this order Martin Luther later came. These Augustinians are to be distinguished from the Augustinian Canons or Regular Canons, which date to the middle of the eleventh century.

The thirteenth century was the heyday of monasticism. It declined at the end of that century and throughout the fourteenth. There was some reform in the fifteenth century. The Reformation destroyed most of the monasteries of northern Europe and seriously curtailed the activities of those in central Europe. Though monasticism continued to prosper in Roman Catholic countries, the French Revolution and the Napoleonic conquests dealt it a very severe blow. A resurgence of monastic orders began in the mid-nineteenth century in most countries of Western Europe (except Scandinavia) and in North America. Monasticism continued to prosper in the Orthodox East until the onslaughts of Islam and more recently Marxism.

FOURTEEN

Decline of the Medieval Church
The Church from 1305 to 1517

Reasons for Decline of the Medieval Church

Rise of nationalism
Backlash against the Inquisition
Reaction against money-raising efforts of church
Moral laxity
Secularization of the church during Renaissance
The Crusades
Babylonian Captivity of the papacy
Papal schism

THE period of the decline of the medieval church may be dated between 1305 and 1517. The first date marks the beginning of the Babylonian Captivity of the papacy, which is discussed below; the latter is the year Luther posted his theses on the church door at Wittenberg and launched the Protestant Reformation.

There were many reasons for the decline of the papacy. *First, there were the rise of national monarchs and the decline of feudalism;* correspondingly, there was a developing sense of nationality and increased loyalty of the people to their rulers. The church claimed a supra-national loyalty, which would certainly suffer with the spread of the new intense nationalism. As strong monarchs arose, they became jealous of the immense wealth and power that the church held within their monarchal borders. An example of what could happen occurred during the pontificate of Boniface VIII (1294-1303).

In 1296 Boniface VIII issued the bull *Clericis laicos*, which prohibited taxation of the clergy by secular princes. Aimed especially at Philip IV of France and Edward I of England, it immediately drew fire from both of them. Edward placed the English clergy outside the protection of the law until they obtained permission to give him the taxed amounts. Philip merely confiscated all moneys being sent from France to Rome.

Second, the rigid enforcement of doctrine and practice, especially by means of the Inquisition, stirred up opposition and dissent.

Third, the increasing cost of maintaining the hierarchy and the employment of oppressive means of securing money alienated many.

Fourth, there was an increasing moral laxity among churchmen, especially during the fifteenth century.

Fifth, moral relaxation was accompanied by a general secularization of the church during the fourteenth and especially fifteenth centuries. Secularization of all of life was in process, a feature of the Renaissance. The Renaissance was not just a rebirth of knowledge; it was a rebirth of the classical spirit, with its rationalistic outlook on life. The classical world had formulated its ethics by means of philosophy and custom and therefore found them to be relativistic; it did not follow an unchangeable revealed standard.

Moreover, the Renaissance marked the rise of the middle class with new wealth, commonly spent on art, literature, education, and the like, rather than on the church. Spurred by the thought patterns of the classical world and an improved economic climate, men of the Renaissance subscribed to a humanistic orientation to life. Man instead of God increasingly became the measure of all things. There was a desire to make this world a more fit place for human beings instead of concentrating all efforts on preparing for the life hereafter.

The heady individualistic spirit of the Renaissance also weakened the corporate orientation and demands of the Roman church. An important phenomenon of the Renaissance was the invention of printing, which facilitated not only the distribution of Scripture and a return to New Testament Christianity, but also the spread of satirical or critical writings that often ridiculed the church.

Sixth, the Crusades contributed in many ways to the decline of the church. For example, hordes of Europeans who had lived within sight of their lord's manor house, without education, bred on superstitions of the times, learned that life elsewhere was different. The new ideas and ways of life with which they came in contact in the East weakened the ties of many to the church.

Last, the Babylonian Captivity of the church and the Papal Schism did much to weaken the power of Rome in Western Europe.

The Babylonian Captivity

The Babylonian Captivity was a period of approximately seventy years (1305-1377) when the pope ruled from Avignon, just outside the southern border of France. It was called the Babylonian Captivity by Italian patriots such as Petrarch and Dante because they likened this period when the pope presumably was a virtual prisoner of the French king to the seventy years when the Hebrews were captive in Babylonia.

The captivity came about partly because of rising nationalism and partly because Pope Boniface VIII over-reached himself. Boniface, in his famous bull *Unam Sanctum* (1302), insisted that all rulers were subject to him and that it was "necessary for salvation" for every human being to be subject to the pope. Philip IV of France (1285-1314), who was having a running battle with Boniface, sent representatives to Italy to arrest the pope. Rescued by the townspeople at his home in Anagni, Italy, Boniface died a month later. His successor, Benedict XI (1303-04), lasted for only eight stormy months, and the papal chair remained vacant for eleven months thereafter. Finally it was filled by Clement V, a French churchman who was under constant pressure from King Philip. Trying to remove himself from the direct presence of the French king and threatened by unsafe conditions in Italy,[17] Clement settled down at Avignon in 1309.

Whether or not later popes were under French control, Clement was, and all popes of the period were Frenchmen. Political rulers and many of their subjects of the later part of the captivity seemed to feel that papal interests were closely identified with those of France. Such a belief was found to have significant effects. For example, during the Babylonian Captivity the Hundred Years War broke out between France and England, greatly weakening the power of the papacy in England. During the war, the pope demanded the surrender of Wycliffe, the great reformer; but a powerful party at the English court protected him. Furthermore, the papacy gained a reputation for extravagance in expenditure and offensiveness in taxation during this period.

The seven Avignon[18] popes do not appear to have been bad men or even bad popes, but they were not the spiritual leaders that the times demanded. As Frenchmen they often allowed their nationalistic feelings to influence their policies, thus alienating both England and Germany. Most of them were sincere and well-intentioned; but they gained a reputation as a group for being luxurious, bureaucratic, and rapacious, as wolves rather than shepherds of the flock. Their conduct contributed to a growth of anticlericalism, mysticism and heresy.

The Avignonese leadership was not out of step with the general condition of the church in their day, however. The clergy generally seem to have been more interested in their economic well being than in the spiritual well being of their parishioners. Even in the monasteries rules tended to be relaxed. Under such conditions it is not surprising to see the growth of mysticism (among those who sought spiritual satisfaction in a privatized faith) and heresy (among those who denied the doctrinal authority of a corrupt clergy).

The Papal Schism

The Papal Schism (1378-1417) hurt the papacy even more than the Babylonian Captivity. The schism resulted from the total incompetence of Pope Urban VI, who within a few months of his election in Rome (1378) had alienated the entire college of cardinals. Ultimately all the French cardinals slipped out of Rome, declared Urban's election void, and elevated Robert of Geneva to the papacy as Clement VII. When Urban refused to be deposed, the French cardinals and Clement moved to Avignon and the rupture was complete. Naturally, the princes of Europe lined up behind the pope of their choice, and Christendom was split.

When the Council of Pisa (1409) tried to settle the

problem by deposing the two existing popes and installing a single one in their place, all it succeeded in doing was electing a third pope; so for several years there were three popes anathematizing and excommunicating one another. Christendom was utterly confused, and reforming parties grew rapidly. During this period Hus preached with great success in Bohemia, and the Lollards (followers of Wycliffe) secured a large following in England and Scotland. Finally the Council of Constance managed to depose all three popes in 1417 and elect a new one, who henceforth would permanently reside in Rome.

Some have called the last part of the fifteenth century the paganized stage of the papacy. The Renaissance was taking its toll in the secularization of some of the top clergy. Pope Nicholas V (1447-1455) was a great lover of classical literature and the founder of the Vatican library. He spent considerable sums on his pet project and on the repair of numerous classical structures in Rome. Julius II (1503-1513) is known as the patron of artists, especially Michelangelo, who painted the Sistine Chapel ceiling from 1508 to 1512. And Leo X (1513-1521), pope when the Reformation began, was very extravagant. His court life was a constant round of banquets, theatrical shows, and balls. As builder of St. Peter's in Rome, he used the revenues of the papacy on art, architecture, and the like. It should be remembered that his conflict with Luther came over the sale of indulgences—designed to raise money for the building of St. Peter's.

Conclusion

So at the beginning of the sixteenth century, the medieval papacy was sick. Some within the system began to make prescriptions for cure of the illness. These, coupled with the disruption brought about by the Reformers, stirred the church to make changes that permitted a strong resurgence of power in later years.

PART IV

♦

The Church in the Reformation

FIFTEEN

Forerunners of the Reformation

LONG before Luther fired his verbal salvo against indulgences and launched the Reformation, others had sniped at the theological position of the Roman Catholic church. In fact, there always had been some within the Roman church who did not agree with its teaching, and many had even broken away into separate religious communities.

Forerunners of the Reformation

Peter Waldo
John Wycliffe
John Hus
Savonarola
Brethren of the Common Life

Peter Waldo

Peter Waldo, one of the most effective of the

pre-Lutheran Reformers, was a wealthy merchant of Lyons, France. Impressed with the way of poverty and service to Christ as the path to heaven (based on Matthew 19:21), he sold most of his holdings in 1176 and gave the proceeds to the poor. He retained some property to care for his wife and daughters, however. Within a year or so, he was joined by others, men and women, who called themselves the "Poor in spirit," and undertook an itinerant ministry of preaching repentance and living from the handouts of listeners.

As good Roman Catholics, they appealed to the Third Lateran Council in 1179 for permission to preach but were refused because they were thought to be ignorant laymen. Convinced that they, like early believers, should obey God rather than men, Peter and his followers continued to preach. In 1184, Pope Lucius III excommunicated them for their disobedience. This act brought them numerous supporters, and the movement spread into southern France, Italy, Spain, the Rhine Valley, and Bohemia. It is hard to know whether all the individuals classified as Waldenses were part of the movement or whether contemporary Roman Catholic opponents merely used the term as a blanket descriptive for many disaffected individuals who opposed the official church.

At any rate the true Waldenses seem to have taken the New Testament as a rule of faith and life and appear to have used it in a rather legalistic sense. They went about two by two, wearing simple clothing, preaching repentance, engaging in frequent fasting, and living from the gifts of others. They rejected purgatory and masses and prayers for the dead and held to the necessity of using vernacular translations of Scripture. They insisted on the right of both laymen and laywomen to preach, but they did have an organization with bishops, priests, and deacons. Perhaps it should be noted that Waldo (also Valdez or Valdes) seems never to have become fully evangelical in the best sense of the term. But in pointing to the Scripture as the source of religious truth, he opened the door for his followers to become truly evangelical.

The Waldenses were severely persecuted for centuries. Part of the reason for their widespread distribution in Europe was that they were driven from their homeland. In Bohemia they ultimately became part of the Hussite movement. In the mountain fastnesses of the Cottian Alps between France and Italy, their real homeland by the time of the Reformation, they met in historic conclave with representatives of the Genevan Reformation in 1532 and adopted the theology and government of the Swiss Reformers. Subsequently, in 1545, some three to four thousand of them were massacred in Provence (France). Finally, in 1848, they won toleration in the kingdom of Sardinia and subsequently in a united Italy (where they now number some 20,000). They are the only late medieval separatist group to survive to the present, though of course numerous changes in organization and teaching have taken place among them.

John Wycliffe

Like Peter Waldo, John Wycliffe (1320?-1384) was a biblical reformer, bringing to bear the teachings of Scripture on the practices of the Roman church. He also engaged in Bible translation, and it was largely through his efforts that the first English version was produced. Though he personally translated or supervised translation of much of the Bible, his version was not completed until after his death, by Nicholas of Hereford and John Purvey. Without doubt, its widespread use had an influence on the development of the English language. Descended from a noble family, Wycliffe was educated at Oxford and later became master of Balliol College at the university. He was therefore able to reach some of the upper-class English. But he addressed himself largely to the common people, sending out lay evangelists to instruct them.

After 1375 Wycliffe's reforming views developed rapidly. Pope Gregory XI condemned him in 1377 for his efforts, but he was protected by some of the nobles and the powerful John of Gaunt, who was duke of Lancaster and son of Edward III. These were the days of the Hundred Years War (between England and France), and it was unthinkable that Englishmen would surrender one of their most outstanding countrymen to a pope at Avignon, who was considered to be under the domination of England's French foes. The power of Wycliffe was at least threefold: his intense patriotism, his deep piety, and the belief of many that he had no scholarly equal in England.

To Wycliffe, Scripture, which he interpreted literally, was the sole authority for the believer. Decrees of the pope were not infallible except as based on Scripture. The clergy were not to rule, but to serve and help people. Eventually he reached the conclusion that Christ and not the pope was the head of the church; in fact, the pope, if he were too eager for worldly power, might even be regarded as the Antichrist. Ultimately he came to repudiate the entire papal system. He also attacked transubstantiation (the view that the bread and wine in the Eucharist become the body and blood of Christ) and seems to have come to a position similar to Luther's. Moreover, he condemned the dogma of purgatory and the use of relics, pilgrimages, and indulgences. He seems to have been deeply influenced by St. Augustine. It is not clear how evangelical Wycliffe was personally, but under the influence of biblical teaching, his followers increasingly moved in that direction.

The followers of Wycliffe were suppressed by force in 1401. Thereafter those who held his views went underground and no doubt helped to prepare the way for the Lutheran and Calvinistic teachings that invaded Britain about a century later. Bohemians studying at Oxford in Wycliffe's day carried his ideas to their homeland, where they influenced the teachings of John Hus.

John Hus

John Hus (1372?-1415), professor of philosophy at the University of Prague and preacher at Bethlehem Chapel, did not slavishly depend on Wycliffe, however. The old view that he was influenced by Wycliffe to the point that he simply adopted the views of the Englishman as his own must now be abandoned. A Czech reform movement, dating to about the middle of the fourteenth century, paralleled Wycliffe's efforts. Hus was in the tradition of the native movement and a product of it. But during the early fifteenth century indigenous and imported varieties of reform joined to form a single development.

At any rate, Hus's approach was similar to that of Wycliffe, and his influence on the Continent was greater than that of the Englishman. It should be remembered that Luther was greatly impressed with the reformer from Prague. Hus's great work was entitled *On the Church*.[1] In it he stated that all the elect are members of Christ's church, of which Christ rather than the pope is head. He argued against simony, indulgences, and abuses of the mass. He demanded a reform in the lives of clergy, and he asserted the right of laity to take both the bread and wine in the Communion.

Hus became the leader of a reform movement that spread across Bohemia. Almost the whole nation supported him in his reform program, in spite of the fact that he was excommunicated by the pope. After Hus's death this reform agitation did not cease, and about the middle of the fifteenth century the Bohemian Brethren rose out of the embers of the fire Hus had lit. They still exist as the Moravian Brethren.

When the pope summoned Hus to the Council of Constance to stand examination on his views, the emperor Sigismund ordered him to go and promised safe conduct to and from the council. But when the council condemned him as a heretic and burned him at the stake, Sigismund did not interfere.[2] Like Luther, Hus came to blows with the pope over the issue of indulgences (among other things); but Europe was not so ready for the Reformation in 1415 as it would be a century later.

Savonarola[3]

Girolamo Savonarola (1452-1498) was a forceful preacher against the worldliness and corruption of church and society in Florence. A Dominican, he was transferred to the priory of San Marco in Florence in 1482 and gradually rose in influence and power in the city. His studies in the Old Testament prophets and the book of Revelation helped to make him a powerful preacher against the evils and corruption of society.

Savonarola served as the spiritual leader of the democratic party that came to power in Florence with the invasion of Charles VIII of France and the flight of the Medici in 1494. Exercising virtual dictatorship over the city, he tried to reform both the state and church there. The new constitution of 1495 was similar to that of the Republic of Venice.

With the passage of time opposition to Savonarola heightened and his power began to slip. His opposition and ultimate downfall resulted as much from his political and social involvements in the city as from his religious tangle with the Roman church. Pope Alexander VI excommunicated him in 1497, and in April of 1498 he was arrested and tried for sedition and heresy and cruelly tortured. Finally on May 23 he was hanged and his body burned.

Although Savonarola demanded reform in the church, he never took the more advanced position of Wycliffe and Hus. He had no quarrel with the teachings or the organization of the church, but personally seems to have believed in justification by faith. He was characterized by religious zeal and personal piety. Because he openly condemned the evil character and misrule of Pope Alexander VI and the corruption of the papal court, he won the undying opposition of the papacy and suffered execution.

Brethren of the Common Life

Contemporary with Wycliffe and Hus was a mystical movement that flowered in Holland, Belgium, northern France, and northern Germany during the latter fourteenth and the fifteenth centuries. Emphasizing Bible reading, meditation, prayer, personal piety, and religious education it produced such outstanding figures as Jan Van Ruysbroeck (d. 1381), who wrote *The Seven Steps of Spiritual Love,* and Gerhard Grote (d. 1384), who was instrumental in founding the Brethren of the Common Life. The principal aim of the Brethren was to secure a revival of practical religion. The Brethren gathered in private houses rather than monasteries, held property in common, worked to support themselves, and avoided the approbrium of the community by not seeking tax exempt status or begging. They generally established good relations with the townspeople but sometimes incurred the suspicion or opposition of the clergy or monks. They did, however, attend the parish churches and had no peculiar doctrinal positions. This movement is commonly called the "new devotion" (*devotio moderna*); they were sort of cells of devotion or true piety in the community.

The Brethren were deeply devoted to the cause of education. They established several schools in the Netherlands and Germany that were outstanding for scholarship and piety. Four of their best-known students were Nicholas of Cusa, Erasmus, Luther, and Thomas à Kempis, who is credited with writing the widely distributed *Imitation of Christ*.[4]

Other Religious Movements

Many other religious movements, for which there is no space here, spread across Europe during the fifteenth century, demonstrating how widespread was the demand for church reform there. In fact the Continent was a seething kettle by 1500—ready to boil over. In the realms of economics, society, politics, intellect, and religion, the time had come for an eruption. All that was needed was someone who could mold these explosive elements into a single movement. Such a movement would blitz Europe. It was Martin Luther who provided a channel for all this explosive energy in what is now called the Protestant Reformation. For a clearer understanding of Luther's place in the history of Europe, it is necessary to survey the various facets of life on the Continent on the eve of the Reformation.

SIXTEEN

Europe on the Eve of the Reformation

IN GIVING reasons for the decline of the papacy during the later Middle Ages we have noted some of the properties on the stage of Europe while the drama of the Reformation unfolded. Much more needs to be said on the subject.

Politics

The political map of Europe was a crazy quilt composed of hundreds of principalities, evidencing extreme decentralization. But around the fringes, in Portugal, Spain, France, and England, national states were rising, challenging the supranational power of the papacy. In central Europe the Holy Roman Empire (now essentially a German entity) had an emperor checkmated by numerous states with slight allegiance to him. Not only was the emperor hampered by these semi-independent vassals, but Muslim hosts knocked at the doors of the empire soon after Luther nailed his theses on the church door at Wittenberg. After toppling Constantinople and the Byzantine Empire in 1453,[5] the Muslims (in this case Ottoman Turks) advanced across Eastern Europe until they stood before the gates of Vienna in 1529 and again reached the vicinity of the city in 1532.

What had really happened was this. Charles, a Hapsburg with holdings in central Europe and king of the Netherlands and Spain, was elected in 1519 as Charles V of the Holy Roman Empire. Francis I of France, almost surrounded by the holdings of Charles and defeated by him in 1525, made an alliance with the Ottoman Empire in 1526 to apply a pincers movement against his enemy. Charles needed the help of all his German vassals to defeat the Turks. As some of the German princes became supporters of Luther, Charles was not able to put religious pressure on them, because then they would not give him political and military support. Thus Charles was not able to force Frederick of Saxony (one of his most powerful vassals) to surrender Luther when the pope demanded the Reformer.

Meanwhile Europe was expanding. A few years after Luther's birth Columbus reached the New World (1492) and launched the Spanish Empire in the West; shortly after Luther posted his theses, Magellan's expedition sailed around the world. At the same time, the Portuguese were establishing outposts of empire in Brazil, Africa, India, and the Far East.

Intellect

A new world of thought was discovered long before 1492. The full tide of the Renaissance had rolled in. Rediscovering the literature and thought patterns of the classical age, it contributed to a greater secularization of life.

Humanism and Individualism

Humanism was one of the main features of the Renaissance, involving a new emphasis on man and his culture and an effort to make the world a better place in which human beings might live. The pull of the future life was not so great for the true child of the Renaissance as it had been for his forebears during the Middle Ages. He would rather eat his pie now than have it in the sky by and by.

In harking back to the literature of the classical age, the humanists put new emphasis on the study of Greek (and some of them, Hebrew) in an effort to read the classics in the original languages. The greatest of all ancient documents was the Bible, and the renewed emphasis on ancient languages led many to the Scripture. The humanism of northern Europe seemed to put more stress on the form and analysis of classical literature, the humanism

A few years after Luther's birth, Columbus reached the New World; shortly after he posted his theses, Magellan sailed around the world.

of southern Europe seemed to emphasize the philosophy embedded in that literature.

The literary humanists included a good deal of biblical study in their academic diet, and it was in the north that the Reformation gained most headway—Zwingli, Calvin, Melanchthon, and Erasmus are examples of the more biblical of the literary humanists. That Erasmus, among others, was a great satirist of the evils of the institutional church, as well as of the evils of society in general, underscores the fact that criticism of Romanism by Renaissance leaders contributed to the success of the Reformation.

Also advancing the effectiveness of the Reformation was the Renaissance spirit of individualism, which paved the way for Luther's emphasis on the priesthood of the believer and its attendant ideas of the right of believers to go directly to God and to interpret the Scriptures for themselves.

The Spread of Printing and Growth of Universities

Another important facet of the intellectual development of Europe on the eve of the Reformation was the invention of movable type and the spread of printing.[6] Without it the Reformers could not have had the same effect. In fact, the tremendous literary activity of the Reformers was largely responsible for building the printing trade in many areas.

Last, an important phenomenon of the period was the rapid growth of universities, which provided education for a larger number of people, fostered the critical spirit, and provided a means whereby the leaders of the new generation could be reached with Reformation principles and wherein they could be trained to promulgate them.

Religion

The religion of Europe was in a condition of decay. The evils of the church were many—simony, economic oppression, the purchase of salvation through indulgences, immorality of many of the clergy, and so on. The effects of the Babylonian Captivity and Papal Schism had been great, as noted earlier. The wave of secularism that engulfed Europe during the fifteenth century affected all levels of church life: the parishioners, lower and higher clergy, monks, and even the successors of St. Peter.

The decadence of the church led to numerous calls from within for its reform. Symptomatic of this concern were such movements as the Observant Franciscans in England, the Oratory of Divine Love in Italy, and the

Brethren of the Common Life in the Lowlands. Books of devotion found wide audience. Mendicant friars preached an emotional religion. Evidence of the religious concern of the populace at large is considerable; a religious ferment emphasized the emotions and provided a basis for popular support of the Reformation.

Society and Economics

European society and economics were in flux. Feudalism was on the decline and was largely extinct, and it was paralleled by the rise of towns and nation-states. In these new towns and states a new middle class emerged, as did a degree of social mobility not known for more than a millennium. Compared with the old nobility, these striving, successful people were social, political, and economic outsiders; naturally they wanted to become social, political, and economic insiders. Traditionally, what really mattered in society were the titled nobility with their great holdings in landed estates.

But members of the rising middle class, with their wealth in financial and commercial interests, felt they were the equals of the old aristocracy and sought social recognition and political power. Peasants were generally restless, looking for a way out of their economic and social oppression. Both national governments and the middle class needed a ready supply of cash. Kings and nobles had to support armies and navies, finance public improvements, and promote the general welfare of their people. Businessmen needed to have capital reserve for new economic ventures. All this naturally hindered the flow of wealth to the church, and efforts of the church to drain money from an area were met with something less than enthusiasm by king and middle class alike.

SEVENTEEN

The Lutheran Reformation
Germany and Scandinavia

The Reformation in Germany

The Background of Martin Luther

TO SUCH an age as this, one seething with unrest and vexed with a host of problems and longings, came Martin Luther.[7] He was a voice speaking for a multitude who had been voiceless. In fact, as he began his reformation activities, many hoped he would become their spokesman in political, economic, and social, as well as religious matters.

Born the son of a miner in 1483,[8] Martin Luther lived in a day when men were able to better their fortunes. Hans Luther gradually amassed a fairly adequate estate and was able to provide his son Martin with an excellent education. After early studies at Mansfeld, Magdeburg (where he was taught by Brethren of the Common Life), and Eisenach, Martin matriculated at the University of Erfurt,[9] where he earned his B.A. and M.A. degrees. He was second in a class of seventeen when he took the M.A. in 1505. Thereafter, on his father's urging, he entered the law school of the university.

But in July of that year, when thrown to the ground by a flash of lightning during a very bad storm, he vowed to enter a monastery if spared from death. But that was not the only reason for his decision. Apparently,

Luther hoped he would find at the Augustinian monastery in Erfurt the peace for his soul that he could not find on the outside. As Luther pursued the monastic life, he saw Christ as a stern judge, and he spent days in fasts and bodily mortification, seeking release for his sinful soul. During his struggle he came under the influence of Johann Von Staupitz, vicar-general of his order, who urged him to think on God's love for the sinner as evidenced in Christ's death. Luther assiduously studied "the Bible with the red binding" that he had been given on entering the monastery.

Meanwhile, Staupitz had become dean of the faculty of theology at the newly founded University of Wittenberg (in Saxony), and he arranged for Luther to join the faculty of the university in 1508, as a visiting professor for a year. Then he returned to Erfurt, from which in 1510 he went to Rome on a business trip for the Augustinian order. The following year he joined the Wittenberg faculty for good. When in 1512 he received his doctor of theology degree, he succeeded Staupitz[10] as professor of theology, which position he held until his death in 1546.

During 1513-1518, Luther lectured on Psalms, Romans, Galatians, Hebrews, and Titus and sometime during that period came to an acceptance of the doctrine of justification by faith.[11] He was a Saul turned Paul. He abandoned the prevailing Scholastic and allegorical interpretation for a more strictly literal and grammatical interpretation. His students responded enthusiastically to his pedagogical method. Luther's influence expanded as he was given charge over eleven monasteries in 1515. In the same year the town council of Wittenberg called him to the pulpit of the City Church, where he continued to minister the rest of his life. From that vantage point, he could carry his views directly to the laity.

The Issue of Indulgences

The issue that brought Luther to the attention of all Europe was indulgences. Initially, an indulgence provided for the remission of punishment imposed by the Roman Catholic church on someone who was guilty of a specific sin. An indulgence was based on the principle that sinners were unable to do sufficient penance to expiate all their sins. Hence it was necessary for them to draw on the "treasury of merits," to which Christ, the Virgin Mary, and the saints contributed and which could be dispensed by the pope. In earlier days one might gain an indulgence for risking his life in fighting the infidel during the Crusades. Gradually however, financial sacrifice was accepted in lieu of physical risk. And the financing of the building of churches, monasteries, hospitals, and the like could be designated by the pope as warranting indulgences. During the later Middle Ages, indulgences came to involve not only remission of punishment imposed by the Roman church, but also absolution of all guilt incurred before God.

Pope Leo X (1513-1521), like his predecessor Julius II, sought to raise funds for the building of St. Peter's in Rome by indulgence sales. His needs coincided with those of Albert of Hohenzollern, then only twenty-three, who had gone heavily into debt to buy from the papacy the archbishoprics of Mainz and Magdeburg and the bishopric of Halberstadt. So it was decided that indulgences would be offered for sale in Albert's domains and the proceeds split equally between the archbishop and the pope.

Luther did not know about the pope's involvement in this financial arrangement. What bothered him was the promise of full remission of sin and punishment in purgatory for living persons and what was worse, the assurance to purchasers that their dead loved ones in purgatory could be forgiven their sins without confession or contrition.

Frederic of Saxony (Frederick the Wise) forbade the sale of indulgences in his domain; so there was none of the traffic at Wittenberg. But Wittenberg citizens traveled to other towns to buy indulgences. When Luther observed the effect of this sale on the moral and ethical standards of his parishioners, he decided to post his famous Ninety-five Theses (or topics for debate) on the door of Castle Church at Wittenberg on October 31, 1517, in protest against the indulgence sale.[12] Printed copies quickly flooded Europe, and popular enthusiasm was engendered everywhere.

A conservative, faithful son of the church, Luther believed the authority of the pope and the validity of the sacrament of penance were at stake in the way the indulgences had been sold. He sent a copy of the theses and a letter of explanation to Albert. Early in 1518, still not believing that the abuse in the indulgence sale had been approved by the pope, Luther sent an explanation (the *Resolutions*) to Leo X. In trying to squelch Luther, Leo preferred to put pressure on him through local agencies (e.g., the Augustinian order), but members of the higher echelon of papal power in Rome persuaded the pope to demand Luther's appearance in Rome as a suspect of heresy.

Luther then appealed to Frederick the Wise of Saxony for advice in handling the complicated proceedings and requested that the hearing be held in Germany. Nationalistically minded Frederick arranged a meeting at Augsburg in 1518; this ended in a standoff between the two parties. In subsequent years, polarization of the two camps increased. Luther gradually turned his back on the authority of the pope and councils and planted himself squarely on the teachings of Scripture alone.

The pope became increasingly determined to get his hands on Luther; but he could not, because Frederick protected him. The new emperor, Charles V, was reluctant to come to Leo's aid and thus alienate Frederick, because Saxony was the most powerful state in Germany at the time and the emperor needed all the support he could get for his war against the Turks.

The Excommunication of Luther

Finally, in 1521 Luther went to the Diet of Worms (a parliament of the empire) under an imperial safe conduct. There he uttered the famous words: "I cannot and will not recant anything, for it is neither safe nor honest to act against one's conscience. God help me. Amen." On the way back Frederick's men kidnapped Luther to protect him, and put him in the Wartburg Castle, where he translated the New Testament into idiomatic German in the unbelievably short time of eleven weeks.[13] While there, he was informed of extremism and violence at Wittenberg; so he returned to quell the disturbance.

With Luther excommunicated by the Roman church and living under an imperial ban that deprived him of physical protection, what began as a reformation became in effect a revolution. Luther, with Frederick's protection, launched a new religious movement. During these years the pope was still trying to stop Luther.

At the Diet of Speyer (1529) it was resolved to forbid further spread of the Lutheran movement. A number of German princes and free cities entered a *protest* against this action. Subscribers came to be known as protestants, and soon the name *Protestant* passed on to the whole movement. In the following year the Protestant princes got together in what was called the Schmalkald League. Already hard pressed by the Ottoman Turks, who had appeared before the gates of Vienna in 1529, the emperor Charles V finally granted religious freedom to the princes in 1532 and did not interfere with Lutheranism for several years.

Meanwhile, the Roman Catholics became alarmed by the spread of Protestantism and banded together to form the Holy League. War broke out in 1546, the year Luther died. After initial victories by the Roman Catholics, the Protestants finally defeated the imperial forces. The Diet of Augsburg (1555) ended the struggle and provided for a recognition of Roman Catholicism and Lutheranism as legal religions in the Holy Roman Empire, with the stipulation that the religion of the prince was to be the religion of the people. In other words, Catholic and Lutheran state churches were to be established in each of the principalities of the Empire and minorities were not to be tolerated. The establishment of state churches was to be the order of the day in all the countries where the Reformation was successful. Religious liberty and religious pluralism, so much taken for granted in contemporary America, were not accepted concepts in sixteenth century Europe and were not products of the Reformation.

Luther's Able Associate

Luther's right-hand man at Wittenberg was Philipp Melanchthon (1497-1560), who directed the organizational, educational, and publishing side of the Reformation. He is often called the teacher of Germany.

He aided in establishing primary and secondary schools and did all he could to train the clergy. Recognizing the need for organizing the church that Luther had brought into being, he prepared a manual for that purpose. He also wrote a systematic theology, commentaries on New Testament books, and was largely responsible for preparing the various statements of faith that the Lutherans presented at some of the diets where they met papal foes.

Luther's Success and Distinctives

Luther was a popular and dynamic leader in an age that was looking for such leadership. He was an indefatigable critic of Roman Catholicism in an age that became increasingly critical of Roman Catholicism. He played on the national interests of the Germans in such pamphlets as his "Address to the Christian Nobles of the German Nation" in an age when nationalism was gathering momentum rapidly. He offered a message of hope and faith to a people lost in the darkness of sin and looking for light. For all these reasons, Luther was successful.

Great Distinctives of the Lutheran Reformation

Justification by faith alone
Salvation by grace alone
The Bible alone as the authority for
doctrine and practice
The priesthood of the believer
Promotion of congregational singing

But often he has been criticized because he did not go far enough in his reforms (he retained the crucifix, candles, and other elements of Roman Catholicism), because he placed the church under the control of civil authority, and because he failed to cooperate with the Swiss Reformers and thus present a solid block of Protestants against Roman Catholic power in Europe.

In his preaching Luther set forth three great distinctives: *sola fide* (justification by faith alone); *sola gratia* (salvation by grace alone); and *sola scriptura* (the Bible alone as the source of the believer's authority for doctrine and practice). He also had much to say about the priesthood of the believer. Every believer was a priest and had the right to go to God directly; Christ was the only mediator between God and humanity. Moreover, all believers had the right to interpret the Scripture for themselves under the guidance of the Holy Spirit. God spoke directly to the believer-priest through His Word; believers could address God directly in prayer and especially in their songs. Luther gave the German people not only a Bible in their own tongue, but also a hymnbook. In his hands the hymn became a powerful spiritual weapon, and he became the father of evangelical hymnody.

The Reformation in Scandinavia

Although Lutheranism spread early to many countries of Europe and later to the New World, it became the dominant faith of Scandinavia. When Luther posted his theses at Wittenberg, Sweden and Norway were united to Denmark (as they had been ever since the Union of Kalmar in 1397). But in 1517 a Swedish revolt was trying to throw off Danish control. This nationalistic effort was opposed by the Roman church, and the archbishop of Upsala won the title of Swedish Judas Iscariot. Ultimately, Gustavus Vasa was successful in winning Swedish independence and, because of national antipathy to Roman Catholicism and because of his personal preferences, he had little difficulty in setting up a national Lutheran church in the 1520s. Because Finland was a possession of the Swedish crown, Lutheranism was soon established there too.

Spread of Lutheranism

Germany
Scandinavia
Baltic States
England
New World

The advance of Lutheranism in Denmark (and Norway, which was linked to it) is much more complicated and would require considerable space to describe. Suffice it to say that Frederick I (1523-1533) set up a national church with definite Lutheran leanings. After a period of civil war, Christian III came to the throne (1536-1559) and at once reorganized the Danish church and made it distinctively Lutheran. Roman Catholic and Anabaptist dissenters were suppressed. In Iceland, which belonged to Norway, the policy was to force Lutheranism on a reluctant populace. After suppression of a midcentury revolt against Norwegian authority, Lutheranism was established there by royal decree in 1554.

At the eastern end of the Baltic, in Estonia, Latvia, and Lithuania, Lutheranism spread rapidly after 1539. And in 1561, Sweden annexed Estonia, which fact strengthened Lutheranism there. About 1525, the grand master of the Teutonic Knights established Lutheranism throughout East Prussia.

EIGHTEEN

The Swiss Reformation
Zwingli and Calvin

Zwingli[14]

HULDREICH Zwingli (1484-1531) sparked the Reformation in German-speaking Switzerland. After study at the universities of Bern, Vienna, and Basel, he was ordained and became parish priest at Glarus, where he remained for ten years. At Glarus he studied extensively the classics in the original languages, thus laying the foundation for his future Reformation work. During those years he also served as chaplain to Swiss mercenaries in Italy and began a campaign against Swiss mercenary service. This effort brought him many enemies in some of the poorer areas of the country, where that means of employment was thought to be necessary. Such animosity would be important in the later factionalizing of the country. He also fell under the influence of Erasmus during the Glarus period.

In 1516 he moved to the monastery church of Einsiedeln for a three-year ministry. There he studied the Greek New Testament published by Erasmus. He later claimed that at Einsiedeln in 1516 he had begun to found his preaching on the gospel. Because the monastery church had a well-known image of the Virgin Mary, it had become a pilgrimage center. To such comers Zwingli began to preach against the belief that religious pilgrimages were a means of obtaining pardon.

After becoming priest in the cathedral of Zurich (1519) Zwingli gradually became more open about his views. He broke with the pope and married, and preached openly against celibacy. Popular feeling was roused to such a point that the city council felt that it was necessary to appoint a public meeting for the discussion of religious subjects. When it convened, Zwingli presented his Sixty-seven Articles and was so convincing that the council declared that thereafter all religious teaching was to be based on the Bible alone and that the state would support this principle. The council also dissolved the Zurich monasteries and took control of the Great Minster (the Cathedral). Tremendous changes followed; many priests married and set aside the mass. Some thought the evangelical movement had gone too far, but the city council stood behind the Reformation and eventually abolished the mass and image worship altogether (1525).

Switzerland was a network of thirteen small states, or cantons, loosely federated and generally democratic. Culturally, the northern and eastern regions were German in language and orientation, the western part French, and the southern part Italian. Geographically the country was divided between mountain or forest and valley cantons. Gradually, the Reformation spread from Zurich, the chief city of the chief canton, to other cities of German Switzerland until the valley cantons were won. But that did not mean they were willing to join with Zurich in a united front. Some did not want to risk domination by Zurich. Several forest or mountain cantons remained militantly Roman Catholic and being poor farming areas, found Zwingli's antimercenary patriotism to be a threat to their economic life. At the time of the Reformation there were under a million people in

Switzerland and the population was largely rural. Zurich had an estimated 6,000 inhabitants.

As political tensions heightened, some Protestant cantons formed a Christian Civic League; the Roman Catholic cantons organized also and allied themselves with Ferdinand of Austria. A desire to avoid war led to the First Peace of Kappel in 1529. But two years later the five Roman Catholic cantons attacked Zurich, which was totally unprepared for war, and defeated her forces. Zwingli fought as a common soldier in the battle and died on the field on October 11. The Second Peace of Kappel (1531) prohibited further spread of the Reformation in Switzerland. Heinrich Bullinger,[15] Zwingli's son-in-law, now took over leadership of the Protestant cause in Zurich and enjoyed tremendous influence in many places on the continent. The military struggle had assured the virtual independence of the several cantons and therefore made it possible for the western canton of Geneva to go its separate way in following the lead of John Calvin a few years later.

Zwingli directed the Reformation in Switzerland along civic lines, with a view to establishing a model Christian community. He persuaded the city council to legislate the various details of the Reformation and supervise the carrying out of its decisions. In other words, he aimed at political as well as spiritual regeneration.

Zwingli's theology put great emphasis on the sovereignty of God and His election unto salvation. He held that the Lord's Supper contributed nothing to the elect; it was merely a symbol or remembrance of the sacrifice of Christ. He could not agree with Luther, who held that the body and blood of Christ were really present in the Communion. This was the rock on which the negotiations of the German and Swiss Reformers broke at Marburg in 1529. During his last years Zwingli moved away from his earlier position toward a doctrine of the spiritual presence of Christ in the Supper. The same may be said of Melanchthon. The Zwinglian movement merged into Calvinism later in the sixteenth century.

The Anabaptists

By no means did all those who broke with Rome agree with Zwingli, or with Luther or Calvin, for that matter. As early as 1523, in Zurich, Protestant separatists Conrad Grebel and Felix Manz questioned a number of the teachings and practices of Romanism and began to insist on adult baptism. Their activities caused the city council to persecute them, and many of their followers and fellow preachers were exiled, spreading the movement into Germany and Moravia.

In time, *Anabaptist* became a general term applied by Zwinglians, Lutherans, Roman Catholics, and others to those who would not fellowship with any of those communions, who rejected a connection between church and state, and who rejected infant baptism or for some reason insisted on rebaptism later in life. Persecution of Anabaptists was severe and often cruel in many countries of Europe.

The term *Anabaptist* was a general descriptive, and widely diverse views were held among them. Some were pantheistic, some extremely mystical, some anti-Trinitarian, some extremely millenarian, and some quite biblical. Modern Baptists who like to place themselves in the Anabaptist tradition need to remember that some groups of Anabaptists were not truly biblical. Furthermore, many of them, although they insisted on water baptism after a conversion experience, did not baptize by immersion. Moreover, the doctrinal position of biblical Anabaptists is more closely related to the modern Mennonite viewpoint than to Baptist theology (see below).

Today there is a tendency to describe the Anabaptists as the left wing of the Reformation, or better, the radical Reformation, and to find at least three major groups among them: Anabaptists proper, spiritualists, and religious rationalists. Generally, all of them opposed meddling with the religious affairs of the citizenry by the state or state churches, though a few tried to set up a revolutionary theocracy or accepted protection of the state.

Rationalists sought to put intuitive and speculative reason alongside Scripture as a basis of religious authority or a source of religious information. From this seedbed came the anti-Trinitarian efforts of Socinus and Servetus, as well as various pantheistic or transcendental approaches that involved a spiritual contemplation of the order of nature or allegorized the Bible into a cosmic philosophy.

Spiritualists put much emphasis on the future. They either sought revolutionary change in society as they set up communities designed to be utopias of sorts, or quiescently awaited the end of the age or the dawn of a millennial day.

The true Anabaptists were quite ascetic, tended to communal holding of goods, were pacifistic, opposed the use of oaths and capital punishment, favored the free will of man as opposed to predestination, stressed individual faith and witness, insisted on water baptism after a conversion experience, and taught separation of church and state. Primarily they were the spiritual antecedents of modern Mennonites rather than modern Baptists.

As may be suspected, by no means can all groups of radical Reformers be neatly categorized under one of the three headings suggested here.[16]

John Calvin[17]

John Calvin (1509-1564) was the great second generation Reformer. Thus, he could benefit from the work of such leaders as Luther, Zwingli, and Bucer. He began in the Roman church and gained a couple of benefices early in life because his father was in the service of the bishop of Noyon (France), but he was never ordained to the priesthood. His father wanted him to study law and he completed the degree in that discipline, but he also took university training in literature. His intellectual pursuits took him to the universities at Paris, Orléans, and Bourges. At the latter he came under the influence of Wolmar, with whom he studied Greek and Hebrew and the New Testament in the original language.

His conversion probably dated sometime during 1533. Calvin says it was sudden, through private study, and because he failed to find peace in absolutions, penances, and intercessions of the Roman Catholic church. Soon thereafter he and some of his friends were caught up in an anti-Protestant drive. Early in 1534 he was imprisoned for his faith twice. Late in the year Francis I of France imprisoned hundreds of Protestants, burning thirty-five of them at the stake, and executing Calvin's own brother.

For three years Calvin wandered about as a refugee in France, Germany, and Switzerland. During this period in his life, he met Martin Bucer, the great Reformer of Strasbourg, who later taught at Cambridge and aided Cranmer in English Reformation activities during the reign of Edward VI. And at Basel in 1536, at the age of only twenty-six, Calvin published the first edition of his *Institutes of the Christian Religion;* the last edition (1559) was four times the size of the original. Later in 1536, Calvin decided that after paying a last visit to his native France he would settle in Strasbourg.

But he passed through Geneva (a city of about 10,000 at the time) on the way, and William Farel persuaded Calvin to remain and help him with the Reformation there. In 1535 the Geneva city council had broken with the Catholic church and had confiscated its properties. The following May it committed the city to "live according to God's law and God's word and to abandon idolatry," and it instituted laws against drunkenness, gambling, dancing, and the like. So when Calvin came the city was ready for a new religious order. He prepared a catechism and articles of faith and insisted on the right of the church to exercise discipline over unworthy communicants.

At this point a tension developed with the magistrates who had for centuries controlled much of the social behavior of the populace through sumptuary laws and did not want to surrender that control to the church.[18] There was also a controversy over whether Geneva would follow the church program, liturgy, and discipline of Calvin or that of the city of Bern. Farel and Calvin worked very hard from 1536 to 1538 to establish the community on a theocratic basis. But in February of 1538 elections brought into leadership a faction more favorable to the Bernese pattern of reform. This development, coupled with opposition of those who wanted a less rigid moral control, led to the expulsion of the reformers in April—Farel going to Neuchatel and Calvin to Strasbourg (Spitz, 214-215).

The interval at Strasbourg[19] seems to have been a happy one for Calvin. He pastored a congregation of about five hundred French refugees at St. Nicholas church, wrote his commentary on Romans, produced the text for a hymn book, met with reformers in Germany, lectured in the academy, and married a widow. But a son born to them lived only a few days. He was made a citizen of the city in 1539. Meanwhile, back in Geneva the church fell into confusion, and the Roman church had put on a campaign to bring the city back into its fold. This threat made some Genevans look to Calvin for help to prevent it. This development, together with the rise of his friends to power in the city government, led Calvin to return reluctantly in 1541.

For the rest of his life Calvin worked tirelessly in his adopted city. Though he held no government office and did not even gain citizenship in Geneva until 1559, Calvin dominated the city. He exercised strict discipline over the morals of the community and drew up a new form of government and liturgy for the church. Moreover, he was largely responsible for a system of universal education for the young and programs to care for the poor and aged. And he established the Academy, later to be the University of Geneva.

The major event that marred the administration of Calvin at Geneva was the Servetus incident. Michael Servetus was a Spaniard under sentence of death by the Inquisition for his unitarian views. He staged a sensational escape from the prison of the French Inquisition near Lyons (France) and passed through Geneva on his way to Zurich and thence to Naples. Evidently he had been warned ahead of time that if he went to Geneva it was at his peril. In Geneva he was put on trial and ultimately judged guilty of subversion of religion and the general welfare. Genevan authorities consulted with other Swiss leaders (such as Bullinger) and Melanchthon, who supported the accusations against Servetus and recommended the death penalty. Finally, on October 25, 1563, he was judged guilty on fourteen counts and condemned to death by fire, contrary to provisions of the city ordinances, which limited punishment to banishment.

Although this act must be lamented, it is to be remembered that the age was an intolerant one. Roman Catholics executed thousands of Protestants throughout the century, and they probably would have burned Servetus at the stake if he had not escaped from them. Calvin took part only in this one execution; and he argued for a more humane form of execution. Moreover, the event had political overtones. Calvin's enemies sought to use Servetus to overthrow Calvin and expel his friends from power in the city government. In spite of all that, Calvin's reputation has been forever tarnished by the event.

Spread of Calvinism	
Switzerland	France
Germany	Scotland
Holland	Hungary
England	New England

Calvin's Influence

John Calvin was probably the most influential leader of the Reformation era. He put much stress on education. His catechetical system for the young has been carried all over the world. And at the school in Geneva men were trained who spread Presbyterianism all over Western Europe. In part his influence rose from the fact that Geneva generously welcomed refugees from almost every country in Europe. Often they returned home to spread the variety of Christianity they had come to know in Geneva. It was Calvin's theology and form of church government that triumphed in the Protestant church of France, the Reformed church of Germany, the Church of Scotland, the Reformed church in Hungary, the Reformed church in Holland, and in Puritanism in England and New England.[20]

Calvin's biblical and theological writings also have been very influential. He wrote commentaries on every book of the Bible except the Song of Solomon and Revelation. His *Institutes of the Christian Religion* became the dominant systematic theology of the Reformation in all except Lutheran lands. And he wrote numerous pamphlets on current issues. His literary output was so prodigious that he influenced the development of modern French; he has been credited along with Rabelais as being co-founder of modern French prose. And Calvin is often called the father of the historical-grammatical method of biblical study—a method that attempts to discover what the Scripture meant to those who wrote it, and what it means according to the common definition of its words and its grammatical intent. Contemporary evangelical students have so taken this method for granted that they have little realization of the part that Calvin had in its development and of the fact that it was virtually nonexistent in the church before the Reformation.

NINETEEN

National Reformations
France and England

The Reformation in France[21]

The Rise of the Huguenots

AS THE sixteenth century wore on, the Roman Catholic church in France fell into a progressively deplorable condition. In addition to the general slackness it experienced during the Renaissance era, the Roman church suffered increasingly from the effects of the Concordat of Bologna (1516). This agreement between Francis I of France and Pope Leo III gave the French monarch the right to appoint the 10 archbishops, 38 bishops, and 527 heads of religious houses in the realm. Henceforth the church became part of a vast patronage system, and individuals won positions in the church not for ability or religious zeal but for service to the crown or by purchase.

Conditions became indescribably bad. For instance, it is asserted that standards for parish priests declined to the point that only some 10 percent could read. Whether or not this percentage is correct, it seems safe to say that only a minority were literate. The king had in fact become the head of the church, and his great dependence on its patronage system and revenues helps to explain why Francis I and Henry II were so zealous in their persecution of Protestants. They could not afford to permit the system to crumble. They certainly were not zealous for the Roman Catholic faith.

Impetus for the French Protestant movement came from Geneva, and its advance was achieved especially through the printed page—the French Bible, Calvin's *Institutes*, and numerous other publications.[22] Naturally the most literate element of the population was more largely won. Converts were especially numerous at the universities and among lawyers and other professionals, the merchant classes and the artisans, the lower clergy and the friars, and the lesser nobility. The illiterate peasantry was hardly touched.

In addition to the positive attraction of the gospel, special forces worked to propel many into the Protestant camp. Lawyers and other professionals were traditionally anticlerical, merchants and financiers were discontented because of the financial strain of Francis' Italian wars, and many of the lesser nobles were in revolt against a social and political system of which they were victims. Dunn claims that about two-fifths of all French nobles joined the Huguenot cause. Few of them were authentically converted but sought to use the Protestant movement to weaken the trend toward royal absolutism.[23]

In spite of persecution the Protestants increased rapidly. At the beginning of the reign of Henry II (1547-1559) they probably numbered in excess of four hundred thousand. By the end of his reign they had come to be known commonly as Huguenots (meaning uncertain), and the total number of their congregations stood at 2,150 in 1561, with roughly two million adherents—about 10 percent of the population. The Presbyterian system of church government gave a firm organization and discipline to the Huguenot movement.

Conditions affecting the French Reformation

In order to understand the course of events that the French Reformation took and to see why it became embroiled in the civil wars, it is necessary to look at political and social conditions of the times. First, that many of the younger nobility joined Protestant ranks is of very great significance. Entitled and accustomed to carry swords, they became protectors of Huguenot congregations during the turbulent years of mid century and later. Often they protected church meetings against hostile bands of Roman Catholics. Naturally, their concerns became mixed up in the affairs of the church, and their quarrel with the crown very much affected the actions of the church.

Second, it is important to note that there were three major groups of mutually jealous nobility in the realm. The Bourbons, heirs to the throne if the ruling house of Valois should die out, controlled most of western France. Their leadership was largely Huguenot. The powerful Guises, staunch Roman Catholics, had extensive holdings in the east. The Montmorencys controlled much of the central part of the country; their leadership was divided between Protestants and Roman Catholics.

Third, when Henry II died, he left behind him three young sons (Francis II, who ruled 1559-1560; Charles IX, 1560-1574; Henry III, 1574-1589) who were dominated by his queen, Catherine de Medici. She was determined to maintain her personal control and advance the power of her sons and the central government. She was opposed by many of the nobility who were jealous of their old feudal rights and wanted to restrict the power of the monarchy.

Fourth, foreign affairs furnished another ingredient to the mix. As civil war boiled, the English and

Spanish sent aid to appropriate factions to serve their respective national interests.

Fifth, as already intimated, the rising middle class, as political and social outsiders and put upon by heavy financial exactions, opposed the crown for reasons of their own. The fact that they were also largely Huguenot only complicated their antipathy to the establishment.

The Peak of the Conflict

Such animosities provided the tinder to ignite armed conflict. In fact eight wars were fought between Roman Catholic and Protestant forces in France.[24] Leading the Protestants early in the conflict was Gaspard de Coligny. But he lost his life along with some fifteen to twenty thousand other Protestants in the massacre of St. Bartholomew's Day, August 24, 1572, at the instigation of Catherine de Medici. Thereafter Henry of Navarre, of the Bourbon family, led the Protestants. His military activities were successful, and ultimately, with the death of others in the royal line, he became heir to the throne of France. Because he did not have quite enough strength to complete his conquest, he turned Roman Catholic and won the crown as Henry IV. Judging from his conduct, Henry's religious principles sat rather lightly on his shoulders. His switch to Catholicism was obviously for political reasons, and perhaps he sought to turn off the blood bath that was drenching France.

At any rate, in 1598 Henry published the Edict of Nantes, a grant of toleration for the Huguenots. It guaranteed them the right to hold public office, freedom of worship in most areas of France, the privilege of educating their children in other than Roman Catholic schools, and free access to universities and hospitals. The edict was the first significant recognition of the rights of a religious minority in an otherwise intolerant age. Though the Huguenots enjoyed a period of great prosperity thereafter, they became a defensive minority, and finally Louis XIV revoked the edict in 1685. Then thousands were driven into exile to the benefit of England, Holland, Prussia, and America.

The Reformation in England

Reformation in England

Henry VIII, break with Rome
Edward VI, Protestant development
Mary I, back in Roman fold,
persecution of Protestants
Elizabeth I, establishment of Anglican Church;
Pilgrim, Puritan opposition
James I, King James Version,
heightened Puritan opposition

Henry VIII and the Break with Rome

The marital problems of Henry VIII especially led to England's break with Rome. Not only was he tired of Catherine of Aragon and enamored with Anne Boleyn, but he was concerned that Catherine had not provided him with a male heir. This could well have led to civil war after Henry's death. The dynasty was only in its second generation. It was his father, Henry VII, who had ended the thirty-year War of the Roses and established the Tudor line in 1485. So he sought annulment of his marriage at the hands of the pope. But Clement VII, under the influence of the powerful Charles V of Spain (nephew of Catherine) and the Holy Roman Empire, would not agree. In the midst of the struggle

Henry managed to install Thomas Cranmer as archbishop of Canterbury and to win from him annulment of his marriage to Catherine.

Though the rupture with Rome resulted from Henry's marital difficulties, the Reformation came to England for more complex reasons. Social, economic, political, cultural, and theological factors combined with personal matters to contribute to the success of the movement. The general spirit of anticlericalism, antipathy to Cardinal Thomas Wolsey, Tyndale's New Testament (1525), Erasmus's humanism, the influence of Lollardy, the contributions of the New Devotion, and the impact of numerous Lutheran converts were additional specific elements that helped to spark the Reformation and make it a success. In other words, popular religious feeling from below combined with official governmental changes from above to bring about the English Reformation.

The break with Rome came in 1534, when Parliament passed the Supremacy Act, making Henry head of the Church of England. Soon thereafter Henry, in need of money and afraid of a fifth column in the realm, closed the monasteries of England. But Henry did not provide a Protestant theology for England; he merely changed the headship of the English church. His efforts were always directed toward political control rather than theological change. Evidently he sought the degree of political absolutism, or at least control over the church, that was being achieved by such contemporary sovereigns as Ferdinand of Spain, Francis I of France, and Gustavus Vasa of Sweden. That he wanted no change in church doctrine is evident from his promulgation of the *Act of the Six Articles* (1539), a very Catholic creed, and his severe persecution of individuals of a Lutheran per suasion. His one innovation was the publication of the Great Bible (1537) and its installation in the parish churches of the realm.

King Edward VI and Protestant Gains

There was a marked change, however, during the reign of Edward VI (1547-1553). Coming to the throne at a very early age, he was ruled by regents who were of Protestant persuasion. The liturgy was changed, services conducted in English, a prayer book composed, marriage allowed for the clergy, images done away with, and the mass abolished. Archbishop Cranmer and others composed the Forty-two Articles, which later became the Thirty-nine Articles of the Church of England. A blend of Lutheran and Calvinist teachings, they were subscribed to by the king but not by Parliament. During his reign a stream of refugees and immigrants came to England from the Continent, most of them inclined to Zwinglian or Calvinistic views.

Queen Mary I and the Catholic Reaction

Edward died in the midst of a Roman Catholic reaction. So when Mary I (1553-1558) took the throne as a Roman Catholic, she was well received. In 1554 she married Philip of Spain but had no children, so no serious question of the union of the two nations ever arose. Edward's religious policy had been too sudden in one direction, and Mary's was too strong in the other. In fact Mary brought the English church once more within the Roman fold.

Many Protestants fled the country; some three hundred were martyred (252 is a commonly-accepted figure), including such outstanding leaders as Cranmer, Ridley, and Latimer. Of special importance to the future of religion in England is the fact that many of the Marian exiles went to

Geneva. There they were converted to Calvinism and later returned to England to help launch a Puritan opposition to Elizabeth's establishment. Though Mary enjoyed some success in restoring the Roman Catholic church in England, she experienced considerable opposition in Parliament. Though the Parliament of 1554 consented to her marriage to Philip of Spain, it refused to allow Mary to disinherit Elizabeth and bequeath the crown by will, and it rejected the restoration of laws against the Lollards, the reinstatement of the Six Articles, and the reestablishment of the monasteries.

Queen Elizabeth I and the Establishment of the Church of England

After the persecutions during Mary's reign and the unpopular Spanish alliance, the reign of Elizabeth I (1558-1603) was well received by the English people. Persecution came to an end, as did the Spanish alliance. The Church of England was reestablished, a prayer book drawn up, and the Forty-two Articles revised to Thirty-nine and adopted by Parliament. Queen Elizabeth loved an ornate service, and under her influence the Church of England developed its liturgy in that direction.

The Puritans and the Separatists

In this development Elizabeth was opposed by the Puritans.[25] The Puritans, who are known to have existed as early as the days of Edward, stressed rigid morals, church discipline, and a conversion experience as a prerequisite to church membership; they de-emphasized ritualism. At first they did not oppose a church government controlled by bishops. But the oppressive measures of Elizabeth and the return of Marian exiles with their Calvinist views changed the character of English Puritans.

Ultimately a great many of them argued for a presbyterian form of church government, insisted that only Christ could be considered Head of the church, and called for a general purification of the church and English society. Some of them came to prefer a congregational form of church government and were called Congregationalists or Independents. Some Congregationalists (Brownists or Separatists, later Pilgrims) held to complete separation of church and state.

At about the end of Elizabeth's reign the Baptists appeared,[26] drawing members from the ranks of the Puritans and Separatists. Baptists insisted on separation of church and state, the congregational form of church government, and a conversion experience prior to church membership and baptism. Normally, they also held that baptism should be by immersion.

The Success of Elizabeth's Middle Way

To what extent Elizabeth intended to follow a middle way (*via media*) or a compromise in establishment of the Church of England or was forced to do so by circumstances is open to question. Suffice it to say that the Anglican establishment was a compromise between elements of Catholicism and Protestantism. The liturgy, the prayer book, and the church government were largely Catholic; the Thirty-Nine Articles and the theology generally, the preaching, and the service in the vernacular were Protestant elements.

The success of the establishment was due to many factors, but to none more than the longevity of Elizabeth's reign. During that long period of forty-five years (1558-1603) the English populace knew nothing but the establishment she had brought into being. By the end of her reign, for most English that meant only their grandparents could remember a time when a different religious system existed.

Parenthetically, there was an important political by-product of the English Reformation. Both Henry VIII and his daughter Elizabeth sought the approval and support of Parliament in their Reformation activities: Henry in the break with Rome and Elizabeth in the formal establishment and regulation of the Church of England. These actions gave a power and prestige to Parliament that it did not previously have and set the nation on a new course politically. The rise of Parliament would be important for England, her American colonies, and the future United States.

King James I, the Puritans, and the Bible

James VI of Scotland became James I of England in 1603[27] and is significant to Protestants for his interest in the Bible translation that bears his name (published in 1611). James is also important because he increased the opposition of the Puritans to the crown by arranging for Sunday sports and by encouraging Arminianism in England. This animosity grew until in the days of Charles I it erupted in civil war (1642-1646).[28] Prior to the outbreak of the war, many Englishmen had given up hope of any appreciable change in English religious life. Some, as Separatists (Pilgrims), had gone to Holland and/or Plymouth, Massachusetts, and others (Puritans) had established the Massachusetts Bay Colony.

From 1640 to 1660, Parliament and Oliver Cromwell ruled the nation. The Puritan divines worked with the commissioners of the Church of Scotland to compose the Westminster Confession, which was adopted by the Church of Scotland in 1647 and in part by the English Parliament in 1648.

TWENTY

National Reformations
Scotland and the Netherlands

The Reformation in Scotland[29]

PROBABLY in no country of Europe were the Roman Catholic clergy more depraved than in Scotland at the time of the Reformation. This fact, taken in conjunction with remaining influences of Wycliffe, the old Celtic church, and the infiltration of Lutheran and Calvinistic ideas, greatly contributed to the rise of the Reformation in Scotland.

The pioneer Reformer in Scotland was Patrick Hamilton, who had been influenced by Luther's views while a student in Paris and had returned to his homeland to preach. He was burned as a heretic in 1528. The second great leader of the Scottish Reformation was George Wishart, who had a Zwinglian and Calvinistic orientation. Wishart was martyred in 1546. Martyrs' blood stirred many a heart in bonnie Scotland—and many a temper, too. By the time Cardinal Beaton presided over the martyrdom of Wishart, he had made so many enemies that a band of nobles (only one of whom was Protestant) entered his castle at St. Andrews and killed him.

The Influence of John Knox

Wishart's most ardent follower was John Knox—a leader with all the enthusiasm and popular power of

Luther and the steadfastness of Calvin. Knox had just completed his university training at St. Andrews about the time of Wishart's martyrdom; and in great personal danger, he fled for safety to the castle of St. Andrews, where the assassins of Beaton and an increasing crowd of Protestants were holed up. After some months, a French fleet, coming to the assistance of the Scottish queen, took the castle, captured its occupants, and sold Knox as a galley slave. After nineteen months the English rescued him, and he ministered in England during the days of Edward VI.

Leaving England when Mary Tudor (Bloody Mary) came to the throne, he ministered briefly among English exiles in Frankfurt and then became pastor of a group of English exiles in Geneva. His chapel was only a stone's throw from the cathedral where Calvin regularly preached. In 1555 he made a brief visit to England where he married, and subsequently preached in Scotland for nine months with great courage. Then he returned to Geneva for another three years.

The Scottish Reformation as a Mass Movement

Meanwhile the Reformation message spread widely in Scotland. Of prime importance to its success was the fact that in 1543 Parliament legalized the reading of the Bible in English or Scots. Moreover, a great amount of Protestant doctrinal literature was coming into the country. Actually, the Reformation was successful among all classes of the population. Many of the nobility supported it. The common people flocked by thousands to the cause. Of special importance in winning them were the plays, ballads, and pamphlets that blanketed the country. Lyrics on sacred themes taught doctrine, cast ridicule on the papacy, and provided a hymnody for the masses.

Recent scholarship has shown that the rising middle class was also heavily involved. Students were constantly moving to and from centers of learning on the Continent, where they came in contact with the writings and ideas of Hus, Luther, Calvin, and others. John Knox himself said in his History[30] that "merchants and mariners" had a prominent role in bringing religious books and ideas from the mainland. Amazingly, all this Reformation development was going on when there were hardly any Protestant preachers in Scotland and not even a semblance of a church organization.

The Scottish Political Situation

It should be remembered that after the death of James V (1542), Scotland was ruled by his wife, Mary of Guise, of a noble French family and virtually a tool of the French. Her daughter Mary, when six years old, was sent for education to France where she was married to the Dauphin, the crown prince Francis, son of Henry II and Catherine de Medici. For seventeen months (until Francis' death in December, 1560) Mary Stuart was queen of France.

Meanwhile, in an effort to maintain her position, Mary of Guise even had French troops stationed in Scotland. Many of the nobles, because they were both Protestants and good Scots, banded together to expel the French. Aided by an English fleet sent by Elizabeth, they defeated the French in 1560. In the midst of this conflict Mary of Guise died, and Scotland was without a ruling sovereign. Her daughter, Mary Stuart (Mary Queen of Scots) was occupied as queen of France.

Organization of the Scottish Reformation

John Knox had returned to Scotland in 1559, and he set about to organize a reformation that already had become a reality. The Roman church had virtually ceased to function. Without waiting for the absent queen to express an opinion, Parliament approved the First Scottish Confession and established the Church of Scotland in August of 1560.

Mary Stuart came back to Scotland in 1561. From the outset, she experienced the opposition of Knox, whose outspoken denunciations destroyed the possibility of persuading her to moderate or forsake her Roman Catholicism. Her determination to restore Romanism in Scotland brought her many enemies. But her love affairs with worthless men sealed her downfall. The refusal of the nobles to permit her third husband, the Earl of Bothwell (evidently a murderer), to rule as king led to a military confrontation, her defeat, and her imprisonment in 1567. Mary abdicated in favor of her son James VI; and her half brother, the Earl of Moray, became regent. After Mary fled to England for safety and was imprisoned there, plots against Elizabeth I began to swirl around Mary's head. Finally, in 1587 Elizabeth was pressured into executing Mary.

Protestantism was firmly established by Parliament. Knox had done his work. His impress may still be seen on the Church of Scotland and the educational system of the land. When Knox died (1572), Andrew Melville took over the work and perfected the system Knox had established. Though Knox had tolerated the episcopal form of church government, Melville opposed it. And after a lengthy conflict between the episcopal and presbyterian systems, presbyterianism finally won out completely.

The Reformation in the Netherlands[31]

The teachings of Luther and especially of Calvin were readily accepted in the Netherlands. And the great humanist Erasmus did much of his work there, writing devastating satires on the Roman church and other institutions of contemporary society under such titles as *The Praise of Folly* and *Familiar Colloquies*. Moreover, the Bible had been translated into Flemish several years before Luther was born. The Brethren of the Common Life were another important factor in the advancement of the Reformation in the Netherlands.

Spain controlled the Netherlands during the Reformation, and it was the great Charles V who first had to deal with Protestants. There were many martyrdoms in his days, especially of Anabaptists. Because Charles had been born in the Netherlands, the populace tended to put up with his policies. With his successor, Philip II (1556-1598), conditions radically changed however.

To begin with, he was looked upon as a Spanish foreigner in a day of rising nationalism in the Lowlands. He had the poor judgment to appoint almost exclusively Spanish administrators instead of using some of the local talent. Second, his autocratic ways were greatly resented by the more moderate Netherlanders. Third, his severe financial exactions threatened economic ruin of the fairly well-to-do burghers of the region. Fourth, Philip's introduction of the Inquisition and the stationing of the Duke of Alva and numerous Spanish troops in the Lowlands proved to be the last straw. Alva's "Council of

Blood" is credited with executing well over six thousand Lowlanders.

Thus there erupted an eighty-year war of independence, which evidently was not merely a struggle between Protestants and Roman Catholics. This is clear from the fact that in its early stages the Protestant north (Holland) and Roman Catholic south (Belgium) united to expel the hated Spaniard. Ultimately however, the Spanish were able to drive a wedge between the northern and southern provinces, and the Dutch fought on alone.

Actually, this statement requires some explanation and modification. The Netherlands or Lowlands consisted of seventeen autonomous provinces governed by the States-General with about as much power as the Continental Congress of the early United States. The merchant oligarchs controlled the provincial governments as well as the States-General. Philip II tried to tighten up the political structure as well as to reorganize the church and improve its machinery for inquisitorial activity. He nominated all the new bishops himself. This attempted political and religious absolutism galvanized the Netherlands into fierce opposition to him.

Initially the ten southern provinces (modern Belgium) were more Protestant and more rebellious than the northern provinces. In the summer of 1566 the Protestants ravaged hundreds of churches and destroyed their images. The Duke of Alva came in 1567 with 10,000 Spanish troops and nearly crushed Netherlands' resistance, killing thousands of suspected heretics and confiscating their property. Then he went on to mobilize a force of 65,000 men, which had to be paid and supplied from Spain. The failure to keep the salary of all these men up-to-date led to numerous mutinies that often paralyzed Philip's battle plans.

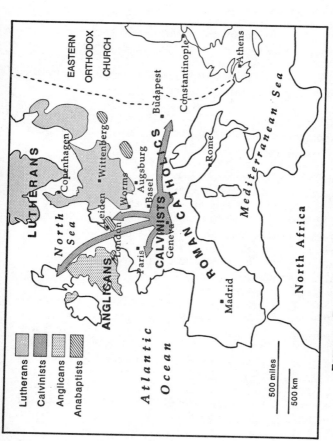

EUROPE DURING THE REFORMATION, c. 1550

The rebels had a hard time giving up the autonomous political structure in order to form an effective opposition to the Spanish. William of Orange, leader of the resistance movement, sought almost singlehandedly to mold the Netherlands into a nation. A decisive point in the struggle occurred in 1572. In April some rebel ships staged landings in the northern provinces of Zeeland and Holland and captured a number of ports; the Spanish were never able to dislodge them. Gradually a larger percentage of the population of the northern provinces became Protestant.

And as the Spanish achieved military victories in the south, large numbers of Protestant refugees fled north, with the result that gradually the north became almost solidly Protestant and the south almost solidly Catholic. The Spanish began to appeal to the southern provinces to dissociate themselves from the north on religious grounds; and in 1579 the new Spanish commander, the Duke of Parma, organized the south into the Union of Arras, and William organized the north into the Union of Utrecht.

The latter declared full independence as the United Provinces or the Dutch Republic in 1581. Religious refugees continued to flee northward. Finally in 1584 Parma achieved the assassination of William and the patriot cause went through dark days. At that juncture Queen Elizabeth of England sent a small force, and the Anglo-Dutch army held the Rhine River line from 1585 to 1587. Then with the defeat of the Spanish Armada in 1588 it became clear that Dutch independence was ultimately assured.

The Dutch were able to expel the last of the Spanish in 1609 and to win independence officially in 1648 with the Peace of Westphalia. The Reformed church was established as the state church of the Netherlands.

While still technically at war with Spain, the Dutch settled a colony at New Netherland (New York) in the 1620s and likewise moved into the East Indies to take over former Portuguese territory. They felt justified in occupying Portuguese holdings because Philip II had moved into Portugal and annexed both it and its empire. In struggling to gain their independence, the Dutch found themselves engaged in a world war with the Spanish. Subsequently they planted a settlement at the Cape of Good Hope as a halfway station between their homeland and their colonies in the Far East. Thus the Dutch Reformed church gained a foothold in North America, Africa, and the East Indies.

TWENTY-ONE

Counterattack

The Counter-Reformation and the Thirty Years War

Counter-Reformation

Renewal within the religious orders;
origin of the Jesuits
Inquisition
Council of Trent
Spiritual writings and spiritual movements

The Counter-Reformation[32]

THE term *Counter-Reformation* is misleading. The Roman Catholic church, like a sleeping giant, was not suddenly awakened to new life and vigor by the Protestant menace alone. Calls for reforming the teachings and practices of the church could be heard throughout the fifteenth century and earlier. And in some quarters, reforms of sorts were undertaken long before Luther posted his theses at Wittenberg in 1517. But it is undeniably true that the threat of Protestant successes spurred the Roman church's efforts to set her house in order. And she did counterattack at numerous points to regain areas lost or in danger of being lost to Protestants.

The Roman church was successful in these efforts

for many reasons, among which must be included the following:

- As state churches were established in Protestant lands, the church increasingly came under the dominance of the political arm and was forced to serve the interests of the state. Thus Protestant churches began to suffer the same kind of fate as the Roman church had at the hands of a Francis I or Henry II of France.
- The early evangelical enthusiasm declined, partly because of political involvements and partly because enthusiasm cannot be maintained at a high level for long.
- The controversial spirit arose among Protestants—state-church people against dissenters, and divisiveness among members of the dominant group.
- The papacy had the advantage of a thoroughly organized system.
- The papacy was supported by Romance peoples—among whom there was little reformation.
- The Roman church learned from the Reformation and set its house in order somewhat.

Religious Orders New and Renewed

There were at least four aspects to the Counter-Reformation. The first of these concerned the religious orders. There was renewal within the older orders such as the Franciscans, Dominicans, and Benedictines. Reform among the Franciscans led to the founding of the Capuchins in 1528; their aggressive work among the peasants of Italy held them for the Catholic church. New orders included the Theatines (1524) with the chief aim of recalling the clergy to a godly life and inspiring the laity to the same; the Ursulines (1535), an order for women who cared for the sick and needy and concerned itself with the Christian nurture of girls; and especially the Jesuits.

The Jesuits (Society of Jesus) were the most important of the new orders. Founded in Paris in 1534 by Ignatius of Loyola (but officially recognized by Pope Paul III in 1540), the order demanded slavish obedience of all its members for the furtherance of the interests of the Roman church. They were absolutely unscrupulous in their methods, holding that it was permissible even to do evil if good might come of it. The Inquisition could win back individuals where the Reformation had slight effect. In other areas the Jesuits set up schools to convert the minds of the populace, sought to infiltrate governmental office, or used every means fair or foul to advance the cause of the church. Their power became so great and their methods so immoral that the order was suppressed by the papacy from 1773 to 1814 as a result of appeals from various governments.

It should be noted, however, that when Ignatius began his spiritual odyssey in 1521 and when he later launched the Society of Jesus, a counterattack against the Reformation was not in view. He himself was characterized by a missionary zeal and especially by a desire to convert Muslims. The three major goals of the Jesuits were to convert pagans, combat heresy, and promote education. Military features of the order derive from the fact that Ignatius had been a soldier before he decided to devote his life to the church.[33]

The Inquisition

The Inquisition was another feature of the Counter-Reformation. The medieval Inquisition, discussed earlier, was revived during the sixteenth century, especially in Italy (launched by Pope Paul III in 1542) and Spain and her dependencies. Though the Netherlands was subjected to a terrible persecution, Protestantism triumphed there. But in Italy, Spain, Portugal, and Belgium the Inquisition was fairly successful in extirpating the effects of the Reformation.

The Council of Trent

A third aspect of the Counter-Reformation was papal concern and the Council of Trent. The cardinals elected a Dutch theologian Adrian VI as a reform pope in 1522. He frankly admitted that the Lutheran troubles may have come upon the church because of the sins of the church, from the papal office on down (Spitz, 296). Paul III in 1536 appointed a blue ribbon panel of cardinals to prepare a report on the condition of the church. That report gave Luther a lot of grist for his mill. Successive popes were increasingly concerned about calling a council to deal with the issues raised by the Lutherans, and Lutherans looked forward to the convoking of such a council.

The Council of Trent was that council. It met in a total of twenty-five sessions, under three popes, from 1545 to 1563. The majority of participants came from Italy, Spain, France, and Germany. The council decided a host of issues, including the validity of the seven sacraments in bestowing merit on the believer and the necessity of some of them for salvation; the value of tradition as a basis of authority alongside the Bible; the canonicity of the apocryphal books of the Old Testament; the existence of purgatory; the value of images, relics, indulgences, and invocation of saints; and the importance of confession to a priest. It also defined more specifically the sacrificial aspects of the mass and decided that only the bread should be distributed to the laity.

The council's work constituted a statement of faith by which true Roman Catholics could determine their orthodoxy. No such comprehensive statement existed before. If it had, perhaps the force of the Reformation would have been blunted in some places. What the Council of Trent did, in effect, was to make official dogmas of the church the various positions Luther had questioned in his break with the church.

A New Spirituality

A fourth aspect of the Counter-Reformation was a new and vigorous kind of spirituality that bloomed in a remarkable series of writings and movements.[34] Some little spiritual books from this movement, such as the *Imitation of Christ* and the *Spiritual Exercises*, have received proper attention, but many have not. This new kind of devout life was characterized by a systematized examination of conscience, prayer, contemplation, and spiritual direction. Its roots lay deep in the Middle Ages with such groups as the Carthusians, who put special emphasis on the contemplative life and the practice of spiritual exercise. The *Devotio Moderna*, which made its appearance in the Low Countries during the fourteenth century, gave the movement greater impetus and was at the background of the Brethren and Sisters of the Common Life. In the same context fits the Italian Oratory of Divine Love. One can go on and on listing sixteenth century Italian or Spanish masters of spiritual cultivation. For instance there is the Italian Dominican Carioni, the Theatine Scupoli, the Spanish Dominican de Granada, and the writer de Cisneros.

This magnificent and massive development deserves extensive new exploration for the benefit of contemporary lay movements. Though some of the developments noted here date earlier than the sixteenth century, it seems proper to include them. As noted above, there were signs of new life in Roman Catholicism before Martin Luther's attacks. Probably it is better to speak of a Roman Catholic Reformation than merely a Counter-Reformation.

The Thirty Years War[35]

The Reformation period closed with a bloodbath that is known as the Thirty Years War. This conflict was really a combination of three antagonisms wrapped into one: Protestants versus Roman Catholics in Germany, emperor versus princes in the Holy Roman Empire, and France versus the Hapsburgs for the domination of Europe. The ambitions of other princes and states became involved; for example, Sweden and Brandenburg-Prussia.

The war is normally divided into four phases, with slightly varying dates and titles given to each:

Bohemian (1618-1623)

At the background of this struggle is the fact that only Lutheranism had been recognized at the Peace of Augsburg in 1555, and Calvinism had rapidly advanced in the empire subsequently. In 1618 the Bohemians refused to recognize the newly elected Roman Catholic emperor, Ferdinand II, and elected Frederick V of the Palatinate of Germany, a Calvinist, as their king. This could only lead to open warfare. The imperial and Roman Catholic forces were victorious and crushed Protestantism in Bohemia, Moravia, Austria, and the

Palatinate and engaged in a ruthless policy of reconversion and confiscation of Protestant property.

Danish (1624-1629)

Christian IV of Denmark entered the struggle with English subsidies. Imperial and Roman Catholic forces were again victorious, and Protestantism in central Europe lay virtually prostrate.

Swedish (1630-1634)

German princes, fearing the increasing power of the emperor, became involved in a squabble that weakened the imperial and Roman Catholic cause. At that point the great Gustavus Adolphus, "Lion of the North," landed an army in Germany. Evidently he believed he was fighting for the sake of the gospel, but he was also interested in expanding the Swedish empire. For that reason some German Protestant princes were reluctant to join forces with him. Cardinal Richelieu of France (virtual prime minister) sought to use Gustavus's successes to weaken the power of the Spanish and Austrian Hapsburgs to the benefit of France and provided the Swedes with French subsidies. Gustavus won major victories, but was killed in battle in 1632; his army continued to fight.

International (1635-1648)

The last phase of the war was a struggle for advantage by German states and foreign powers. Armies crossed and recrossed Germany, creating havoc and destruction.[36] Finally, after years of negotiations the Peace of Westphalia was signed in 1648. Calvinism was recognized as a legal religion along with Lutheranism and Roman Catholicism. Each prince of the empire was permitted to determine the religion of his state, according to the status of 1624. The Holy Roman Empire was further weakened by allowing the three hundred German political entities local autonomy. Holland and Switzerland officially won independence. Sweden gained holdings in Germany. Brandenburg-Prussia expanded her territory. France won Alsace and Lorraine from the Holy Roman Empire, which fact raises a hint of future international conflict.

Europe was now officially divided religiously. England, Scotland, Holland, Scandinavia, part of Germany, and part of Switzerland had established Protestant churches. The Roman church retained its hold everywhere else in the West. The Russian Orthodox church was the state religion in Russia. Other orthodox groupings in the Balkans had fallen behind the Muslim curtain. Though Richelieu had restricted Huguenot power and freedom in France, that significant minority clung to a degree of toleration for a few more decades.

Other Considerations

In reply to those who criticize Christianity for the many wars it presumably fought during the Reformation period, it must be observed that in every case the political, economic, and social considerations were often as important as the religious. Much of the time, there was no clear-cut struggle between Roman Catholics and Protestants. Let it be remembered that both Protestants and Roman Catholics were found in the armies that opposed Mary Queen of Scots. The Reformer Henry of Navarre was supported in his bid for the throne of France both by Protestants and Roman Catholics. And during much of the Thirty Years War, Roman Catholic France was allied with Protestant Sweden.

PART V

◆

The Church in Modern Europe

TWENTY-TWO

An Age of Orthodoxy
The Seventeenth Century

THE seventeenth century was a century of orthodoxy. Both Protestants and Roman Catholics were concerned with dogmatic formulation of their positions for the purpose of catechizing their adherents. Although some of this orthodoxy stressed Christian experience, much of it emphasized right thinking. The drying up of the wellsprings of vitality in religion had started by the beginning of the seventeenth century, but the process accelerated in certain areas of Europe that lay prostrate as a result of the Thirty Years War.

Cold orthodoxy will not long satisfy. It will produce at least three reactions or results: rationalism, biblical revivalism, or extreme forms of mysticism. In other words, some will turn from ineffective supernatural Christianity to a religion based on human reason or to no religion at all; others will return to a healthy combination of doctrine and experience; still others will substitute the authority of experience for the authority of creeds, catechisms, and sometimes Scripture itself.

Forms of Mysticism

The Quakers

Prominent among the inner light or mystical groups of the seventeenth century were the Quakers. The originator of the movement was George Fox of Drayton, England. Following a religious experience in 1646, he began a forty-year ministry of itinerant preaching, including journeys to Ireland, the West Indies, and North America. The Quaker movement spread very rapidly across England and, after its organization in 1660, to the Continent, Asia, Africa, the West Indies, and North America. There William Penn founded a haven for them in Pennsylvania in 1682, after it had become evident that New Jersey would not offer them adequate protection.

The Quakers were severely persecuted, not only because of their great difference from the confessional churches on many points, but because of their open criticism of other faiths, their refusal to pay taxes for the support of the state churches in some places, and their occasional disruption of services of the state churches.

Quakers emphasized the work of the Holy Spirit: that the revelations of the Spirit, or the inner light, were equal to the Bible, but not contradictory to it; that since the Holy Spirit speaks to all, special training and ministers were unnecessary; that the Spirit could speak through women as well as men, and therefore they could teach and preach on an equal basis with men; and that formal worship was an abomination to God. They insisted on complete separation of church and state and did not practice the sacraments, take oaths, or do military service.

Their frequent imprisonments acquainted them with conditions in English jails and led them into prison reform. Later they launched a campaign against slavery and entered other forms of social service. In more recent times many Quakers have abandoned the traditional service, in which people sat silently until "moved by the Spirit" to share with those gathered, and have turned to a simple service led by a pastor. There are about 200,000 Quakers (or Friends) in the world today, of which approximately 80,000 live in the United States.

The New Jerusalem Church

The teachings of the Swedish scientist Emanuel Swedenborg (1688-1772) led to the founding of the New Jerusalem Church. He claimed to have had a revelation that enabled him to communicate with the world of spirits and angels; and during his various communications with that world, he claimed to have learned the secrets of the universe. Instead of rejecting the Bible, he spiritualized or allegorized it. The theological system he developed had some similarities to Gnosticism. He seems to have denied the Trinity, original sin, the vicarious atonement, and the bodily resurrection.

But some individual congregations of the New Jerusalem Church do not appear to be quite so unorthodox. Actually, Robert Hindmarsh launched the New Jerusalem Church in London in the 1780s, and Swedenborgian churches were established mainly in England, Sweden, Germany, and North America. Membership in the New Jerusalem Church in the United States has shrunk to 2,245 in the General Convention of the New

Jerusalem and 2,143 in the General Church of the New Jerusalem.

Quietism

Within Romanism there was also a reaction to the rationalization of dogma, which expressed itself in an extreme mystical movement. Known as Quietism, it held that God can act on believers to meet their spiritual need only as they surrender themselves utterly. When the soul is completely passive, the way is open to receive impartation of divine light from God. At that point the individual rests in the presence of God in pure faith in a kind of mystic death or sinless state, and all that the person thinks or does is supposed to be the work of God. Some of the Quietists were pantheistic in approach, teaching that contemplation of the divine would lead to absorption into the divine.

Michael Molinos in Spain and Madame Guyon and Francis Fénelon in France were three of Quietism's leading writers. Recognizing that Quietism seemed to need none of the externalities of the Roman church and that it was therefore a danger to the system, the Jesuits mounted an effective assault on the movement, first in Spain and then in France. It is strange that some modern evangelicals are attracted to the writings of Madame Guyon when she was so far from the mainstream of orthodox faith.

Biblical Revivalism

Jansenism

A contemporary Roman Catholic reaction that stressed experience, though not of the same type, was Jansenism. So named for its leader Cornelius Jansen, it sought to return to the teachings of Augustine, to stress greater personal holiness, the necessity of divine grace for conversion, and performance of divine commandments. As a reform movement, Jansenism attracted numerous outstanding scholars, among them Blaise Pascal.

The Jesuits launched a violent attack on the Jansenists, and Pope Innocent X condemned their teachings in a papal bull in 1653. Louis XIV, also engaged in some controversy with the papacy, defended the Jansenists. But the Jesuits continued the attack, and in 1713 Pope Clement XI issued another papal bull against them, this time condemning 101 statements from one of their writings—many of them direct quotations from St. Augustine.

Pietism

A seventeenth-century evangelical corrective to the cold orthodoxy of the Lutheran church was Pietism. Although its main center was in Germany, it claimed many adherents in Switzerland and Holland as well. In Holland, the revolt was against the Dutch Reformed church. Pietism emphasized the need for a regeneration experience on the part of all, promoted a living Christianity wherein the love of God would be expressed, and encouraged practical church work and Bible study on the part of laypersons. It also sought better spiritual training for ministers and a greater fervency in the preaching of sermons.

The great leaders of German Pietism were P. J. Spener and A. H. Francke; the latter was especially important for his training schools and institutions for the needy at Halle (e.g., an orphanage, a hospital, a widows' home). Spener and Francke did not want to found a new church but only to form evangelical groups within the established Lutheran church to leaven the larger community. Its lack of organization made it somewhat ineffective in perpetuating its message and ministry, however. And the almost pharisaical attitudes and austere legalism of many of its adherents did not provide the winsome attractiveness to a more elevated Christianity that Spener and Francke had desired.

Arminianism

While Pietism reacted primarily against Lutheranism, Arminianism reacted against the Reformed Church of Holland. Calvinism in Holland had grown much more harsh and severe than it was in Calvin's day; so the Arminians in 1610 (a year after the death of Jacobus Arminius, their leader) addressed a *Remonstrance* to the States-General of Holland. In it they emphasized the opportunity and responsibility of man in salvation: that one faces a choice of salvation or condemnation and is actually free to do so, that predestination is conditioned on God's foreknowledge of one's faith and perseverance, that although grace is indispensable it is not irresistible, and that to stay saved one must desire God's help and be actively engaged in living the Christian life.

Perhaps it should be noted that in the ongoing debate between Arminianism and Calvinism both groups have grown more extreme than the views set forth by their founders. Much misunderstanding of both positions and much quibbling between groups holding these divergent positions today could be stopped if there were a wider reading and understanding of the works of Calvin and Arminius. At any rate, the Dutch church did not welcome the Arminian *Remonstrance*, but at the

Synod of Dort in 1618 set forth the five points of Calvinism in response to it: total depravity of man after the Fall, unconditional election, limited atonement, irresistible grace (divine grace cannot be rejected by the elect), and perseverance of the saints (they cannot fall from grace).

Rationalistic Response: Socinianism

One of the more important rationalistic movements of the seventeenth century was Socinianism, so named for its founder, Faustus Socinus (1539-1604). Originally from Italy, Socinus spent most of his years of teaching and preaching in Poland. There he espoused an essentially anti-Trinitarian system, a rationalistic interpretation of Scripture, and separation of church and state. He taught that Christ was a man who lived a life of exemplary obedience and who ultimately was deified. One becomes a Christian by following Christ's example of devotion to God, renunciation of the world, and humility. Christ's death was not substitutionary, but merely an example of ultimate devotion.

After a couple of generations of success in Poland, the Socinian movement was broken up by the parliament under pressure from the Jesuits, and its followers were banished. Many found their way to Holland, where they were welcomed by Arminians and others and where they injected a considerable liberal influence into the theology of the country. Some went to England, where they also joined with Arminians to infuse Anglicanism with a liberalizing tendency. Others went to Hungary and Prussia.

TWENTY-THREE

An Age of Rationalism
The Eighteenth Century

The Rise of Rationalism

IF THE seventeenth century was an age of orthodoxy, the eighteenth was an age of rationalism. In part, rationalism was a reaction to or an outgrowth of cold orthodoxy. And in part it grew out of the great emphasis on faith and emotion during the seventeenth century. Many of the groups that stressed spiritual experience did not strive hard enough to meet the intellectual needs of their constituency. In their emphasis on emotion, they neglected a doctrinal basis of their faith. Note for instance that Immanuel Kant, a watershed in the history of philosophy, was the son of Pietistic parents and that he was educated as a Pietist until 1740.

Secular philosophy

The rise of rationalism also resulted from the place given to philosophy in the universities. During the Middle Ages philosophy and theology had been wed in the system called Scholasticism; but with the decline of Scholasticism and the church the two were divorced, with the result that philosophy became an enemy of theology. Western philosophy was now free to discover answers to the big questions of life by means of human reason alone. In such a frame of reference there were no absolutes, and thought processes clashed head on with theological systems in which the answers to the big questions of life came by revelation and in which there were numerous divinely-prescribed absolutes.

The New Science and Empiricism

Furthermore, the rise of rationalism was fostered by scientific developments. Copernicus (1473-1543) was responsible for developing the view that the sun instead of the earth was the center of the universe. Galileo (1564-1642) trained the telescope on the heavens and used observation to support Copernicus's view of the solar system. Descartes (1596-1650) propounded the concept of a mathematically ordered universe governed by natural law, and Isaac Newton (1642-1727) furnished the principle that the law of gravity held the universe together and caused it to function as it did.

In another connection, Descartes taught that one ought never to allow himself to be persuaded of the truth of anything unless on the evidence of reason. And Francis Bacon (1561-1626) introduced the inductive method, according to which a scientist accepted nothing on the basis of authority alone, but developed his theories by observing phenomena. So knowledge was tied to what the senses could discover and what the reason could deduce. Revelation tended to take a back seat to reason and to knowledge gained by sense perception.

The Natural Religion of Deism

The new scientific developments led to the view that the universe was a closed system of cause and effect, ruled by universal and dependable laws. God was considered to be a necessary first cause to start the system going; but once He set the universe in motion, He no longer interfered with its natural processes. Miracle, providence, prayer, and revelation were ruled out. The natural religion of deism took over. God was still viewed as Creator, but He had little to do with the universe, which He as a kind of watchmaker had wound up and let run according to natural laws.

Since He did not interfere in this universe, there was no such thing as revelation. Thus the Bible was a human book with some elevated ethical principles and spiritual lessons that had value for humanity. The greatest revelation of all, God's self-revelation in His Son, and the greatest miracle of all, the incarnation of the Son, were rejected out of hand. Thus, Jesus was only a human with an amazing God-consciousness and a superior ethic to be emulated. Deism made great inroads in England, France, Germany, and other countries of Europe, as well as in America.

John Locke and the Philosophes

From the same context as deism rose a new social philosophy whose proponents included John Locke and the philosophes, or social philosophers. Locke (1632-1704) taught that just as the universe was governed by natural law, so men (as part of nature) were guaranteed certain natural rights. His political philosophy was an important facet of the political theory of the eighteenth century and was written into the American Declaration of Independence and the French Declaration of the Rights of Man. His religious views were significant too. In *An Essay Concerning Toleration, The Reasonableness of Christianity*, and in his four letters on toleration he argued that no one could be saved by a religion that was forced upon him and that he did not believe. Therefore, he called for religious toleration and the separation of church and state.

The philosophes, a group of middle-class French intellectuals of the eighteenth century, broadened Locke's views and popularized them in France. Voltaire ("prince of the philosophes"), Diderot, and others taught that just as the universe was governed by natural law, so society was governed by natural laws. And just as men could discover the laws of nature and bend it to the service of mankind, so they could discover the laws of society and make it a more equitable and reasonable structure. In doing so, they held that the institutions of the past, or "debris," which had impeded human progress, had to go.

One of the most important of these restrictive institutions was the church. And the church in France, home of the philosophes and of the Enlightenment, was the Roman Catholic church. Thus began open warfare between "science" and theology in the West. Voltaire and other leaders of the Enlightenment were vocal in their opposition to the church and the orthodox view of the Bible. Voltaire (1694-1778) in his *Questions of Dr. Zapata* helped to lay the foundation for rationalistic higher criticism of the Bible. What began in the eighteenth century developed into a formal system of biblical criticism late in the nineteenth century.

One of the most influential writers of the century was David Hume (1711-1776), a Scottish philosopher and historian. He is especially remembered for his skeptical attacks on miracles, which appeared in his famous "Essay on Miracles," published in his *Philosophical Essays Concerning Human Understanding* (1748). He is also important for his *An Enquiry Concerning the Principles of Morals* (1751), in which he argued that moral judgments were the product of passions rather than of reason.

The Methodist and Moravian Counterattack

Attack and counterattack are characteristic both of the eighteenth and nineteenth centuries. Forces at work during the nineteenth century will be discussed later. The attack during the eighteenth century was launched by rationalism, a counterattack by such groups as Moravians and Methodists.

The Moravians

The Moravian movement was an outgrowth of Pietism. Its leader, Count Nikolaus von Zinzendorf, had spent several years in one of the Pietist schools at Halle. In 1722 he invited exiled Protestants from Bohemia and Moravia to settle on his estate in Saxony, where they organized as the "renewed fraternity," dedicated to a religion of the heart and an intimate fellowship with the Savior. Zinzendorf himself developed a very keen interest in world evangelization, but he was especially concerned with establishing an international fellowship of true believers belonging to various religious bodies. Therefore he did not want to start a new denomination. His own colony he kept within the Lutheran church.

As Moravian missionaries became active in preaching the gospel and in organizing groups of believers within the established churches of Europe, they had great success in founding fellowships elsewhere in Germany and in Holland, Denmark, England, Switzerland, and North America. When Zinzendorf fell into the disfavor of the Lutheran church and hence the Saxon government, he was exiled for over ten years. During those years, much against his will, the Moravians organized as a separate denomination known as the Unity of the Brethren (1742), and won recognition from the

Saxon government. In England they became known as Moravians. Their doctrinal position was basically that of the Lutheran Augsburg Confession.

The Moravians have been famous for their church music, which owes its original inspiration to Zinzendorf, who himself wrote many hymns. He is credited with the authorship of more than 2,000 lyrics.[1] There are about 510,000 Moravians in the world today, 55,000 in the United States and 60 percent of the total in Tanzania and South Africa, reflecting the missionary thrust of the denomination.

Methodism

The Moravians had a direct influence on the establishment of the Methodist movement, which was founded by John and Charles Wesley[2] and George Whitefield.[3] Moravian missionaries exposed the Wesleys to the gospel message while the latter were on a fruitless missionary journey to the New World and had not yet been converted. Later, another Moravian, Peter Boehler, brought the Wesleys to Christ. Shortly thereafter, John Wesley visited Zinzendorf in Germany and then embarked on his lifework. *Methodist* was the name applied to the "holy club" at Oxford to which the Wesleys and George Whitefield had belonged; they had founded the organization because of their concern over the spiritual condition among the students. Because of the strict rules and precise spiritual methods of the group, they were nicknamed "Methodists"; subsequently the name passed on to the movement begun by the three.

John Wesley (1703-1791) and George Whitefield (1714-1770) were the great preachers; Charles Wesley (1708-1788) though also a preacher, was the hymn writer. Having composed some 7,270 hymns, he is ranked by many as the greatest hymn writer of all ages.[4]

As the Wesleys carried on their revival efforts, they received little encouragement from the Anglican church, of which they were members. Shut out of many Anglican churches, they took a cue from Whitefield, who had had great success in outdoor preaching in America. Tremendous crowds constantly gathered for their meetings.

Early Methodism was characterized by the preaching of present assurance of salvation, development of the inner spiritual life, belief in the attainability of Christian perfection in this life, and a dignified ritual. The Wesleys were Arminian in their theology, but Whitefield was Calvinistic. Originally, John Wesley did not wish to organize the Methodist church as a separate denomination; he set up societies within the Anglican church. But the success of the American Revolution demanded a separation there, and the Methodist Episcopal church was established in 1784. In England, Methodism separated from the Anglican church about the same time.

As well as having a wide spiritual impact, Methodism proved to be a very real answer to the social ills of the day. Spiritually, Methodism was the answer to deism in England, especially among the lower and middle classes. And it met the needs of the new laboring classes in the cities, for whom the Anglican church did not assume much responsibility. Socially, in large measure it retarded forces that in France led to revolution: it provided medical dispensaries, orphanages, and relief for the poor; it stood at the front of the movement for prison reform, the abolition of slavery, and the regulation of industry.[5]

TWENTY-FOUR

An Age of Science
The Nineteenth Century

IF THE seventeenth century may be characterized as the age of orthodoxy and the eighteenth as the age of rationalism, the nineteenth may be characterized as the age of science. But science took over after about the middle of the century; other forces were at work in the early part of the century. The Enlightenment of the eighteenth century had gone too far in its rationalism and in its effort to eradicate religion and remove feeling from all of life. The first part of the nineteenth century saw in Romanticism a reaction to that extreme.

Romanticism

Romanticism was characterized by a new emphasis on feeling, faith, individualism, and communion with nature divine and untamed. There was a new emphasis on feeling in all phases of life—music, poetry, drama, and certainly religion. Faith—not necessarily orthodox faith—was considered to be good. Individualism manifested itself in a new impatience with society's laws and rules of conduct and sought expression in personal religion and individualized education.

Moreover, there was a new emphasis on the organic view of history and society. That is, it was felt that the present must be understood in connection with the past and the future; and that there is slow, not radical, development of the social organism. This intellectual context is important for the appearance and impact of Darwinian thought.

But it was important, too, for the development of Hegelianism, Marxism, and nationalism. Georg Hegel (1770-1831), a professor of philosophy at several German universities, finished his career at the University of Berlin. He taught many things, but his very influential *Philosophy of History*, published posthumously in 1837, saw a spiritual or non-material force moving through history and evolving by means of a dialectical process (clash of opposites) to establish freedom in a utopia on earth.

Karl Marx (1818-1883) borrowed from Hegel and others to teach a materialistic philosophy; that is, he saw a materialistic force moving through history by means of the dialectic of the clash of classes to establish the utopia of a classless society. Marx, commonly regarded as the founder of modern scientific socialism, did much of his writing in England, where he attacked the evils of capitalism. His great works were the *Communist Manifesto* (1847) and, in collaboration with Friedrich Engels, *Das Kapital* (3 vols., 1867, 1885, 1893). Marx's views were not destined to catch fire in the nineteenth century.

The nationalistic spirit was advanced by such writers as the German Johann Herder (1744-1803) and the Italian Joseph Mazzini (1805-1892). Herder spoke of a *Volksgeist* or spirit of a people or national character that enabled an individual nation to make its contribution to civilization. This romantic individualism fed into the stream of national thought in such writers as Mazzini, who founded the Young Italy movement and in his *On the Duties of Man* saw individuals realizing their potential and fulfillment in the formation of a country. In his *Duties* he said, "O my brothers, love your Country. . . . It is only through our country that we can have a recognized *collective* existence." He worked hard for the unification of Italy.

One facet of the Romantic reaction was the revival of religion of all types. Some took the aesthetic approach and found a delight in vesture and symbol and stained glass and stately organ music. Others turned from rationalistic apologies for Christianity to emotional experience of a more or less orthodox faith. Napoleon made a concordat with the papacy (1801) and restored the Roman Catholic church in France. Schleiermacher, in Germany, redefined religion as feeling—man's feeling of dependence on God as he comes to realize how finite, limited, and temporary he is in comparison with the eternal principle indwelling the world. Schleiermacher's rationalized Christianity has influenced such more recent movements as neo-orthodoxy and existentialism.

An evangelical revival moved through the Church of England during the first third of the century under the leadership of such well-known saints as John Newton and William Wilberforce.[6] Meanwhile Methodist, Baptist, and other dissenter groups grew rapidly in number. The Sunday school movement spread across England like a prairie fire,[7] and several Bible societies were founded in Europe and America, including the British and Foreign Bible Society, the Berlin Bible Society, and the American Bible Society. At the same time, the foreign missions movement continued to expand. In fact the nineteenth century has been called the "Great Century of Protestant Missions."

Early British Missionaries

William Carey, Henry Martyn, Alexander Duff—India
Samuel Marsden—South Pacific
Robert Morrison, Hudson Taylor—China
Robert and Mary Moffat, David Livingstone—Africa

The Beginnings of the Modern Missionary Movement

The modern missionary movement is usually considered to have begun with William Carey (1761-1834), whose efforts led to the founding of the Baptist Missionary Society at Kettering, England, in 1792.[8] The following year Carey set out for India. As reports of his work reached home, members of other denominations banded together to form the London Missionary Society (1795). Other societies followed in rapid succession. Carey taught himself several languages of India and became a leader in Bible translation. He was followed there by the Anglican Henry Martyn and the Church of Scotland's Alexander Duff. Samuel Marsden pioneered for over forty years in Australia, New Zealand, and the Pacific Islands.

The London Missionary Society sent Robert Morrison to open up the work in China, and Robert and Mary Moffat and their son-in-law, David Livingstone, to Africa. Morrison provided a Chinese dictionary and a Chinese translation of the Bible for later missionaries there. Moffat translated the Bible into important tribal languages of South Africa. Livingstone opened up central Africa. In 1865 J. Hudson Taylor founded the China Inland Mission (now known as Overseas Missionary

Fellowship), one of the great interdenominational faith missions. His writings and extensive travels led to the establishment of several other faith missions.

England and Scotland were not the only European countries sending out missionaries during the nineteenth century. In 1821 the Basel Evangelical Missionary Society and the Danish Missionary Society were founded. Three years later, in 1824, the Berlin Missionary Society and the Paris Missionary Society came into being.

Impact of the Scientific Revolution

Although the beginnings of the scientific revolution can be traced to the sixteenth century, science did not make its full impact on society until the nineteenth century. It was the harnessing of technology and science that drastically changed the way people lived. Though the factory system began to reshape the English countryside and herd masses of humanity into foreboding aggregations called cities during the late eighteenth century, the industrial revolution was not so widespread in other countries until the nineteenth century. About the middle of the century, the rapidity of new technological breakthroughs started to accelerate. The rubber and petroleum industries began to develop about that time. New technological improvements resulted in the lowering of the price of steel by one-half between 1856 and 1870. New alloys and synthetic fabrics joined the long list of developments that suddenly changed human existence and speeded up the growth of cities.

As people moved into the cities, they found their lives to be hard indeed. Whole families worked for pittances from dawn to dark in factories without safety devices, and they lived in impossible tenements. They were reduced to concentrating all their energies on making their livings—on keeping bodies and souls together. Increasingly their interests were centered in organizations that would better their way of life.

As unions and governmental agencies took over functions and provided social outlets previously furnished by the church, society became increasingly secularized. Materialism overspread all things. Sunday was the workers' day off, and they used it as a day for recreation. In many cities, had they wanted to go to church there would not have been enough churches for them to attend, because denominations often failed to keep up with the need. It may be said that the real enemy of religion was the science of the shop rather than the science of the laboratory.

The Theory of Evolution

Yet the impact of the science of the laboratory was tremendous. The publication of Darwin's *Origin of Species* (1859) and *The Descent of Man* (1871) culminated a long history of increasing acceptance of the concept of evolution in the natural sciences. In the hands of its popularizers (Thomas Huxley, Ernst Haeckel, and others) Darwin's teachings were somewhat modified and became widely accepted. Man was no longer viewed as the creature of God, but as the product of an infinite process of development necessitated by the demands of environment. Creative intelligence had been banished from the universe; there was no longer any need for God.

The reaction of established religion to Darwinism was threefold: some capitulated and turned their backs on Christianity; others repudiated the claims of science; the majority worked out some sort of compromise between their faith and the new science. The struggle was especially vehement because at the time Darwin's publications hit English bookstores the country was largely controlled by adherents of a biblical orthodoxy that interpreted the Bible literally.

Not only did the concept of evolution invade the fields of the natural sciences, cultural interpretation, and social theory, but it invaded the field of religion as well. That man started out with no religion and finally advanced to the elevated viewpoint of monotheism was commonly taught. The Bible was not a product of revelation, but a collection of myths, legends, and a few historical facts; this collection developed over the years and finally was edited and put in the form we now know it.

The Tübingen and Wellhausen schools of thought were two of those that subscribed to the evolutionary and higher critical viewpoint in religion. The German biblical critic Julius Wellhausen (1844-1918) was a pivotal figure in the rise of liberal scholarship. His *Prolegomena to the History of Israel* (1878) gave him a place in biblical studies considered by many comparable to that of Darwin in biology. Building on a long development in German scholarship, he denied Mosaic authorship of the Pentateuch and concluded that it was postexilic. The Old Testament, he believed, was put together by later editors using a variety of source materials. He applied to religion and the Old Testament the same evolutionary principles that Darwin and others were applying to the natural sciences. The system he constructed was destined to have impact worldwide during the twentieth century.

The Resurgence of Biblical Christianity

But while industrialism, antisupernaturalistic science, theological liberalism, and spiritual indifference made great inroads against Christianity during the nineteenth century, opposition forces were at work also. The Roman church asserted itself under the leadership of Pius IX (1846-1878), who issued the Syllabus of Errors (1864) and called the first Vatican Council (1870). The former condemned almost all the tendencies of the age, including pantheism, naturalism, rationalism, socialism, and Communism. The Council declared the dogma of papal infallibility, which extended to official pronouncements of the pope on faith and morals.

Attacking higher criticism were such scholars as E. W. Hengstenberg and Franz Delitzsch in Germany and Abraham Kuyper in Holland. The latter founded the Free University of Amsterdam, destined to become a great center of orthodoxy.

To meet new social and religions conditions brought on by the industrial revolution, William Booth organized the Salvation Army, George Williams started the YMCA, and the Anglican church launched the Church Army. New mass evangelism efforts of D. L. Moody and Ira Sankey and others sought to reach the unchurched masses that had come to inhabit the cities.[9]

In short, throughout Western Europe there were individuals and groups who landed telling blows on behalf of biblical Christianity. And it would take pages to list the Spirit-sent revivals that fell on England and the Continent during the century.

TWENTY-FIVE

An Era of Settlement
The Seventeenth Century

The Spanish

WHEN Columbus sailed westward in 1492, he was not merely looking for a new route to the Indies. He hoped to discover new sources of wealth to finance another Crusade against the Muslims and to link up with leaders of the Far East to establish a massive pincers movement against the Muslim Middle East.[1] Moreover, when he came upon the non-Christian tribes of the New World, his religious inclinations predominated again. He and Ferdinand agreed that measures should be taken to protect, convert, and educate the Indians.

Soon Spanish priests began to accompany the explorers and conquerors. A bishopric was established at Santo Domingo in 1512, another in Cuba in 1522, with others following in rapid succession. The University of Mexico and the University of San Marcos, in

Lima, were both founded in 1551; others were built elsewhere in Latin America as the need arose. When one recalls that the Spanish usually sent their sons back to Europe for education, it will be clear that these New World institutions were especially for the training of the natives.

Admittedly, the Spanish oppressed and maltreated the Indians over the centuries, but it is nevertheless true that the church and crown made sincere and expensive moves to protect the natives in the early days. Shortly after the death of Luther, the Spanish settled Florida (St. Augustine, 1565) and then advanced into New Mexico and Texas. They were establishing their missions in California while Jefferson was writing the Declaration of Independence. Portuguese settlement in Brazil began in 1532, and of course the Roman church was established there. Thus, all of Latin America and part of the present area of the United States responded to the religious efforts of Spanish and Portuguese priests.

The French

Although the French became interested in North America very early, they were not able to establish a permanent colony until 1608—at Quebec. Thereafter, French explorers and missionaries ranged across the northern part of the continent and throughout the Mississippi valley down to the river's mouth in Louisiana. They set up mission stations, trading posts, and forts wherever they penetrated, and established friendship with many Indian tribes. But the paucity of French settlers in the New World, inadequate colonial policies, and the defeat of French forces ultimately brought an end to the French Empire in North America (in 1763) and the effects of French Jesuit work everywhere except in Quebec and Louisiana.

The English

At Jamestown in 1607, the English established their first successful colony. Planted by the Virginia Company, the colony was basically an economic venture; but the Anglican church was established there to meet the spiritual needs of the colonists, who were members of the Church of England. About the same time, a group of Pilgrim separatists, persecuted in England because of their religious views, took refuge in Holland. Finally they made arrangements with the London Company to settle in Virginia. But the *Mayflower* and the Pilgrims landed at Plymouth, Massachusetts, instead, introducing Congregationalism to New England in 1620.

A decade later the Massachusetts Bay Company came with its charter, stockholders, and board of directors to plant colonies at Salem, Boston, and the immediate vicinity. These Puritans sought to escape the despotism of Charles I and to found a "wilderness Zion," but economic reasons for colonization were much greater than religious historians often have been willing to admit. Like the Pilgrims, the Puritans were Calvinistic in doctrine; and they ultimately also accepted the congregational form of government. In 1691 the Pilgrim and Puritan settlements amalgamated to form Massachusetts, and Maine was included as part of the union until it became a state in 1820.

Meanwhile, primarily because of economic advantage, settlers of a Congregational conviction spilled over into Connecticut on the south and New Hampshire and

Vermont on the north. Separatists like Roger Williams moved to Rhode Island, where Baptist churches were first organized on North American shores and where separation of church and state was practiced in an atmosphere of almost complete religious liberty.

Both Puritans and Anglicans were interested in an educated ministry and founded colleges for that purpose. In 1636 and 1701 respectively, the Puritans launched Harvard and Yale. In 1693, the Anglicans chartered William and Mary in Williamsburg. Because denser population in towns permitted it, the New Englanders also built public elementary and secondary schools to provide religious instruction for the populace and to train them for intelligent citizenship. The Middle Colonies organized parochial schools for similar reasons.

About the time Massachusetts settlers were spilling over into Connecticut (1630s), Lord Baltimore was planting a colony in Maryland. Although Baltimore designed his colony as a haven for persecuted Roman Catholics, not too many came, even on the first boatloads of settlers. Therefore, in order to maintain a successful economic venture and to protect Roman Catholics against an unsympathetic Protestant majority, he permitted religious toleration. Puritans came to Maryland in large numbers, but Anglicanism was established at the end of the century, when Maryland became a royal colony.

The Germans and The Dutch

Because Quakers were persecuted in both England and New England, William Penn sought to provide a haven for them in Pennsylvania during the last decades of the seventeenth century. And because Quakerism did not lend itself to exclusiveness and because Penn wanted a profitable colony, he threw open the doors to all who would come. Penn advertised widely in Europe with good success, and Germans came in droves to Penn's Woods. There were Lutherans, Moravians, and other German sects. West Jersey, too, became a Quaker settlement.

In 1623 New Amsterdam was founded on Manhattan Island. Although the Dutch did not profess any religious motivation for colonization, they naturally favored the Reformed church, the first of which appeared in 1628. New York developed a cosmopolitan character, however, and the efforts of Dutch governors to enforce religious conformity were never successful. After the English took over New Netherland, they established the Anglican church there in 1693—at least in New York City and surrounding counties.

Lutherans settled in New Amsterdam almost as soon as the Dutch Reformed, but they did not fare very well under Dutch rule. The Lutherans were more successful, however, in the Swedish colony on the Delaware, planted in 1638. This too fell into the hands of the Dutch and finally into the hands of the English.

The first permanent English Presbyterian church was also established in New Netherland—on Long Island in 1640. But in the early days the Presbyterians were most numerous in East Jersey and Pennsylvania. Religious developments in the Carolinas were somewhat uncertain in the early days. The proprietors, who received their grant in 1663, gave considerable freedom to settlers, who had spilled over the border into North Carolina from Virginia and who came into South Carolina in considerable numbers from the West Indies.

The Puritans

It is not the purpose of this brief survey to discuss in detail any one movement or individual. Certainly it is not the goal to provide a history of Christian doctrine. But one seventeenth-century group often referred to and almost as commonly misrepresented and vilified are the Puritans. The goal here is not to defend them or even to explain them in any detail. Certainly it is impossible to provide any definitive statement when many library shelves are filled with books about them. It is important, however, to try to understand somewhat a people as significant as the Puritans.

Theologically, they emphasized the sovereignty of God and human depravity. Individuals were elected to salvation and needed to put their faith in Christ for salvation. Believers had a responsibility to live holy lives for the glory of God, and their concept of the "holy calling" (that one's occupation, whatever it was, was a calling from God) gave dignity to all the callings or careers or walks of life people pursued. Their philosophy of history saw God working sovereignly in human affairs to accomplish His purposes.

Socially, they took a corporate view. The whole of society was to be ordered for the glory of God and for human welfare; the individual was to be subordinated to the will and the betterment of the community. That meant control of public morals, insistence on church attendance, establishment of a system of public education for knowledge of Scripture and performance in one's "holy calling," and an application of biblical principles to human conduct.

Economically, they may have been more prosperous because of a desire to serve God with a job well done or to live worthy of the "holy calling"; but in fact they had laws controlling *maximum* wages and prices to protect the public at large.

Permissive modern Americans have labeled the Puritans as extremely legalistic, as people who had no fun and were determined to see to it that others did not have any either. And they tend to snicker at them a bit. Some have looked at the Puritans through Victorian eyes and have made them out to be something they never were. They did not commonly wear dark clothes. They opposed the celebration of Christmas as a "popish holiday," but they had their fun on election day or commencement at Harvard or on other occasions. One of the main activities in the common house at Plymouth was brewing (beer/ale); the Puritans had their well-stocked wine cellars. Harvard graduates had an allotment of wine for commencement weekend.

> *For the Puritans, the whole of society was to be ordered for the glory of God and for human welfare; laws set maximum wages and prices to protect the public.*

To be sure, there were lots of regulations controlling society at large. But the fact needs to be put in larger perspective. The Catholic church had more social controls in Western Europe during the Middle Ages and early modern times than most people are aware of. And the kind of regulation of life in seventeenth and eighteenth century America thought to have been typically "Puritan" was not. For example, in "secular" Virginia there were laws on the books against absence from church, sabbath breaking, swearing on the sabbath, and the like, and those laws were enforced. I have in my files many cases from the county court records of Virginia, dating well into the eighteenth century, in which individuals were fined for absence from church, for swearing oaths on the sabbath, and other minor infractions.

Contemporary Americans with their castigation of the Puritans as a rather somber lot also need to rethink the past. Life was hard in colonial New England. There was no central heating. There were no microwaves, washing machines, or power equipment. Back-breaking toil was the lot of both men and women all day long on most days. There were no miracle drugs or serums either. It was not at all unusual for a man to bury two wives and sometimes half or more of his children—perhaps five or more out of ten if he had that many. A special scourge was smallpox epidemics which sometimes carried off nearly the entire young population of a town.

Under these circumstances, one does not expect the more jovial and relaxed lifestyle of a modern American with a gas grill on the patio for his outdoor barbecue, a family doctor, a pediatrician, a dentist, an eye doctor, a pharmacy down the block, a house full of labor-saving devices and a vacation with pay. All this is said not to defend the Puritan way in all its ramifications. The Puritans made their mistakes and provide lessons for modern Christians. They also had a desire to know God and serve Him and provide some good examples for modern Christians.[2]

TWENTY-SIX

Breaking of Ties and Revival
The Eighteenth Century

THE development of the colonies south of Virginia occurred largely in the eighteenth century. In fact, settlement in Georgia did not even begin until 1733. In all these colonies the Anglican church ultimately became the established church. It was established in South Carolina in 1706, Georgia in 1758, and North Carolina in 1765. The eighteenth century was also a time when the Anglican church made a determined effort to reorganize and to improve ministers, morals, and service rendered in the parishes. The famous Society for the Propagation of the Gospel in Foreign Parts took the lead in this effort.

In general it may be said that at the time of the American Revolution the Anglican church dominated the Southern Colonies and the Congregational church the Northern Colonies, while in the Middle Colonies there was diversity. To be more specific, the Anglican church was the established church in Georgia, South Carolina, North Carolina, Virginia, Maryland, and New York City and surrounding counties. The Congregational church was established in Massachusetts (Maine), Connecticut, and New Hampshire. In New Jersey, Pennsylvania, Delaware, and Rhode Island there was no state church.

It is remarkable that although in the rest of the Western world before, during, and after the American

Revolution a state church was everywhere established, in the United States complete separation of church and state was achieved in most states, with the accompanying disestablishment of the church. (An established church is one officially maintained by a government and supported by taxes levied on all citizens. The degree of toleration accorded to minority faiths varies from place to place.)

Reasons for Separation of Church and State in America

Ethnic and religious mixture of immigrants
Proprietary promises
Leveling influence of revival
Pioneering attitudes
Impact of the unchurched
Natural rights philosophy
Impact of the Revolution
Efforts to establish an Anglican bishop

Disestablishment of the Churches

There are several reasons for the disestablishment of the church in the United States. *First, the kind and extent of immigration that flowed into the colonies after 1690 was significant.* It brought about such a mixture of peoples and faiths that ultimately a majority faith existed almost nowhere. First came Quakers and some Huguenots. Quakers settled mainly in Pennsylvania and dominated the colony; their opposition to formal church structure prevented the rise of a state church there. Quaker presence in New Jersey contributed to the religious mixture in that colony, and Pennsylvania's control over Delaware during most of the colonial period insured freedom of religion there. Huguenots found refuge in several colonies. Having suffered from persecution in France, they had no desire to persecute others.

The second great wave of immigrants, in about 1700, consisted of some 200,000 Germans. Though a great percentage of these were Lutheran and Reformed, many smaller sects were represented; and of the total, most were dominated by the Pietistic emphasis on inner, personal religion. Such persons had no desire to dominate the religious expression of others. The Germans went in large numbers to Pennsylvania and northern New York. Last came a wave of about 250,000 Scotch-Irish from northern Ireland—Presbyterians who had been persecuted by the Anglican church there. They spread widely over the Middle and Southern colonies, especially along the back valley of the Appalachians, and contributed greatly to religious diversity. By 1760 there were about 2.5 million people in the colonies, of which about one-third were foreign born.

A second influence favoring disestablishment was the effect of the proprietary colonies. All the colonies established after 1660 were proprietary grants. Something already has been said about the fact that a desire for a successful colonial venture led to religious toleration in Pennsylvania, and especially Maryland. The same was true for New York, Georgia, North and South Carolina, New Jersey, and Delaware, all of which were proprietary colonies at one time. During periods when these colonies were under proprietary control, religious pluralism increased. And even though a state church might have been imposed later, it could not forever endure, because the population was too religiously diverse.

Third, the leveling influence of the great revivals that shook the colonies during the eighteenth century made their impact. The revivals transcended denominational lines, and the revivalists stressed the equality of all in the sight of God.

Fourth, pioneering attitudes made a contribution similar to that of the revivals. The frontier was a leveler. Moreover, pioneers had to become self-reliant individualists if they were to survive. Individualism and religious institutionalism did not mix well. Frontiersmen generally have been suspicious of or opposed to the establishment or the more settled areas (in the United States, the East).

Fifth, the impact of the unchurched was significant. Because the frontier moved so fast and people were spread out in such a thin line, the churches failed to keep up with the needs of the population. Many people were without church membership—in proportion to the population, probably more than anywhere else in Christendom during the first third of the eighteenth century. The unchurched do not have much interest in supporting an established religion.

Sixth, natural rights philosophy influenced many. Something was said in chapter 23 about natural rights philosophy and the rise of deism during the eighteenth century. One of the rights educated people of that day came to accept was the privilege of deciding the kind of religious belief they should follow. John Locke in his *Letters on Toleration* (1689-1706) had argued for the separation of church and state and for the voluntary nature of one's religious affiliation. Many leaders of the American Revolutionary generation, such as Jefferson, were greatly imbued with this philosophy, and they were active in bringing down the church establishment in

Virginia soon after the new nation won its independence.

It should be added that *when the Revolution began, the Anglican church suffered greatly.* Many ministers were loyalist in sympathies and left their churches either by choice or because of intimidation. So did many of their parishioners, for that matter, as the Church of England, the Anglican church, took the brunt of attack from patriot opponents. When the war was over, there were few Anglican ministers left in the country and many churches had been destroyed. Especially in the states south of Virginia the Anglican church had little support, and disestablishment was not difficult there.

Last, agitation for the appointment of an Anglican bishop in America, especially on the part of the Society for the Propagation of the Gospel, *stirred fires of disestablishment.* Cries of dismay rose from the influential Congregational and Presbyterian camps. And coming as it did when the colonists increasingly resented the rule of Parliament, this proposal stirred political opposition as well as religious. If Parliament could establish religion in all the colonies, it could by so much tighten the noose around the necks of a people looking for greater freedom.

Thus it may be seen that disestablishment was almost a foregone conclusion in the United States. With the founding of the new nation, one after another the edifices of state church establishment toppled. The last to go was Congregationalism: in New Hampshire, 1817; Connecticut, 1818; and Massachusetts, 1833.

Reasons for continued church establishment in New England are not hard to find. First, immigration of non-British or non-Puritan stock did not come in significant numbers to the region. Second, the colonial legislatures saw to it that the frontier progressed in orderly fashion, with provision for a church and a home for a minister in each new town that was laid out. Since churches were constructed and church attendance required, there was no significant number of unchurched. Third, outside of Maine, which early came under control of Massachusetts, there were no proprietary colonies in New England, with their provisions for religious toleration or diversity.

The Churches and the Revolution[3]

If there was so much religious diversity and agitation during the eighteenth century, it may be well to ask about the attitudes of the various denominations toward the Revolution and their participation in it. The Anglicans were divided, with a probable loyalist majority. In the North they were generally loyalist; but in the South many of the great planters, among them Washington, favored the Revolutionary cause. The Congregationalists gave enthusiastic support to the Revolution, their ministers preaching sermons in favor of the patriot cause.

The Presbyterians were generally patriot, their struggle with royal governors and the Anglican church in the colonies being something of a continuation of the Presbyterian-Anglican conflict in England. One of the greatest Presbyterian patriots was John Witherspoon, signer of the Articles of Confederation and the only clergyman to sign the Declaration of Independence. Lutherans also enthusiastically supported the Revolution, especially under the leadership of the Muhlenbergs. Though divided, the Roman Catholics generally were patriot.

The Baptists supported the Revolution because, for one thing, they felt that the cause of separation of church and state was at stake. They believed that British victory would bring new political controls and a new religious tightening, accompanied by the installation of an Anglican bishop in America. It should be noted, however, that some Baptists, like some Congregationalists and Presbyterians, were reticent about committing themselves to the patriot cause.

Methodists were suspect because Wesley at the beginning of the war urged neutrality, but native-born preachers seem to have been in sympathy with the Revolution. Although Quakers, Mennonites, and Moravians were conscientious objectors, a large percentage of them were in sympathy with the Revolution and some even joined the army.

The Revolution brought about the dissolution of ties between many religious bodies in America and Europe, necessitating separate organization in America. For other reasons some groups likewise organized. William White and Samuel Seabury, Jr., were responsible for rehabilitating the Anglican church after the war; and it was organized as the Protestant Episcopal Church in 1789, along more democratic lines than the Church of England.

Cut loose from English Methodism by the force of circumstances, the Methodists organized in 1784 as the Methodist Episcopal Church, under the leadership of Francis Asbury. In the same year, American Roman Catholic dependence on British jurisdiction terminated, and in 1789 John Carroll became the first Roman Catholic bishop, with Baltimore as his see. The Baptists formed a General Committee in 1784. And the Presbyterians were in Philadelphia drawing up a constitution for their church at the same time as the national Constitution was being formed in 1787.

The Great Awakening

One of the major events of American Christianity during the eighteenth century was the Great Awakening. With the loss of the evangelical enthusiasm that characterized the first generation of Congregationalists, Presbyterians, and others, and with the increase of the unchurched on the expanding frontiers, religion and morals declined all over the colonies. In fact, even the churches were filled with unconverted. To meet such a need came the Great Awakening. The Awakening began with Theodore Frelinghuysen's preaching among the Dutch Reformed of New Jersey in the 1720s. Of Pietistic persuasion, Frelinghuysen apparently began his revivalistic efforts soon after he came over from Holland in 1720. By 1726, revival fires were burning not only among the Dutch Reformed of the Raritan River valley, but also among the Presbyterians of the area. Frelinghuysen especially influenced the Presbyterian pastors William and Gilbert Tennent, who worked among the Scotch-Irish in New Jersey.

Next the revival spread to the Congregationalists through the preaching of Jonathan Edwards,[4] though there is no evidence that he had any communication with Frelinghuysen or that he was influenced by revival in the Middle Colonies. Under Edwards' preaching a revival broke out in his parish at Northampton, Massachusetts, in 1734. According to his statement, some three hundred of the town's eleven hundred people were converted in about six months. From Edwards' parish at the head of the Connecticut River valley, other revival fires spread down the valley and helped prepare the way for George Whitefield's ministry.

Whitefield, associate of the Wesleys, began his first great American tour in 1739 and preached with tremendous success during that year and the following in New England and the Middle Colonies. Because frequently there were no buildings large enough to hold the crowds, he preached in the open. Subsequently a great revival swept the region in 1741 and 1742. The Awakening spread to Presbyterians in Virginia through the work of Samuel Morris and Samuel Davies after 1740, and to the Baptists of North Carolina in 1755 through the work of Shubal Stearns and his brother-in-law Daniel Marshall. The Baptists had great success in Virginia, too.

Results of the Great Awakening

Widespread conversion
Stirring of missionary interest
Founding of evangelical colleges
Rise of religious liberty
Divisions in Congregational and
Presbyterian churches
Rise to prominence of Jonathan Edwards

On the eve of the Revolution, a revival broke out in the South under the leadership of the Methodists, especially through the work of John King, Robert Williams, and Francis Asbury. Though Whitefield put much stress on emotionalism and incurred considerable opposition during his 1739-1740 tour, he changed his approach when he returned in 1744. Though results were proportionately smaller in New England on that occasion, in Pennsylvania, Maryland, and the South his efforts were tremendously successful. As may be seen from the dates given above, the Great Awakening in its various phases continued from the 1720s to the beginning of the Revolution.

Its results were phenomenal. First, careful study of the church records of New England will show that earlier estimates that at least 10 percent of the population of the area was converted in the Awakening are probably correct. Thousands were swept into the Kingdom in the Middle and Southern Colonies. Baptists in Virginia alone reaped a harvest of some ten thousand souls between 1759 and 1776.

> *At least 10 percent of New England was converted in the First Great Awakening.*

Second, there was a quickening along missionary and educational lines. David Brainerd, Jonathan Edwards, and others preached to the Indians, and some effort was made to reach blacks with the gospel. Among the colleges to rise from the Awakening were Princeton (Presbyterian), Rutgers (Dutch Reformed), Brown (Baptist), and Dartmouth (Congregational). Dartmouth was founded as a training school to prepare Indians to serve as missionaries to their own people.

Third, the revival contributed to the rise of religious liberty because it greatly increased the number of persons outside the established churches.

Fourth, it proved to be divisive in that among the Congregationalists and Presbyterians especially arose groups for and against the revival. Later, many of the

Congregationalists opposed to it slipped into the Unitarian camp.

Fifth, the Awakening brought to prominence Jonathan Edwards, who has been called "America's greatest theologian" and "America's only original theologian." Last, the revival preserved the American religious heritage and assured its perpetuity amid the desolation of the Revolution. And it may be argued that it prepared many individuals for the stresses and strains of the Revolutionary period.

Religious Decline

The Revolutionary War was hard on religious life in America. Because the churches so generally supported the Revolution, the British took out their spite on houses of worship. Moreover, many churches were destroyed when they were used for barracks, hospitals, and storage of military equipment. This was true in part because the constant heating of churches, often with defective or inadequate chimneys, resulted in disastrous fires. Pastors and their people were absorbed in the cause of the Revolution rather than in building up the churches, and French deism and atheism were fashionable because of alliance with France. In fact, rationalism took control in the colleges and other intellectual centers of the land. In some colleges, there was hardly a

Conditions were so bad when the new nation was being launched that politicians and ministers alike virtually gave up hope.

student who would admit to being a Christian.

Conditions were so bad during the years when the Constitution was being written and the new nation was being launched that politicians and ministers alike virtually gave up hope. For example, Bishop Samuel Provoost of the Episcopal Diocese of New York believed the situation so hopeless that he simply ceased to function. A committee of Congress reported on the desperate state of lawlessness on the frontier. Of a population of five million, the United States had 300,000 drunkards and buried about fifteen thousand of them annually.[5] In 1796 George Washington agreed with a friend that national affairs were leading to a crisis, and he could not predict what might happen.[6]

Dark indeed were the closing years of the eighteenth century. It is strange how distorted a view one gets from well-meaning preachers and patriots of the present who paint a rosy picture of conditions at the founding of the nation. There is little good that can be said of those times except that God was not through with the United States.

TWENTY-SEVEN

Revival, Social Concerns, and Liberalism

The Nineteenth Century

Major Nineteenth Century Revivals

Second Evangelical Awakening
Finney Revivals
Revival of 1858
Evangelistic work of Dwight L. Moody

Revival Movements

The Second Evangelical Awakening

HELP was on the way. A few local revivals broke out in the early 1790s, but nothing extensive came until after the Concert of Prayer was launched. The eminent Massachusetts Baptist Isaac Backus and a score of other ministers called for the churches to engage in the Concert of Prayer for spiritual awakening, beginning on the first Tuesday in January, 1795, and continuing once a quarter thereafter. Denomination after denomination took up the challenge. Revivals began to break out everywhere around the turn of the century. The Second Evangelical Awakening was in progress (not only in America, but in Britain, on the Continent, and elsewhere).

Revival fires burned over the entire nation, first in the East (especially Connecticut and Massachusetts) and then on the frontier. The revival was not characterized by evangelists going to and fro to incite churches to activity. There were few great names connected with it. For the most part, services were carried on by the pastors in their respective churches.

In New England the revival was quiet, not accompanied by emotional manifestations as during the Great Awakening. The situation on the frontier was different, however. There the Presbyterians inaugurated the camp meeting, to which thousands came from far and near. Emotional outbreaks were common in these meetings, but they have been greatly misrepresented or overplayed; and they did not seem to hinder the effect of the revival. Presbyterians, Methodists, and Baptists all worked side by side in these great gatherings, and all three benefited tremendously from the effort.

One of the greatest of these camp meetings took place at Cane Ridge, Kentucky, in 1801, where it is said twenty-five thousand gathered in August. As many as five preachers addressed the crowds simultaneously in different places on the grounds. As elsewhere, Presbyterians, Methodists, and Baptists cooperated in the venture. Reportedly the character of Kentucky and Tennessee was completely changed by these meetings.

The effects of the Second Evangelical Awakening were tremendous:

(1) The colleges of the land were largely reclaimed through the overthrow of infidelity.
(2) There was a spiritual quickening in nearly all denominations, with tens of thousands being

added to Baptist, Methodist, and Presbyterian churches.

(3) Lines were more clearly drawn between rationalism and evangelicalism, and there was a split between the Unitarians and evangelicals in the Congregational church.

(4) The midweek prayer meeting and Sunday schools became common features of church life.

(5) Close to a score of new colleges and seminaries were founded.

(6) Missionary endeavor was spurred. The American Board of Commissioners for Foreign Missions came into being in 1810; one of its first missionaries was Adoniram Judson. The American Bible Society was founded in 1816, the American Tract Society in 1825.

The Finney Revivals

As the Second Evangelical Awakening began to lose some of its force, Charles G. Finney[7] came on the scene with his revival efforts. Beginning in New York State in 1824, he conducted very effective meetings in several Eastern cities. The greatest took place in Rochester, New York, in the fall and winter of 1830-31, when he reported one thousand conversions in a city of 10,000. The revival affected adjacent towns as well, with over 1,500 making professions of faith and joining the churches in them (Hardman, 209). At the same time there were about one hundred thousand conversions in other parts of the country from New England to the Southwest. In 1835 Finney became president of Oberlin College in Ohio, where he continued to be an influential revivalist through personal campaigns and the wide distribution of his *Lectures on Revival*.

The teachings of Finney and his associates Asa Mahan and Thomas Upham included entire consecration, sinless perfection in this life, and freedom of the will. Finney is given credit for introducing the anxious bench (the place to which inquirers went forward for conversion) and the cottage prayer meeting (at which non-Christians were prayed for by name in meetings in private homes). Out of the Oberlin School came the Holiness and Pentecostal churches. Not only did Finney's work make a great impact on America, but he also made two trips to Europe, where he experienced extensive success.

The Revival of 1858

Another great revival spread across the country in 1858-1859. It was quite different from other revivals in that it not only did not have a series of great names attached to it, but those most responsible for its success were laymen. Moreover, it was enthusiastically supported by almost all Protestant denominations and was reported favorably by the press—which helped to make it the success it was.

The usual view is that this revival began among the business people of New York City and that the bank panic had something to do with scaring people into a new dependence on God. J. Erwin Orr, in communication with me, presented evidence to show that this view is erroneous. The revival began in Canada in September 1857, and the first outbreaks in the United States occurred in Virginia and the Carolinas among slaves, who did not have any money at all. Ultimately over one hundred thousand blacks were converted in the 1858 revival.

But it is true that the movement gained momentum through the efforts of Jeremiah Lanphier, a city missionary in New York, who distributed handbills calling for weekly noon prayer meetings at the North Dutch Church beginning September 23, 1857. People were invited to come for five or ten minutes or to stay the whole hour if they could. Soon it became necessary to schedule daily meetings at other churches, halls, and theaters; and the movement spread to Philadelphia, Albany, Boston, Chicago, and other cities North and South. It is estimated that there were at least one million conversions in the United States during 1858 and 1859, with proportionately as great a revival in the South as the North, in spite of the slavery agitation of the period.

In 1859 the influence of the revival spread to the British Isles, where it is said that another million made professions of faith. The awakening also touched many European countries, South Africa, India, the East and West Indies, and Canada. The revival continued after the War Between the States and in its later stages was even more visible in the South than the North. During the war, in 1861, a revival broke out among Confederate forces around Richmond and became a general moving of the Spirit by 1863. Though estimates vary, probably fifty thousand or more were converted in this awakening among the troops. Higher figures given in some accounts of this revival seem to be too generous.

D. L. Moody's Evangelistic Efforts

One of the greatest modern revivalists was D. L. Moody,[8] whose preaching was of the old evangelical type: a middle-of-the-road Calvinism rather than the

Arminian approach of Finney and the Holiness preaching of the century. He urged predominantly the love of God as the great reason for repentance. Starting out in the YMCA and army camps during the Civil War, he conducted mass evangelism campaigns with the assistance of Ira D. Sankey in the large cities during the last three decades of the century.

Not only did he have remarkable success in this country, but he made several trips to England. One of the most notable of these was the 1873-1875 campaign, during which he preached to more than 2.5 million people in London alone. Before the London crusade, he had conducted successful evangelistic efforts in other major cities of England and Scotland.[9]

Moody's ministry with the YMCA and his mass evangelism symbolized a new thrust of the church to reach the unchurched in great urban centers produced by the industrial revolution. Another indication of the new approach was Moody's pitching a tent at the Chicago World's Fair in 1893. One of Moody's better-known accomplishments was the founding of the Moody Bible Institute (1886), which pioneered the concept of Bible institutes and led to the founding of hundreds of similar schools, especially in the United States and Canada. R. A. Torrey (first president of Moody Bible Institute), J. Wilbur Chapman, and other evangelists followed in his train. And revivalism has been a continuing characteristic of American Christianity.

Not the least of the later revivals in the United States was the awakening of 1905. Part of a worldwide movement and apparently especially inspired by British revivals, it touched all parts of the country and made its impact in Canada as well. Northern Methodists reported an increase of over 200,000 in 1905-1906; Lutherans,

167,000; Baptists, 165,000; and Presbyterians, 67,000. Revivals hit college campuses in several parts of the country. Missionary effort was greatly stimulated. The story may be found in J. Edwin Orr's *The Flaming Tongue*.

The Slavery Issue

Revivalism was one very important feature of American Christianity in the nineteenth century; a second was agitation over the slavery issue and dissolution of the union. Widespread antislavery sentiment found expression in the formation of numerous antislavery societies in the latter years of the eighteenth century and the early years of the nineteenth century. After the formation in 1816 of the American Society for the Colonization of the Free People of Color in the United States, interest settled especially on relocation of blacks in Liberia, and anti-slavery agitation virtually came to an end.

Then, about 1830, a new phase of the anti-slavery movement began. By that time the full effects of Eli Whitney's cotton gin (1793) were being felt, and the demand for cotton fastened the plantation system ever more firmly on the South. Southern leaders found support for the institution of slavery in the Bible, "both by precept and example." Meanwhile aggressive anti-slavery propagandists such as William Lloyd Garrison (editor of the *Liberator*), Wendell Phillips, and Theodore Parker arose in the North, especially in New England.

Those radical Boston Unitarians were joined by people such as Harriet Beecher Stowe, Finney's convert Theodore Dwight Weld, the Presbyterian brothers Arthur and Lewis Tappan, and the Quaker sisters Sarah and Angeline Grimké, all from evangelical backgrounds. Soon antislavery societies sprang up in the churches, and some religious bodies began to pass strong antislavery resolutions. In 1833, the American Anti-Slavery Society was organized, and Arthur Tappan was its first president.

But the cause of abolitionism had its problems. In their zeal to emancipate the slaves, the radicals increasingly attacked the Constitution and the Bible, which were often used as supports for the "peculiar institution." Evangelicals, as Bible believers and loyal Americans, could not condone the blanket attacks being hurled against the government and Christianity. By 1845 Garrison had ousted all evangelicals from the American Anti-Slavery Society.

Evangelicals also had problems within their ranks. A great many of them had come to believe that the churches of America had a mission to Christianize the nation and the world. If the issue of slavery were allowed to fracture the churches and the nation, then all was lost. So, many leaders wanted to silence abolitionist sentiment and work out compromises that would at all costs preserve the unity of the church and the unity of the nation.

Perhaps this attitude concerning America's place in world missions and the union of the nation helps to explain why almost every major religious body in the North gave such generous support to the Federal government during the war. In fact, maintenance of the unity of church and the unity of the nation became more precious than abolition of slavery.

In spite of efforts at compromise and conciliation, ruptures along sectional lines took place in one after another of the major religious bodies. The rank and file of American church members in the North did not feel that they had to choose between abolition on the one hand and Christianity and patriotism on the other. They did not buy the whole of Garrison's argument, and Charles Finney in his role of a winner of souls possibly won as many to the cause of abolition as did Garrison. Of course other religious leaders made also their contributions to the rise of abolitionist sentiment.

The gulf widened between Northern and Southern church members. In 1843 the Wesleyan Methodist Connection organized in Utica, New York. Two years later the Methodist Episcopal Church, South, organized in Louisville, Kentucky. In the same month (May 1845), the Southern Baptist Convention was founded in Augusta, Georgia. New School Presbyterians[10] divided in 1858, Old School Presbyterians in 1861, and the Lutherans in 1863. The period following the war marked the efforts of the churches to unite once more.

Social Concerns

Out of the same context as evangelical concern for the plight of the blacks came an interest in alleviating many other ills of society. The perfectionist, or sanctification, preaching of Charles Finney, Asa Mahan, Walter and Phoebe Palmer, William and Catherine Booth, and many others, especially in the Methodist and Holiness camps, promoted concern for eradication not only of personal sin, but also of the sins of society. They believed that only the power of the Spirit of God ultimately could solve the ills of society and that personal holiness led believers to be servants of their fellow men and women.

The social concerns of many evangelicals coincided with those of such liberal leaders as Washington Gladden and Walter Rauschenbusch, who wanted to deal with a host of problems plaguing society during the nineteenth century. But in this movement the preponderance of numbers and wealth lay on the side of the evangelicals.

One of the first social problems to receive attention was alcoholism. In 1836 two nationwide organizations merged to form the American Temperance Union, designed to urge moderation. In 1840 the Washington Temperance Society was founded to encourage total abstinence. The aim of the movement was not to control private behavior, but to reform society; drunkenness was viewed as the prime cause of poverty. State prohibition was first enacted in Maine in 1851.

Various evangelical agencies developed a new concern for those whom the industrial system had relegated to the city slums. Such organizations as the American Sunday School Union and the Home Missionary and Tract societies moved from simple evangelism to the establishment of Sunday schools and mission churches, job placement, distribution of food and clothing to the poor, and resettlement of destitute youth. Phoebe Palmer[11] did important pioneer work in social welfare projects in New York, engaging in prison ministry at the Tombs, participating in the work of The New York Female Assistance Society for the Relief and Religious Instruction of the Sick Poor, supporting an orphanage, and founding in 1850 the Five Points Mission. The latter marked the beginning of Protestant institutional work in the slums.

In conjunction with this settlement house, Morris Pease established the Five Points House of Industry, which by 1854 supported five hundred people. Mrs. Palmer also helped to organize in 1858 the Ladies Christian Association of New York, which pioneered in programs that the YWCA was later to carry on. About the same time, others founded a home for the deaf and a shelter for black orphans in New York. Missions to immigrants and sailors were established in New York, Boston, and other cities. William E. Boardman served as executive secretary during some of the most effective years of the United States Christian Commission, organized in New York in 1861 to meet both spiritual and physical needs of servicemen.

During and after the Civil War the churches became more alert to their social obligations. City rescue missions, orphanages, hospitals, homes for the aged, and other agencies were established to meet the needs of various groups. The YMCA and YWCA movements spread rapidly across the country to provide for city youths lodging, social activity, and Bible study.

At the end of the war, in 1866, the several church-sponsored freedmen's relief associations united as the American Freedman's Union Commission to aid freed slaves. One could go on and on with names of organizations and individuals, but these examples will suffice. Some of the most effective and best-known efforts took place in New York, Philadelphia, and Boston, but the churches rallied to aid the needs in many centers of the land.

Rise of Liberalism

As noted above, by no means all those engaged in social action were evangelicals. And even some of the evangelicals in time neglected their biblical underpinnings, continuing to feed the hungry but forgetting to do it in the name of Christ.

Walter Rauschenbusch

The name most commonly associated with the rise of the Social Gospel is Walter Rauschenbusch[12] (1861-1918). Pastor of a Baptist church in New York (beginning in 1886), where he came to know human need firsthand, he later joined the faculty of Colgate-Rochester Theological Seminary, where he wrote influential books: *Christianity and the Social Crisis* (1907), *Christianizing the Social Order* (1912), and *A Theology for the Social Gospel* (1917).

Though he started out early in life with a belief in original sin and personal salvation, by the time he got to his last book he viewed sin as social and impersonal and taught that social reform would come with the demise of capitalism, the advance of socialism, and the establishment of the kingdom of God. Rauschenbusch's views found ready acceptance by such spokesmen as Shailer Matthews and Shirley Jackson Case, both at the University of Chicago.

Channing, Parker, and Bushnell

The impact of Rauschenbusch must be added to other threads in the development of liberalism during the nineteenth century. At the beginning of the century Unitarianism made deep inroads under the leadership of such outstanding spokesmen as William Ellery Channing (1780-1842) and Theodore Parker (1810-1860). Channing's sermon "Unitarian Christianity" (1819) receives credit for launching the Unitarian controversy.[13]

Another influential figure of the century was Horace Bushnell[14] (1802-1876). Bushnell published his *Christian Nurture* in 1847 and argued that a child should grow up in a Christian home as a child of the covenant, never knowing he was anything but a Christian. His idea of growth into grace made a profound impact on generations of Christian educators and muted the requirement of a conversion experience in the preaching and teaching of numerous church groups.

In addition to his support of Unitarianism, Theodore Parker also did much to introduce German biblical criticism into American Christianity. Thus the way was prepared for the impact of Darwinian evolution and the ideas of Julius Wellhausen (see chap. 24). Wellhausen's views, especially as interpreted by such English scholars as S. R. Driver, drew an exceptionally large following. A theological liberalism grew up, based on the twin postulates of the evolution of religion and the denial of the supernatural, and teaching such concepts as the fatherhood of God and brotherhood of man and the institution of the kingdom of God as an evolutionary outcome of the efforts of churchmen and women in society.

Schleiermacher, Ritschl, and Harnack

Also important to American liberal development during the nineteenth century was the work of three German scholars: Schleiermacher, Ritschl, and Harnack. Friedrich Schleiermacher (1768-1834) made experience or feeling the basis of the faith, rather than the Bible and one's relationship to Christ. Religion involved a feeling of absolute dependence on God. Doctrine was for him contingent on religious experience, not experience on revealed doctrine. Jesus showed the way of absolute dependence on God and of love to man.

Albert Ritschl (1822-1889) taught, among other

things, that Christ's death had nothing to do with payment of a penalty for sin, but resulted from loyalty to His calling. It was His objective to establish the kingdom of God. He would share with humanity His consciousness of sonship and help them to realize God's goal of living together in mutual love. The practice of religion in community was of vital importance because Christ could best communicate Himself to people through the community He had founded (the church). Ritschl's strong social emphasis contributed to the Social Gospel of the time, and his impact on numerous scholars was great.

Especially was Adolf Harnack (1851-1930) a follower of Ritschl. Like Ritschl, he saw Pauline Hellenism as an intrusion on early Christian thought and chose to emphasize the ethical aspects of Christianity. While professor at Berlin in 1901 he published his influential *What Is Christianity?* This focused on the human qualities of Christ, who preached not about Himself but about the Father; the kingdom and the fatherhood of God; a higher righteousness; and the command to love. The views of these men soon washed ashore in America and helped to further the ideas of the fatherhood of God and brotherhood of man and the gradual establishment of the kingdom of God in cooperation with the deity.

The Conservative Reaction

The churches did not take lightly the liberal attacks on conservative theology.

Protestant Reaction

Charles A. Briggs, professor at Union Theological

Seminary in New York, was put on trial before the
Presbytery of New York and suspended from the ministry in 1893. Henry P. Smith of Lane Seminary in
Cincinnati was likewise defrocked by the Presbyterian
church in 1893. In the same year A. C. McGiffert was
dismissed from Lane for his liberal views. Other denominations also had heresy trials and dismissed or disciplined
offending persons. Probably the most famous conflict of
the twentieth century concerned Harry Emerson Fos-
dick, who in 1925 was forced out of the pastorate of
First Presbyterian Church of New York City and became
an influential spokesman for liberalism from the pulpit
of the Riverside Church of New York until his retire-
ment in 1946.

Roman Catholic Reaction

Roman Catholicism likewise suffered the inroads
of liberalism and reacted strongly against it. Alfred
Loisy, founder of Roman Catholic modernism in
France, was dismissed in 1893 from his professorship at
the Institut Catholique in Paris and excommunicated in
1908. The English Jesuit George Tyrrell was demoted
in 1899 and died out of fellowship with the church.
Liberalism also invaded American Roman Catholicism.
To silence the threat worldwide, Pope Pius X issued the
decree *Lamentabili* in 1907, and in 1910 he imposed an
antimodernist oath on the clergy.

Evangelical Efforts

In contesting with rising liberalism, evangelicalism
had a number of able scholars during the latter part of
the nineteenth century and the early part of the twentieth. Charles Hodge defended a supernaturally inspired
Bible during his long tenure as professor of biblical

literature and later of theology at Princeton Seminary (1820-1878). A. A. Hodge ably succeeded his father at Princeton (1877-1886). In 1887 B. B. Warfield followed Hodge as professor of theology at Princeton. At home in Hebrew, Greek, modern languages, theology, and biblical criticism, he staunchly defended an inerrant Scripture and cardinal evangelical doctrines in a score of books and numerous pamphlets. In 1900 the scholarly Robert Dick Wilson joined the Princeton faculty, and J. Gresham Machen came to the faculty in 1906. In 1929, when a liberal realignment occurred at Princeton, Machen and Wilson joined Oswald T. Allis, Cornelius Van Til, and others in founding Westminster Theological Seminary. Of course other scholars could be mentioned, but these were some of the most vocal and the most prestigious.

While some evangelical scholars were standing for the faith in academic circles, a large number of faith missions came into existence to propagate the gospel on foreign fields. A few of them include: Africa Inland Mission, 1895; Central American Mission, 1890; Scandinavian Alliance Mission (now The Evangelical Alliance Mission), 1890; The Regions Beyond Missionary Union, 1878; Sudan Interior Mission (now SIM International), 1893).

New Groups and Conclusion

Meanwhile, other groups that differed to a greater or lesser degree from mainline positions appeared on the American religious scene. The Mormon movement came into being in 1830, the Seventh-Day Adventists[15] the following year, Spiritualism in 1848, Russellism (or Jehovah's Witnesses) in 1872, and Christian Science in 1876.

American Christianity has been characterized by full religious freedom, the separation of church and state, the voluntary principle of church membership, a democratic approach both in government and in lay participation, a high degree of informality in worship services, and a tendency toward the multiplication of denominations and sects.

PART VII

♦

The Church in the Contemporary World

TWENTY-EIGHT

External Opposition to Christianity

HOW do we stand some two thousand years after Christ delivered the Great Commission?[1] Christianity is still a minority faith. Various sources put the Christian population of the world in 1991 at about 1.76-1.79 billion, for about 33.3 percent of the total world population. Thus it currently stands at slightly less than its peak of about 34.4 percent in 1900. The Lausanne Statistics Task Force estimates that in 1993 there are about 540 million Bible-believing Christians, about 10 percent of the world's population. Although Christianity has been making tremendous advances in Africa, Latin America, and elsewhere, these are somewhat offset by the effects of materialism in Europe and America, the impediment of atheistic Communism behind the Bamboo Curtain, and the high birth rate in the Muslim world and in India.[2]

Not only is Christianity still a minority faith, it is

also still under assault. Such a condition is to be expected, because Jesus never promised that His followers would win the world with the preaching of the gospel or establish a utopia. Only the return of Christ in person will achieve that. Moreover, He never promised that His church would be immune from attack: "the world . . . hated Me; . . . therefore the world hates you" (John 15:18-19). Though opposition to Christianity will certainly come in all periods of history, it assumes new forms in each age. External forces contending with the church have been at least fourfold in recent decades: Communism, nationalism and national or pagan religions, cults, and social assault.

External Opposition to Christianity

Communism
Nationalism
Cults and Eastern religions
Social assault

Marxism

Karl Marx formulated his economic, political, and religious philosophy about the middle of the last century as an antidote to a rampant capitalism. He appealed to the downtrodden workers in industrial nations to throw off the bondage with which they were yoked and to introduce a new classless society. But in industrial nations the lot of the worker slowly improved through the efforts of labor unions and reformers and through governmental intervention. So, it was in the great agrarian nation of Russia, unresponsive to change and the needs of the masses, that Communism, as reconstructed or reinterpreted by Lenin, first caught fire. Communism engulfed over 1.6 billion people at its height in the 1980s; and though it has lost its grip in Eastern Europe and the former Soviet Union and Ethiopia, it still controls over one billion two hundred fifty million people in China, North Korea, Southeast Asia, and Cuba.

Wherever it has gone, this atheistic system has sought utterly to uproot Christianity—either by direct onslaught or by subversion. Although Communism was not able to obliterate Christianity in the countries where it won control, it surely proved to be a formidable enemy. In the former U.S.S.R. and China and some other countries, official churches of sorts were permitted, both to provide some impression to the world of freedom of religion and to control more effectively religious expression. The true church largely went underground in all Communist countries.

Opposition to or persecution of Christianity in most Marxist-dominated states has been covert. Christians have been prohibited from attendance at university and from advancement into prestigious positions. Sometimes they were even fired from menial employment. Efforts were made to choke off a supply of trained leadership of churches by severely restricting the numbers permitted to matriculate in theological seminaries. In order to prevent adequate places for meeting, building permits often were denied to churches or tied up in bureaucratic red tape for long periods of time. Pastors might be intimidated, as was true in the fall of 1982 in Romania when four leading Baptist pastors were accused of embezzling church funds for affirming separation of church and state and for opposition to state interference in church affairs. It was also common in the former Soviet Union for Christians to be accused of having mental illness and to be assigned to mental hospitals for "treatment."

Of course not all the opposition is covert or indirect. As a case in point, in Marxist Ethiopia late in 1982 authorities in Wollega Province closed 284 of the 350 churches of the Lutheran Ethiopian Evangelical church there. And as is well known, the Cultural Revolution in China (1966-1969) openly made war on Christianity and tried by every means to destroy it.

It is hard to discover how many believers may be in prison for their faith at any one time in a given country, but the research center at Keston College in England reported that there were 307 known Christian prisoners in the Soviet Union at the beginning of 1981. According to another report, there were 63 Christians being held in Chinese prisons or under house arrest for religious reasons early in 1991. Then in the latter part of 1991 reports reached Hong Kong of "large-scale arrests" of believers in the provinces of Zhejiang, Anhui, and Jiangsu, and the cities of Guangzhou, Shanghai, and Shenzhen. As the bastions of Communism collapse elsewhere, the Chinese seem determined to maintain their own defenses. Strong evidence indicates that Christians and other dissidents provided some of the slave labor that built the gas pipeline from Siberia to Western Europe.

Nationalism

Nationalism and national religions also vie with Christianity for mastery. Where nationalistic movements have resulted in the creation of new independent states, the religious body with the largest number of adherents has tended to assume leadership and establish a state religion. For example, Muslims predominate in Pakistan, Indonesia and Sudan, Hindus in India, and Buddhists in Burma (now Mayanmar). Therefore Christian work does not enjoy the freedom that formerly existed under friendly British or Dutch governments.

Moreover, in many countries Christianity has been linked in the minds of the people with Western imperialism. Now that those countries have cut the cord that binds them to a foreign power, they find it more difficult to accept the religion of that power. And strongly nationalistic peoples do not care to be evangelized from abroad; such activity puts them on an inferior level.

The impact of nationalism or new national conditions on Christianity is evident from such examples as the following. In 1973 the Somali Republic nationalized all mission programs and facilities; Singapore nationalized all private schools; the Pakistani government took over the Protestant and Roman Catholic colleges of the country; and President Amin of Uganda expelled fifty-eight European missionaries and ordered Africanization of the country's churches.

In 1975 the government of Mozambique proclaimed religion to be a divisive force and confiscated all missionary funds and property; President Tombalbaye of Chad severely persecuted Christians in a continuing effort to return the country to its traditional animism (but his assassination stopped the persecution); President Ngeuma of Equatorial Guinea campaigned against all believers in God and turned many churches into warehouses; and President Mobutu Sese Seko of Zaire continued his moves against Christianity by forbidding religious instruction in the country's school system, 90 percent of which was operated by religious organizations.

In 1980, evangelical radio programs were totally banned in Mexico. On December 3, 1990, Rev. Hossein Soodmand, the only ordained evangelical Protestant minister from Islamic background who chose to remain in Iran during the Islamic Revolution, was hanged by Iranian authorities. In 1991 the Shariah Act was adopted in Pakistan; it calls for law enforcement based on the traditional Islamic law. This act will probably take Christians out of the mainstream of society and force the church to go underground. During 1992 several Christian organizations reported that Turkish secret police and postal authorities were preventing delivery of Bible correspondence courses.

Cults and Eastern Philosophies

A third threat to true Christianity is the cults and Eastern philosophies and religions. However, it may be said that the cults tend to breed where Christianity has failed; untaught or disenchanted adherents of Christianity rather than the completely unchurched constitute the most fertile ground in which cultists may plant their seed.

Jehovah's Witnesses

In the United States at least, Russellism (Jehovah's Witnesses) spreads most rapidly among the unsophisticated. There are now about 3,500,000 Jehovah's Witnesses worldwide, including 915,000 in the United States (1992 statistics). Their work is carried on in 210 countries and on March 27, 1991 they became a legally recognized religious organization in the former Soviet

Union after being opposed by the government for years. In 1993, in Japan their Kingdom Halls (churches) had a total weekly attendance of 400,000, compared with an estimated 250,000 in attendance in the country's Protestant churches on any given Sunday.

Mormonism

Mormonism has gained especially in the Northwest, but has been successful among all classes in various parts of the country and abroad. The Mormons (Church of Jesus Christ of Latter-day Saints) have been extremely successful in winning converts. Beginning the century with 250,000 followers, they increased to 1,000,000 by 1950, doubled to 2,000,000 by 1964, and more than doubled again to reach 5,000,000 in 1982. At the beginning of 1994 they claimed about 8,400,000 members worldwide, with 4,485,000 in all branches in the United States. Missionaries went to several countries of Eastern Europe in 1991 as they provided religious liberty and for the first time to Botswana and Cote d' Ivoire in Africa. Congregations of the church had been established in 130 countries as of 1991. During 1990 they claim to have made and baptized 330,000 converts. Other groups do not demonstrate the same degree of aggressive evangelism as the Jehovah's Witnesses and Mormons and thus do not so greatly threaten orthodox Christianity.

Eastern Religions

It is not quite so easy to quantify the impact of Eastern religions in the West in general, or in the United States in particular. Transcendental meditation, with its roots in India, makes its influence felt broadly in American society. The *Tao Te Ching*, the sacred book of

Taoism, often may be purchased at the corner bookstore and *The Tao of Pooh* by Benjamin Hoff seeks to bring the principles of Taoism to even the youth of America.

Writings of the Hare Krishna movement, which comes from the context of Hinduism, often may be picked up at an airport, especially in Los Angeles, New York, or London. The some 110,000 members of the Baha'i faith support their magnificent temple in Wilmette, Illinois, which dwarfs the temple at the international headquarters of the religion in Haifa.

The Influx to the West

Of especially great importance for the redrawing of the American religious landscape was the immigration legislation of 1965. In that year Congress rescinded the Asian Exclusion Act and redistributed immigration quotas, permitting Asian, Eastern European and Middle Eastern countries to send larger numbers than ever before. As a result, Eastern religions have increased their presence in America greatly. Young adult Americans have converted by the thousands to Buddhism and guru-led Hindu religions. Over 100 different Hindu denominations and 75 forms of Buddhism have come into existence since 1965 and each now claims three to five million adherents.[3] The year 1987 saw the naming of the first Buddhist chaplain in the American armed forces and the formation of the American Buddhist Congress. Hindus are represented in the Hindu Vishwa Parishad.

The Rise of Islam

The new immigration legislation permitted immigration from Islamic countries for the first time in significant numbers. In the United States Muslims now number some four million, mostly as a result of immigration, though converts continue to increase in number. The Islamic Center in Washington, D.C., has been the leading Islamic center of the United States for a number of years, but the $17 million center on 96th Street in Manhattan opened in the spring of 1992. There are about 400,000 Muslims in New York City. The Islamic Center of Greater Toledo (Ohio) and the center in Detroit are among the most prestigious in other large cities of the nation. There are now more than 650 mosques in the United States.

The Black Muslim movement has had varying fortunes since its inception in 1931 in Detroit. Now most Black Muslims have renounced their controversial views on race and religion and, some one million strong, have moved into the mainstream of Muslim orthodoxy. But a few, like the approximately 10,000 members of Louis Farrakhan's Nation of Islam, still cling to black supremacist views. The Islamic community in the United States has now surpassed the Jewish community in size and has become a powerful political force, balancing the Jewish-allied support for Israel in public debates on the Middle East.

The impact of Muslims in Western Europe has been even greater than that in America. Some ten million of them came to the continent for employment during the 1960s and 1970s from North Africa, Turkey, the Middle East, and the Indian subcontinent. Because these aliens cannot gain citizenship there as they can in the United States, they stand apart and constitute an increasing storm center. All over the continent there is a worry that the cohesive nature of national cultures is at risk, as are the jobs of citizens. In a largely secularized France the 1.7 million Muslims there form an especially potent religious force. They are a battleground in Germany too, where about 1.5 million have settled. About 800,000 have immigrated to Britain, over 400,000 to the Netherlands, and about 300,000 to Italy. Currently 50 European cities have an Arab Muslim population of 10,000 or more; 32 are French. Arab World Ministries and at least 14 other missions are beginning to launch outreaches to Muslims in London, some French cities, and New York City. The main hindrance to expansion of this work is lack of trained personnel.

New Age Movement

An especially important threat to orthodox Christianity that borrows heavily from Eastern thought is the New Age Movement. Though the movement began in the 1960s, it especially took form in 1971 with the book *Be Here Now* by Baba Ram Das, the first national periodical *East-West Journal,* and the first national network directories. The movement centers on a personal spiritual-psychological transformation, which in many instances is a kind of crisis experience, but in a majority of cases involves change over a period of time. In any case, in the transformation one is freed from debilitating relationships, boredom, purposelessness, hopelessness and much more and gains a new health, a new meaning to life, and a new excitement.

Elements of Eastern religion and transpersonal psychology provide tools for spiritual transformation and include meditation (Zen or some other transcendental experience), intensive seminars, healing at the hands of a New Age healer (a kind of Indian guru), wearing a crystal, psychological reorientation experiences, and the like. New Agers seek further personal transformation and adopt strategies designed to accomplish that goal.

They subordinate beliefs to experience. For them God tends to be a universal power, a unifying principle, an underlying reality of the universe, discovered by mystical states of consciousness and binding nature and humanity together. This bonding of nature and humanity is well illustrated in Lawrence E. Joseph's book *Gaia*[4] (earth goddess of the Greeks); the earth is seen to be alive and functioning as a superorganism in which living things interact with geophysical and chemical processes to maintain conditions suitable for life.

New Agers believe that eventually there will be one universal religion. And of course they believe that the universal religion, the new way of looking at things, will transform society, will bring about a new age. Others work actively toward a transformation of society with a networking of like-minded individuals to transform education, ecological policy, business organization, national and world politics, and more. They have merged with the holistic health movement. Many of them have joined human rights and animal rights organizations. Since personal transformation requires a long path of growth and cannot be completed in one lifetime, a great many in the movement have subscribed to a belief in reincarnation.[5]

Native American Religious Practices

Yet one more challenge to the church in the United States is the revival of Indian religions. A combination of the desire to give Native Americans their due and an increasing desire of Native Americans to discover or return to their roots has given a new vitality to their non-Christian practices.

Social Assault

A fourth threat to the church is the social assault. Television with its constant discrediting of Christianity and its moral standards, pornography and the increase of sexual looseness, the rise in the divorce rate, the plague of the drug traffic, and the alcoholic craze are only some of the better-known aspects of society that bombard the church, the Christian family, and the individual. The constancy and the intensity of the attack periodically cause the weaker to fall.

The environment of the Christian is increasingly polluted. For instance, a Gallup Poll conducted in 1981 reported that one in four claimed that an alcohol-related problem affected his family life; this was up from one in eight in 1974. Alcohol abuse was cited by one in four as one of the three reasons most responsible for the high divorce rate in the United States.

In a Gallup poll taken in 1987, 24 percent reported that drinking had been a source of trouble in their family. In another Gallup poll taken in the same year only 27 percent of those in the 18-29 age group believed premarital sex was wrong. On June 7, 1991, the Surgeon General Antonia Novello reported on a national survey of junior and senior high school students that found over half of them drank alcoholic beverages and about half a million go on a drinking spree every week,[6] even though under-age drinking is illegal across the nation. The most common reason teens gave for drinking was peer pressure and the fact that parents drank frequently and heavily.

A Gallup poll in 1985 asking teens about their concern over substance abuse at school found the following. Those who said that drinking was a very big problem numbered 24 percent and an additional 23 percent said it was a fairly big problem; 21 percent said marijuana use was a very big problem and an additional 22 percent said it was a fairly big problem; 11 percent said the use of hard drugs was a very big problem and an additional 17 percent said it was a fairly big problem. Surveys showed that marijuana consumption had declined dramatically since 1980 but that drinking and the use of hard drugs had increased slightly.[7]

The social assault of rock music is especially pervasive. It is estimated that between the seventh and twelfth grades the average teenager listens to 10,500 hours of rock music, almost as much as the entire time spent in the classroom from kindergarten through high school.[8] Rock music espouses themes of rebellion, drugs, and sex, and heavy metal has come to embrace outright hatred and rejection. Since adult society has become increasingly sexually and behaviorally explicit, in order for rock music to express rebellion and autonomy, it must take explicitness and even violence to an increasingly higher level.

Certainly the cumulative effect of the message of rock is considerable, but as Brown and Hendee observe, research on the degree and kind of effect is still in its infancy. Music videos apparently make a greater impact than the songs by themselves. It should be some comfort to parents and Christian workers to note the conclusion of Brown and Hendee that, "Healthy well adjusted teenagers . . . may be minimally affected by explicit rock music" (1662).

Christians will find it hard to stand against the social currents. But there is the same power in the gospel today as during the first century. It was to Christians living in a completely pagan society that Paul wrote, "Do not be conformed to [pressed into the mold of] this world" (Romans 12:2).

TWENTY-NINE

Developments Within Christianity
Ecumenical Efforts

Early Efforts

SO MUCH for the external forces that Christianity has to meet today. Now it remains to look at what has been going on within the ranks. Throughout the century there has been great interest in ecumenical or union movements. Part of this effort seemingly has come about because some people honestly felt that the church was too fragmented and that it ought to present a more united front to the world. And part of it seemed to result from the loss of doctrinal distinctives that tended to keep groups separate. The ecumenical spirit especially expressed itself in the United States in the work of the Federal Council of the Churches of Christ in America, organized in 1908.

This body reorganized in 1950 as the National Council of Churches of Christ in America and became a much more comprehensive organization. The Council's member churches (33 communions) now have an aggregate membership of almost 49 million. Some right-wing conservatives organized the American Council of Churches in 1941 as their answer to the generally liberal-minded National Council, but subsequently this group fragmented and became less effective; today it has almost 2 million members. More in the mainstream of American evangelicalism is the National Association of Evangelicals, organized in 1942 as a means of bringing together conservative Protestant churches. This body now has a constituency of more than 15 million drawn from more than 77 denominations.

The World Council of Churches

Then in 1948, after many years of preparation,[9] the World Council of Churches was formed at Amsterdam, with 147 denominations from forty-four countries participating. With the passage of time the Eastern Orthodox church (but not the Roman Catholic church) has joined the world body, but evangelicals generally have not become involved. Today more than 300 denominations from more than 100 countries hold membership.

Both the National Council and the World Council have been criticized for being too theologically liberal and too politicized in favor of leftist causes. The National Council especially has been scored even in the secular press for its leftist leanings and its financial support for revolutionary or at least Marxist-oriented movements. Its employment of revolutionary slogans and rhetoric and its tendency to portray the United States in a bad light while it glosses over the faults of revolutionary movements and glorifies their achievements, have given the Council bad press and increasingly have put it on the defensive. Many have concluded that the church has become too political.

Those who have been worried about theological liberalism and political activity of the World Council of Churches took some consolation in the direction of the Sixth Assembly of the Council in Vancouver in 1983.

After the Fifth Assembly at Uppsala in 1968 supported liberation theologies, sent money to liberation movements, and criticized failures of the West, many evangelicals believed the Council had drifted irretrievably to the left.

At Vancouver, however, there was greatly increased attention to a vigorous Trinitarian theology and evangelistic proclamations, and there was a backdrop of prayer with round-the-clock prayer for the sessions throughout the assembly. A majority of evangelicals present drafted an open letter commending the evangelical concerns at the assembly and calling for evangelical involvement with the World Council of Churches. But a minority opinion saw the evangelical indications at the assembly to be only half the story. They reacted against the continuing theological vagueness, support for liberation theologies, and unbalanced criticism of the West, and urged evangelicals to avoid involvement with the World Council of Churches.

At the Seventh Assembly of the World Council in Canberra, Australia, in 1991, the debate between liberals and conservatives continued. A particularly divisive situation occurred when a woman theologian from the Korean Presbyterian church linked the Christian faith with traditional Korean spirituality and invoked the spirits of martyrs. The Orthodox church particularly took exception to her speech and to the liberalism of the Council's theology and indicated they were considering withdrawal from the Council. As a matter of fact, the Greek Orthodox Archdiocese of North and South America did suspend membership in the National Council of Churches for nine months. The Council welcomed into membership the Chinese Christian Council after Chinese absence from the Council for several decades.

Major American Religions Bodies in 1993

(Protestant and Catholic, membership of over one million in round numbers)

African Methodist Episcopal Church	3,500,000
African Methodist Episcopal Zion Church	1,200,000
American Baptist Churches	1,527,000
Assemblies of God	2,235,000
Christian church (Disciples)	1,022,000
Christian Churches & Churches of Christ	1,070,000
Church of God in Christ	5,500,000
Churches of Christ	1,690,000
Episcopal Church	2,472,000
Evangelical Lutheran Church	5,245,000
Lutheran Church-Missouri Synod	2,607,000
National Baptist Convention, U.S.A.	8,000,000
National Baptist Convention of America	3,500,000
National Missionary Bap. Conv. of Amer.	2,500,000
Orthodox Church in America	1,030,000
Presbyterian Church (U.S.A.)	3,778,000
Progressive National Baptist Convention	2,500,000
Roman Catholic Church	58,000,000
Southern Baptist Convention	15,232,000
United Church of Christ	1,583,000
United Methodist Church	8,785,000

The Moral Majority

While the National and World Councils have been involved in social and political action in a more liberal theological context, the Moral Majority sought to engage in social action in a conservative theological context. The Moral Majority was organized by Jerry Falwell, pastor of Thomas Road Baptist Church in Lynchburg, Virginia, in 1979. It enlisted more than four million members, including 72,000 ministers, at its height. It sought to organize the evangelical and fundamentalist Christians of the United States, as well as others holding to traditional moral values. The movement opposed permissiveness and moral relativism, hoped to restore the sacredness of the family and human life, sought to wage war against illegal drug traffic and pornography, and firmly supported a strong national defense and the state of Israel.

Dr. Falwell disbanded the Moral Majority in 1989 to focus more fully on the work of his church and Liberty University, which he also founded. But when others did not take up the struggle as he had hoped, he founded Liberty Alliance early in 1992 to pursue many of the same goals as Moral Majority. The National Association of Evangelicals also seeks to focus the attention of its membership on social concerns.

Vatican II

A certain amount of hope arose in some circles that all churches might eventually get together, as Roman Catholics launched an ecumenical council, Vatican II, in 1962. Observers who were not Roman Catholics were welcomed and "heretics" henceforth became "separated brethren." In fact, long before the first session of the council met, on May 30, 1960, Pope John XXIII had established a Secretariat for Church Unity to facilitate the reunion of separated brethren into the one fold of Christ.

Some saw a connection between the calling of an ecumenical council and the ecumenical movement. Pope John did not simply invite all others to return to the fold of Rome; he called for a renewal of the Roman church so that it would be more credible to the separated brethren.

The council was characterized by a new spirit of openness. This was demonstrated by the invitation to non-Roman Catholics to attend, by the unprecedented publicity given the event, and by the degree of flexibility and the irenic tone often expressed in dealing with non-Roman Catholics. A new missionary spirit and the responsibility of the church to serve in the world received emphasis.

The council met in four sessions—1962, 1963, 1964, 1965—under John XXIII and Paul VI (about twenty-five hundred delegates came from 136 countries, in addition to Orthodox and Protestant observers). Though Pope Paul was regarded as a liberal, he viewed with alarm the radical character of some of the proposals of the council and intervened to moderate them. But even so, considerable changes occurred, not in basic doctrine, but in approaches and attitudes. Pope John saw that the church had to prepare itself to serve a changed and changing world, and that modernization was necessary to make the church intelligible to modern men and women. The church had to recover its character as a living witness to God's love for humanity.

Results of Vatican II

A total of sixteen constitutions or decrees came out of Vatican II.[10] Of special importance to laypersons was permission to use vernacular languages in the liturgy, adaptation of rites to differing, non-Western cultures, and simplification of the liturgy. The "Constitution on Divine Revelation" changed the basis of authority in the church. Whereas the Council of Trent in 1546 had declared that Scripture and tradition were equal bases of authority, Vatican II did not distinguish between the two, but emphasized their interplay or interrelatedness. The place of the Bible in Romanism had been upgraded by a recent emphasis on biblical studies and the encouragement of Pius XII (1943) to follow literal interpretation of Scripture whenever possible. Now a conciliar decision tends to give greater official support to what has been happening in the church.

In the spirit of greater sharing of authority in the church, the council declared that infallibility of the church resides in the pope and also "in the body of bishops when that body exercises supreme teaching authority with the successor of Peter." Moreover, the "Constitution of the Church" states: "Together with its head, the Roman pontiff, and never without its head, the episcopal order is the subject of the supreme and full power over the universal Church."

Of more importance to the world at large were the decisions on ecumenism. The "Constitution on the Church," as would be expected, defined the church as the people of God who were properly in the Roman communion. But it also included the baptized who "do not profess the faith in its entirety or do not preserve unity of communion with the successor of Peter." The decree on ecumenism, *Unitatis Redintegratio,* declared that both Roman Catholics and Protestants must share the blame for the division among Christians, called on Roman Catholics to play their part in the ecumenical movement, and set forth the importance of renewal as a prelude to unity. This was quite different from the old "return to the Fold" exhortations to Protestants. The "Decree on Eastern Catholic Churches," among other things, underscored the hope of the council for a corporate union of the Eastern churches not in union with the church at Rome. Near the close of the council, a prayer service took place at St. Paul's Outside the Walls, in which Pope Paul, the bishops of the council, and observers and guests joined in prayers for promoting Christian unity.

Supplementary to Vatican II was the Extraordinary Synod of November 25-December 7, 1985. While giving assent to Vatican II, its two documents stressed the duty of every Christian to engage in evangelization and to participate fully in the struggle to build a "civilization of love." The Synod declared evangelization to be the first duty of all Christians, and it called for personal communion that existed between Catholics and other Christians and sought to manifest and increase it as much as possible with a view to eventual restoration of full communion. The Synod also addressed the social needs of the world and spoke of the need to defend human rights, but cautioned against falling into a "this-worldly humanism"; it accepted the principle of inculturation, the regeneration and transformation of culture in the light of the Gospel.[11]

Results of Vatican II

Worship services in language of the people
Both elements in Eucharist distributed to laity
Biblical exposition and congregational
singing common
Cooperation with non-Catholics in
numerous ventures

Thirty years after the calling of Vatican II the Roman Catholic church looks quite different from what it did before the Council. Now worship services are conducted in the language of the people. The priest often distributes both elements to participants in the communion and faces the congregation as he leads them in celebration of the sacrament. Biblical exposition and congregational singing are common elements of Catholic worship services. A Bible in the language of the people may at least be found in most American Catholic homes. Interaction between Catholics and Protestants has been much more pronounced as they have cooperated in social and political action, and as charismatics in both camps have enjoyed a common experience.

Church Unions

In addition to interdenominational cooperation, there has also been considerable organic union of churches in this century. The United Church of Canada came into being in 1925, the National Church of Scotland in 1929, the Methodist Church of the United States in 1939, the Church of South India in 1947, and the United Church of Christ in 1961.[12] In Madagascar the Church of Christ and the Malagasy Lutheran Church merged in 1982 to form a new body with a membership of 1.5 million in a country of about 11.8 million.

The Presbyterian Church (USA) came into being in 1983 with a union of the United Presbyterian Church in the U.S.A. and the Presbyterian Church in the U.S. (known as the Southern Presbyterian Church). The new church had a membership of 3,778,000 in 1991, quite evenly distributed over the United States. The union ended 122 years of separation brought on by the Civil War.

Those who left the Missouri Synod in 1976 formed the Association of Evangelical Lutheran

Churches and almost immediately entered into merger talks with two larger bodies: the Lutheran Church in America and the American Lutheran Church. The three-way merger was completed in 1987 and the new church, the Evangelical Lutheran Church in America, was officially inaugurated on January 1, 1988. Its membership in 1991 stood at 5,245,000.

Roman Catholics and Anglicans are engaging in a dialogue preliminary to merger negotiations. Whether such questions as headship of the church and ordination of women can be settled to the satisfaction of both groups remains to be seen. The decision of the Church of England in November 1992 to ordain women to the ministry may prove to be a major stumbling block to these union talks. Other mergers have taken place at home and abroad; this account is intended only to provide some outstanding examples of church unions. In addition, many denominations are engaged in a wide variety of cooperative ventures.

THIRTY

Developments Within Christianity

Decadence, Renewal, and the Advance of Women

Indications of Decadence

IN RECENT years it has become evident that all is not well within the churches. Worldwide the Roman Catholic church has found it increasingly difficult to control its constituency. Especially in Latin America and Europe, church attendance has been very low. For instance, in France, which is 85 percent Roman Catholic, attendance at mass is only 12 percent on a given Sunday, according to a recent survey; and a full one-third of French youth do not profess to believe in God. Closures of training schools for Catholic leadership have reached the point in some places in Europe that the church finds it increasingly difficult to supply needed personnel. Enrollment in Catholic seminaries in the United States has dropped from 47,500 to 8,000 in the last three decades. There is increasing opposition worldwide to the position of the hierarchy on abortion, birth control, divorce, homosexuality, and clerical celibacy.

Europe

Religion in Europe as a whole is in a decadent

condition. As a leading European evangelical recently observed, "Europe is *the* mission field of the world." Only about 4 percent of the English were in church on a given Sunday as of about 1975. More than 500 Anglican churches were closed during the sixties and seventies. Defections from British Catholic churches are also extensive. Britain has seemed almost to be in a process of de-christianization. The Church of Scotland lost nearly a quarter of its membership during the sixteen years prior to 1983. Less than one-fifth of Scots even nominally belong to the church.

> *As a leading European evangelical recently observed, "Europe is the mission field of the world."*

But Britain is much better off than the Lutheran countries. For example, in Finland, though 92 percent of all adults had been baptized as children by the Evangelical Lutheran Church, in 1986 only 4 percent of parishioners attended Sunday worship services. In Denmark 3 percent, in Sweden 5 percent, and Norway 7 percent of the population attended church weekly in 1986. None of these statistics has fundamentally changed since then. In 1993 only 2 percent of the French were Protestant and less than half of those were evangelical Christians. Only 6 percent of the Catholics actively practice their faith. In West Germany, the Evangelical Church (Lutheran) reported in 1980 that 42 percent of the population belonged to its churches, but that only a little over 5 percent attended worship on Sundays.

But there are signs of spiritual life in Europe. In 1982 British church attendance was up to about 11 percent of the adult population. In 1991 it stood at about 10 percent. One report estimates that fully one-third of all graduates of Anglican seminaries now are evangelical. Luis Palau began his "Mission to London" in October 1983 and planned to extend his crusade there to the summer of 1984; and at the same time Billy Graham conducted crusades in the five other major English cities of Liverpool, Bristol, Birmingham, Newcastle, and Norwich.

Expectancy of spiritual revitalization is in the air in England. "Spring Harvest" has become an annual rallying point for many Protestants who engage in week-long meetings in England and Scotland. In 1990 sixty-five thousand participated in the program, which was billed as the largest teaching event in Europe. Another encouraging development was the elevation of George Carey as Archbishop of Canterbury and head of the Church of England on April 19, 1991. He is a backer of the evangelical wing of the church and an enthusiastic proponent of the Church of England's "Decade of Evangelism."

Evangelicals in Sweden and Denmark are stirring and advocating formation of their own segment of the state Lutheran church. Some hints of new life were evident in Finland in 1980 and 1981. In 1982 Luis Palau conducted a crusade in Helsinki. For the first time in 400 years state and free churches joined in evangelism in a city where only about 1 percent of the people attend church. Over 1,400 responded to the invitation to accept Christ as Savior.

An estimated 3,500 to 5,000 groups of Pietistic believers have been assembling in West Germany in recent years, some with memberships in the hundreds. Wuppertal is the center of this movement. Church attendance among all groups (Catholic and Protestant) in West Germany had risen to 21 percent in 1986. Much missionary effort centered on Spain in the summer of 1992, both at the Summer Olympics and World Expo in Seville. Close to 300,000 visited the Pavilion of Promise at Expo and about 51,000 made first-time decisions for Christ. Sixty tons of Scriptures were distributed at the Olympics in Barcelona; distribution teams visited 90 percent of Barcelona's 600,000 homes. During 1993, under the umbrella of "Project Antwerp," the some 1,000 evangelicals in Antwerp launched a program to reach every resident of the city of 600,000 with the message of Christ and to start 30 evangelistic Bible study groups.

North America

In the United States, though church membership has continued to grow during recent years it has not kept pace with the rate of population increase. For example, it stood at about 131,400,000 in 1974; 132,812,000 in 1978; 133,388,000 in 1980, 134,817,000 in 1981, and 143,926,000 in 1987. The percentage of Americans as members of churches or synagogues has been generally on the decline in recent decades. In 1937 it stood at 73 percent, in 1947 at 76 percent; then it declined steadily to 67 percent in 1982. Going up to 69 percent in 1983, it held at that level to 1988 and then declined to 65 percent, but rose again to 69 percent at the beginning of 1990.

Church and synagogue attendance reached a high point in 1958, when 49 percent of adults attended in an average week; this was up from 41 percent in 1937.

Then a decline set in and attendance remained steady at 40-41 percent between 1972 and 1984; it went up to 42 percent in 1985 but fell again to 40 percent in 1986 and 1987. Roman Catholics suffered the greatest decline, from 74 percent in 1958 to 48 percent in 1988. In 1987 only 24 percent of Jews reported attending synagogue at least once a month; 25 percent said they never attended synagogue. Only 8 percent said they attended weekly, while 26 percent of Protestants and Catholics said they attended church weekly. Canadian attendance on a typical Sunday has declined even more than that of the United States, from 60 percent in 1957 to 31 percent in 1986 and is now below 30 percent. Of adults under thirty only 16 percent were in attendance on a typical week in 1986, which does not bode well for the future. There has been a rapid growth among French-speaking evangelical congregations of Quebec during the last two decades, however.

The religious composition of the population of the United States has changed considerably in recent years. In 1947 Protestants outnumbered Roman Catholics 69 percent to 20 percent. In 1987 Protestants outnumbered Catholics 57 percent to 28. This change is especially a result of the influx of Hispanics but is also due to the higher birth rate among people who are traditionally Catholic. The 1990 census reported that there are now 22.4 million Hispanics in the United States. These constitute 9 percent of the total population; in 1980 the percentage stood at 6.4 percent.

In addition to natural growth and legal immigration, hundreds of thousands of Mexicans slip into the United States illegally each year. The Hispanic increase is more rapid in percentage and total numbers than that of the African American community, which rose from

11.7 percent in 1980 to 12.1 percent in 1990, for a total of thirty million. Apparently Hispanics will soon surpass African Americans as the largest minority bloc in the nation. With current trends among young people, by early in the next century Catholics could vie with Protestants as the dominant religious group in America. Only 52 percent of American teens said they were Protestant in 1987. In 1947, 5 percent of the population was Jewish; in 1989 the percentage had slipped to two.

Decline of Mainline Denominations

Many of the old-line denominations are in real trouble in this country. In turning away from a biblically centered message to social action projects and in turning away from standard services to more contemporary approaches, they have alienated masses of people. Of the ten largest Protestant bodies, seven suffered an average loss of 10 percent of their members during the decade of the seventies.

More specifically, between 1960 and 1979, the Episcopal Church lost 430,000; the Lutheran Church in America, 130,000; the United Presbyterian Church in the U.S.A., 770,000; the United Church of Christ, 520,000; the Christian Church (Disciples), 570,000; and the United Methodists, 1,150,000. The United Methodists lost about 280,000 during the years 1978-1981.

Put another way, between 1973 and 1983 the United Methodist Church lost 8 percent of its members, the Presbyterian Church (USA) 15 percent, and the Christian Church 13 percent. The decline has continued in more recent years. For example, the United Methodist Church dropped from 9,266,000 in 1984 to 8,785,000 in 1991. For the same period the Presbyterian Church

(USA) fell from 3,092,000 to 2,805,000 and the Christian Church from 1,132,000 to 1,022,000.

All of these have emphasized social action almost to the exclusion of evangelism. Now there are stirrings within these denominations to launch evangelistic efforts. They eye with some jealousy the growth of the conservative denominations.

While liberally oriented American denominations have experienced decline in membership, the United Church of Canada has had the same experience. Membership in 1966 stood at 1,062,000. In 1977 it had declined to 930,000; in 1982 to 900,000, and in 1991 to 785,000. Since 1975 Sunday school enrollment has fallen by more than 60 percent. This augurs ill for the future because it means that the church will not have the recruits needed to maintain the membership in years to come.

During the last two decades there has been especially great debate over theological slippage and social and political involvement in four major American denominations: the Presbyterian Church in the U.S. (Southern Presbyterians), the United Methodists, Missouri Synod Lutherans, and the Southern Baptists. Controversy among the Southern Presbyterians led to a defection of 40,000 of them in fourteen states in 1973 to form the Presbyterian Church in America. The new denomination increased to 75,000 in 1980. In 1983 it merged with the Reformed Presbyterian Church-Evangelical Synod, with a combined membership of 130,000 organized in 807 churches.

Meanwhile, the United Presbyterian Church in the U.S.A. (Northern) and the Presbyterian Church in the U.S. (Southern) merged in 1983, giving rise to much internal discussion that led evangelical congregations to withdraw and join other Presbyterian groups or become independent. In part as a result of this action and in part as a result of evangelism, the Presbyterian Church in America in 1991 had 233,000 members organized in 1,167 churches.

The United Methodist defection has moved in various directions, but some of it resulted in the formation of the Evangelical Church of North America in 1968. That denomination has not grown rapidly; its membership stood at 16,000 in 1990.

The Lutheran Church-Missouri Synod

Early in the 1970s the Lutheran Church-Missouri Synod was launched on a doctrinal and political dispute that threatened to wreck the denomination. In 1974 Synod president J. A. O. Preus fired John Tietjen, then president of Concordia Seminary in St. Louis. A total of 45 of the 50 faculty and 400 of the 600 students walked off campus and formed Christ Seminary or Seminex (Seminary-in-Exile). Gradually local churches also broke their ties with the denomination and organized the Association of Evangelical Lutheran Churches, which had a membership of 111,000 in 1982. Seminex graduated about 700 over the years, most of them entering the ministry of the Association of Evangelical Lutherans; but some took positions in the American Lutheran Church and the Lutheran Church in America. Missouri Synod leaders refused to budge from an avowedly orthodox position. Seminex graduated its last class of 25 in 1983 and closed its doors. Most of the faculty was assigned to other Lutheran seminaries.

The 2.6 million-member Missouri Synod has weathered the storm and seems to have turned back the tide of theological liberalism. Enrollment at Concordia has returned to approximately the level it was before the exodus in 1974. All has not been well in the Missouri Synod in recent years, however. In 1989 the board of regents at Concordia Theological Seminary in Fort Wayne, Indiana, dismissed the president, Robert Preus, around whom conservatives in the denomination have rallied. They have attacked Ralph Bohlmann, Synod president, as being too "moderate" and accused him of being behind the actions taken against Preus. At the Synod's triennial conference in Pittsburgh, July 10-17, 1992, the delegates elected conservative Alvin Barry president and ratified an agreement that reinstated Preus as president of Concordia in Fort Wayne. While some classify the squabble as a personality struggle, evidently the battle over the theological direction of the denomination has not yet been resolved.

The Southern Baptist Convention

Southern Baptists, like Missouri Synod Lutherans, have been engaging in considerable debate over theological liberalism in their ranks. A very vocal group of adherents to biblical inerrancy has hurled charges of liberalism against the denominational seminaries and has sought to cut off colleges that in the conservatives' view are now so secular as not to be considered church-related any longer. Many churches have withheld contributions from denominational agencies, and some have broken away to organize evangelical fellowships.

But evangelicals generally have determined to turn the denomination around. They have managed to elect effective evangelicals to fill the office of president of the Southern Baptist Convention for the last several years. The appointment by these men of theologically-conservative trustees is causing the denomination to make an historic turn to the right. Meanwhile Southern Baptists have kept on with aggressive expansion. During 1991 their Sunday school enrollment reached 8,178,000, breaking previous records; and church membership reached a total of 15,232,000. Southern Baptists now support 3,800 foreign missionaries in 121 countries.

Though the Southern Baptist Convention enjoys outward expansion, internal dissension has continued to boil. When conservatives again won the presidency of the Convention in June of 1990, tensions began to rise dramatically. Conservatives moved to replace the heads of several of the church's national agencies and filled the positions with fundamentalists. The conservatives also slapped down guidelines on faculty hiring and promotion at the seminaries. Baylor University, a moderate bastion, amended its charter and became an independent university.

Then in May of 1991, 6,000 disaffected Southern Baptists met in Atlanta to form the Cooperative Baptist Fellowship, which they insisted was not a new denomination; but it certainly was a moderate organization that sought to operate independently of the conservative power structure. It moved toward setting up various organizations parallel to the agencies of the Southern Baptist Convention. John H. Hewett, pastor of the First Baptist Church of Asheville, North Carolina, was elected to head the new Fellowship.

The fight proceeds on the level of the local church as well. Southern Baptist congregations hire and fire their own pastors and terminations have increased dramatically since 1984; a total of 1,390 pastors were fired in 1988 alone—a great many over doctrinal questions. Congregations often are more conservative than their pastors. When they formed the Cooperative Baptist

Fellowship, the moderates said they had given up the political struggle to recapture leadership of the Southern Baptist Convention. Southern Baptists like members of the Missouri Synod had made a historic turn to the right, proving that leftward drift can be arrested in the churches. The latest book-length account of the Southern Baptist struggle is Grady Cothen's *What Happened to the Southern Baptist Convention?* (Smyth & Helwys, 1993).

Renewal Movements in Various Denominations

Doctrinal and numerical slippage in many denominations has led to the rise of renewal movements. Four of the more important of them are the Good News movement in the United Methodist Church, the Biblical Witness Fellowship in the United Church of Christ, the Presbyterian Lay Committee that publishes the *Presbyterian Layman*, and Episcopal Renewal Ministries. Ronald H. Nash has done a great service by editing the book *Evangelical Renewal in the Mainline Churches* (Crossway, 1987), which devoted separate chapters to renewal movements in the Methodist, Episcopal, Lutheran, Presbyterian, American Baptist, Disciples, United Church of Christ, and the United States Catholic Church.[13] Responding to crises facing many historic denominations, a coalition of 21 evangelical renewal leaders from eight denominations met at Wheaton College (IL), March 19-20, 1990, and drafted "The DuPage Declaration: A Call to Biblical Fidelity." This was a three-page document affirming significant theological and ethical standards that are under challenge in their respective communions. The Rev. James V. Heidinger,

Jr., executive secretary of the United Methodist renewal group Good News, moderated the sessions.

Women in the Church*

In many old-line denominations, but unrelated to their decline, there has been a receptiveness to women in places of leadership. They have been ordained as elders and ministers with an increasing frequency. The Church of England decided to ordain women to the priesthood in November 1992. With the exception of some of the Pentecostal and holiness groups, evangelicals generally have not been open to the acceptance of women in places of authority. Roman Catholics refuse to ordain them to the priesthood.

The number of women enrolled in seminaries has increased dramatically, and their involvement in Christian education, church music, missions, and other ministries has risen sharply. More than 31 percent of the students enrolled in 1992 in the 215 seminaries accredited by the American Association of Theological Schools were women. In a few theological schools they are in a majority or have a near majority. Increasing numbers of women have also risen to administrative positions in the various denominations and have received faculty appointments in the theological seminaries. All branches of Judaism except the Orthodox now ordain women as rabbis.

* Though feminism has significant implications for the church, it is a wider social and religious movement that is beyond the scope of this brief study.

THIRTY-ONE

Developments Within Christianity
Evangelical Advance

WITHIN the great denominations and existing as separatist groups are significant and growing numbers of evangelical Christians. This element has become increasingly vocal and respected in recent years.

Advances in Evangelical Education

Evangelical Christianity has benefited greatly from the rehabilitation of the Bible in scholarly circles as a result of New Eastern Studies. An increasing number of evangelicals have trained in the finest universities of the world and now serve as professors and department heads in the universities. Dozens of fully accredited Christian colleges dot the American countryside; and an Accrediting Association of Bible Colleges has come into being with a growing list of fully accredited and associate members. The Christian College Coalition currently has 82 members.

There are now more than 500 Bible colleges and Bible institutes in North America. Evangelical seminaries, instead of withering on the vine, reported expanding and, in some cases, exploding enrollments during the 1970s. But with the smaller number of college graduates, economic recession, and rapidly rising seminary costs during the 1980s, most of those seminaries experienced a leveling off in enrollment or a slight decline. A few of the more successful reported only a slowing in the rate of growth. Nearly all of them were forced to hire admissions recruiters and to increase their advertising budgets.

Advances in Mass Communication

Numerous religious radio stations have been established, and individual programs are aired on national and international hookups. The "electronic church," evangelical telecasting, reaches millions of viewers every week.

Again, mass evangelism is stirring many of the great cities of the world, especially through the efforts of Billy Graham and his team or Luis Palau. Graham's crusades across the United States, Europe, and the Far East have had fantastic success.

Rapid Numerical Growth

Church memberships of evangelical groups continue to expand rapidly. Numerous megachurches have come into existence in the United States. It would be easy to list several with memberships of twenty or thirty thousand or more, but such figures do not provide a true picture of the actual ministry of such churches. More realistic is attendance figures.

Adding up attendance of all major weekly services, including Sunday school, the largest church in the country is First Baptist Church of Hammond, Indiana, with Dr. Jack Hyles as pastor. Between 15 and 30 thousand attend, depending on the season. Second, third, and fourth places go to Willow Creek Community Church, South Barrington, Illinois, with Dr. Bill Hybels as pastor, 14,000; Calvary Chapel of Costa Mesa, Santa Ana,

California, with Chuck Smith as pastor, 12,000; and Thomas Road Baptist Church, Lynchburg, Virginia, with Dr. Jerry Falwell as pastor, 11,000.[14]

On a denominational level, between 1973 and 1983, Southern Baptist membership increased 15 percent; the Assemblies of God, 71 percent; and the Church of the Nazarene, 22 percent. A Gallup poll released in September 1976 indicated that 34 percent of all adult Americans claim to have had a "born again" experience (by projection, some 50 million), and four out of ten believed that "the Bible was to be taken literally, word for word." These were far higher figures than evangelicals ever were willing to claim. Pollsters concluded on various bases in 1989 that 31 percent of Americans claimed to be evangelicals or born-again Christians and 13 percent of Roman Catholics identified themselves as born-again Christians.[15] According to a poll taken in 1988, 31 percent of Americans believed the Bible was "the actual word of God and to be taken literally, word for word."

Advances in Evangelism in the United States

The missionary concern of the American church and of Christians worldwide has increased tremendously. At home there has been the continuing work of such parachurch organizations as the Christian Business Men's Committee, the Full Gospel Business Men's Association, the Christian Business Women's Committee, InterVarsity Christian Fellowship, and Child Evangelism, and the phenomenal growth of the newer ministries of Young Life,[16] Youth for Christ, Navigators, Campus Crusade for Christ, Operation Mobilization,[17] Youth with a Mission,[18] and a host of other works too numerous to mention. Many of these agencies are involved in foreign as well as home missions.

In September, 1992, a two-day forum convened in Chicago to consider how every individual in the United States could hear the gospel of Christ by the year 2000. Representatives from 50 denominations were present and subsequently 41 denominations reported plans to establish 46,182 new churches by the year 2000. The largest goals were those of the Southern Baptists (13,500), the Church of the Nazarene (6,000) and the Assemblies of God (5,000).

Declines and Advances in Foreign Mission Efforts

Between 1950 and 1970, the number of North American Protestant career missionaries worldwide increased from 15,000 to 33,000, serving in 130 countries. The number of full-time North American missionaries stationed abroad in 1988 had risen to 36,000 but in 1992 had declined to 32,634. That does not mean a decline of interest in missions, however. Large numbers serve under "short terms abroad" programs, a new development that permits students, professional or retired people, or others to serve abroad for periods from about two months to two years in length. One estimate put the number of short-term North American Protestant missionaries during 1989 at 120,000. It is difficult to be precise about that figure in any given year. Many sending agencies report fewer "casualties" on the foreign field in recent years as a result of more careful screening of applicants and better training and counseling programs.

A decline in the number of missionaries sent by agencies affiliated with the National Council of Churches was first noted in 1960. Between 1962 and 1979 the number of foreign missionaries supported by major United States denominations declined by the following percentages: Episcopal, 79; United Presbyterian, 72; Lutheran Church in America, 70; United Church of Christ, 68; Christian Church (Disciples), 66; United Methodist, 46; American Lutheran Church, 44. Overall, the number of missionaries from denominations belonging to the National Council of Churches decreased by 51 percent.

During the same period Southern Baptists increased their missionary force by 88 percent and the Assemblies of God by 49 percent. Agencies affiliated with the Evangelical Foreign Missions Association increased their missionaries on the field by 63 percent; and those affiliated with the Interdenominational Foreign Mission Association increased theirs by 19 percent.

Since 1979 all of the mainline denominations listed above have continued to show a decline in the number of missionaries supported. In fact, some of them sharply reduced their missionary staffs in just three years between 1985 and 1988. For example, the United Methodist Church lost about 20 percent and the Episcopal Church almost 40 percent during that brief period. Between 1988 and 1992 the Episcopal Church continued to lose ground while the Methodists maintained their 1988 levels. The Southern Baptists have continued to increase their missionary force and between 1985 and 1988 upped their numbers from 3,346 to 3,839. They have since added to the long-term staff slightly while sending 10,000 short termers. The Assemblies of God also continue to add to their missionary army; between 1985 and 1988 they increased their numbers from 1,237 to 1,530, and between 1988 and 1992 to 1,862. The EFMA and IFMA also have increased their staffs abroad, the former currently having 12,000 and the latter 8,000. As one watches the trends in missionary staffing, it becomes clear that those who have lost their theological moorings have also lost their enthusiasm for spreading the gospel, while those who are energized by the dynamism of a supernatural faith have increased determination to share it.

Third-World Missionary Efforts

In recent years Third World missionaries have begun to respond to the challenge of the Great Commission in substantial numbers. A 1980 survey revealed that there were 13,000 cross-cultural Third World missionaries; 38 percent were Asian, many representing agencies that were 50 to 75 years old. A 1982 estimate put the total of Third World missionaries at more than 15,000 and concluded that the figure had tripled in eight years. This total represents 368 non-Western mission agencies from at least 57 different countries.

Enthusiasm for missions is rapidly building in Asia, Africa, and Latin America. For example, the Japanese evangelical churches (membership about one million) had more than 300 missionaries serving outside Japan in 1990; 260 missionaries from South Korea were commissioned in 1992, with many others preparing for overseas service; there were some 17,000 African missionaries in 1990, Nigeria alone having 30 indigenous mission boards and 3,000 missionaries. Larry Pate of OC International concludes that there were about 49,000 non-Western Protestant missionaries in 1990, that the number would probably rise to 89,000 by 1995, and that by 2000 it would outstrip the total Western missionary force.[19] One estimate puts the Third World missionary force at 150,000 by the year 2000.

Increasing Interest in Foreign Missions

An indication of the upsurge in interest in foreign missions was the InterVarsity-sponsored Urbana, Illinois, conference in December 1973, which registered 14,153, the largest student missionary conference in history to that date. The Urbana conference in December 1976 topped that, with an attendance of about 17,000. At Urbana in 1979, 17,500 attended, with more than 8,000 youths indicating they were serious about answering God's call to a missionary vocation. The three-year Urbana cycle was changed to a two-year cycle in 1981 and 14,000 trekked to Urbana. Thereafter InterVarsity decided to return to the three-year cycle. The 1987 conference drew 18,694 to Urbana, and the 1990 conference topped that with over 19,000 delegates from 99 countries. Over 17,000 attended the 1993 conference, with representatives from 66 countries. Foreign delegates numbered 6,600.

During the 1982 Christmas holiday over 7,000 young people from about 30 European nations met at Lausanne, Switzerland, under the auspices of the European Missionary Association to think, learn, and pray about missions. Messages were translated into twelve languages for more than 650 missionaries.

To consider ways of fulfilling the Great Commission by the year 2000, 2,700 delegates from around the world met in Lausanne, Switzerland, in July 1974. Half the delegates were from Third World countries. The Lausanne assembly established a Lausanne Committee for World Evangelization that has had a continuing impact. For example, in July 1980 a ten-day conference sponsored by the committee met in Bangkok, Thailand. A total of 650 participants from 87 countries met in a working consultation to evaluate "where we are" in the task of reaching the world's 3 billion non-Christians with the gospel. And on April 23, 1982, the Confraternity of Evangelicals in Latin America organized in Panama City, Panama, under the auspices of the Lausanne Committee.

Lausanne II was held in Manila, the Philippines, in July 1989, when almost 200 countries were represented among the more than 4,000 delegates from around the globe who met to discuss strategies for reaching the world for Christ. Meanwhile, "Mission '87" had met in Utrecht, Holland, with 11,000 young people, leaders, and speakers from 40 countries to help European young people "better understand the vision of world evangelization." TEMA (The European Missionary Association) of Lausanne had organized the congress. At a public invitation, more than 1,000 came forward, indicating commitment to missionary service.

New Approaches in Missions

The new approach in foreign missions today is not to concentrate so much on pioneer evangelism, but on the use of all God-given talents in the spread of the gospel. This is true not only because this is the wisest plan that could be adopted, but also because it is necessary. Churches abroad have come of age. Nationalistic fervor in the Third World requires that national churches be free to chart their own destinies. In recent years more and more mission property has been deeded over to national churches with control in the hands of national workers. Missionaries become fraternal workers and provide support or technical know-how for churches abroad.

Of special importance is providing training for foreign nationals so they can more effectively evangelize their own people. The world is being blanketed with a network of Bible schools. And as university training abroad has become available to a larger number of Christians, seminary programs have been instituted in country after country. An example of the new educational opportunities now offered in Europe is the operation of nine Greater Europe Mission Bible institutes all across the continent. In addition, the mission has now launched graduate schools of theology in the Netherlands, Germany, and Belgium. To repeat, this is only an example of what is happening in Europe. It would be tedious and unnecessary to list here all the Bible schools now available to Europeans.

Another new approach in missions today is a tendency to put home missions on a par with foreign missions and/or to achieve an interpenetration between the two. For example, the Central American Mission has started church planting efforts among the Latin population of New Orleans, Los Angeles, San Diego, Tucson, San Antonio, Dallas, and Houston and has plans to begin work in Miami, Washington, New York City, and Toronto. Also, a mission that evangelizes among Muslims abroad conducts summer internships for new missionaries among the Muslims of New York City.

Advances in Missions through Radio

New techniques in missions are speeding the message on its way and making existing work more effective. Missionary radio has virtually blanketed the globe and some television programming is now being offered. The great pioneer in the field is HCJB in Quito, Ecuador; but there are several others, including ELWA (destroyed in the Liberian civil war but still broadcasting), TGNA in Guatemala, CP-27 in Bolivia, WIVV in Puerto Rico,

Far East Broadcasting Corporation (FEBC) in the Philippines, Korea, and the Seychelles, and Trans World Radio with 22 transmitters broadcasting in 100 languages from sites located in Bonaire, Uruguay, Monte Carlo, Cyprus, Swaziland, Sri Lanka and Guam and capable of reaching 80 percent of the world's population. In 1989 Trans World Radio won permission from Soviet officials to establish radio production facilities in the Soviet Union. Trans World has been broadcasting to the Soviet Union from their station in Tangier, Morocco since 1956. In 1992 Trans World reached an agreement to begin broadcasting from Radio Tirana in the capital of Albania.

A specific example of what missionary radio may accomplish comes from a Trans World Radio broadcast from Sri Lanka in 1988. K. P. Yohannan, president of Gospel for Asia, beamed a weekly broadcast in the Malayalam language of India. The broadcast drew 40,000 letters from listeners during the year with more than 3,000 saying they had accepted Christ as their Savior. The Trans World network of stations receives a million inquiries each year. The large number of believers in China and Russia today is presumably at least in part a tribute to the effectiveness of missionary radio. FEBC broadcasts in over 100 languages, in 26 languages to 30 countries from the Seychelles Islands in the Indian Ocean alone. D. James Kennedy of Coral Ridge Presbyterian Church in Fort Lauderdale, Florida, put his "Coral Ridge Hour" on TV in St. Petersburg, Russia in May, 1992, to become one of the first evangelical broadcasts to air locally in Russia. The impetus to the development of missionary radio is the fact that some 60 percent of the world's population lives in countries closed to conventional missionary activity, and radio can be an effective means of spreading the gospel to those nations.

Access to secular stations in Western Europe is increasing. For example, in France over 300 independent radio stations have been established since François Mitterand's Socialist government came to power. Some of these have been willing to broadcast Christian programs. The government-controlled television network is now airing programs for Christian groups. In Spain evangelicals have had some access to state radio and TV since 1982.

In 1980 Christian radio and television stations worldwide were said to number 1,450. By far the largest single bloc was located in the United States. In late 1983 there were 922 radio stations and 65 TV stations owned and operated by evangelicals in the United States, according to National Religious Broadcasters. Though stations come and go, new Christian radio stations were established in the United States at the rate of about one per week and television stations at the rate of about one per month between 1975 and 1983.

Advances in American Religious Television

Religious TV in the United States grew steadily through the fifties and sixties and exploded in the first half of the seventies. By 1970 there were 38 syndicated television programs. By 1975, when growth leveled off, the number had reached 65. In 1972 Pat Robertson operated the only religious TV station in the United States. In 1983 the number of such stations had reached 65, as noted. The total number of Christian radio and TV stations worldwide (full time and part time) in 1991 was 2,340. The 1992-93 directory of the National Religious Broadcasters identified 1,156 full time Christian radio stations and 81 full time Christian television stations in the United States.

Of the major producers of American religious telecasts, a 1983 Arbitron rating service survey put Robert Schuller at the head of the list with an audience of 2,667,000; Jimmy Swaggart second with 2,653,000; and Oral Roberts, Rex Humbard, and Jerry Falwell in third, fourth, and fifth spots. An Arbitron rating for the previous year had put Oral Roberts, Rex Humbard, Robert Schuller, and Jerry Falwell in the top four spots, the first three with more than two million viewers each.

After this high point, televangelism in the United States fell into a devastating period of tumult in the late 1980s. In 1987 Oral Roberts utilized questionable means of raising funds and Jim Bakker was defrocked for sexual lapses and subsequently convicted of fraud and conspiracy and imprisoned. The following year Jimmy Swaggart stepped down from his television pulpit after confessing to moral lapse.

The fall of these giants led the National Religious Broadcasters to impose stricter controls on its members and the Evangelical Council for Financial Accountability to set new standards for religious groups. While the scandals in religious broadcasting hurt some of the titans of television evangelism and temporarily cut contributions to many religious works, the Christian public remains deeply committed to religious broadcasting and a stream of newcomers has produced many programs with smaller followings.

Arbitron ratings of the top 20 religious television programs of February 1992 put the following in the first four places. First was Robert Schuller's *Hour of Power*, with 1,480,000 viewers; second, *World Tomorrow* of the Worldwide Church of God, with 1,433,000 viewers;

third, Charles Stanley's *In Touch*, with 655,000 viewers; and fourth, Kenneth Copeland's *Believer's Voice of Victory*, with 630,000 viewers.

Advances in Missionary Aviation

Missionary aviation is also coming into its own. Mission Aviation Fellowship[20] was organized in 1945 and now has a plane taking off every five minutes or less on the average, around the clock, every day of the year, somewhere in the world. The organization celebrated its forty-fifth anniversary in 1990 with about 260 full-time overseas staff working in more than 20 countries, and dedicated its 88th aircraft in 1992. Wycliffe Bible Translators is another agency using airplanes in a major way through its aviation arm, JAARS. The Moody Bible Institute's Moody Aviation program in Elizabethton, Tennessee, specially contributes to training pilots for missionary work. There are now 12 missionary aviation agencies in the United States.

Advances in Specialty Ministries

Another specialty ministry is Gospel Recordings, Inc., which is producing Bible stories and basic Christian teaching in a very large percentage of the languages and dialects of the world. It has been successful in recording materials for use among peoples who as yet have not had their languages put into writing. PRM International (formerly Portable Recording Ministries) conducts a somewhat similar ministry.

Bible correspondence course programs abound everywhere. The kind of ministry conducted by the Moody Correspondence School is being performed by an increasing number of other schools in many places around the world. Numerous schools are grading scores of thousands of papers every month. Home Bible-study classes are one of the greatest phenomena of the hour; no one knows how many scores of thousands there are in this country—stimulated by the work of the Navigators, Campus Crusade for Christ, local churches, and other agencies. And they are taking hold everywhere abroad. Often this is the only way Christians can function in Communist or Muslim countries.

Religious journalism is a new hope for Christian evangelism. Some successful magazines published in the United States or on the field are *The Latin America Evangelist* (Latin American Mission), *Nuevo Continente* (Luis Palau), *Today's Challenge* (formerly *African Challenge*, published in Jos, Nigeria, by the Evangelical Churches of West Africa), *Africa Action* (Evangelical Fellowship), *Japan Harvest* (Japan Evangelical Missionary Association), *The Quiet Miracle* (Bible Literature International, worldwide focus), and *The Commission* (Southern Baptist, worldwide focus).

Another speciality ministry is Prison Fellowship and Prison Fellowship International, which began in Washington, D.C., in 1976, especially through the efforts of Charles ("Chuck") Colson who had served a prison sentence for his involvement in Watergate. Currently Prison Fellowship is working is prisons in all 50 states and has a staff of about 260. One of every 500 Americans is now in prison. *Inside Journal* is its quarterly journal, distributed in state and federal correctional institutions as a service to inmates. Justice Fellowship, dedicated to restorative justice in society, is a division of Prison Fellowship. Prison Fellowship International is an association of over 45 autonomous national ministries, under the leadership of PFI president Ron Nikkel and directors in Africa, Asia, Europe, and Latin America.

They enjoy the support of more than 50,000 volunteers worldwide. Colson is the director of Prison Fellowship in the United States. In addition to his leadership of the movement, he is known for his ten books, including his best seller *Born Again* (1976) and his 1993 publication, *The Body*.

Yet one more speciality ministry is the floating evangelism of Operation Mobilization's ship ministry. In 1971 OM launched Logos I to train disciples of Christ, to help indigenous churches of the world spread the gospel, and to distribute desperately needed literature. Logos I ran aground off the southern coast of Chile and had to be abandoned, but Logos II was dedicated in London in the spring of 1990 and joined her sister ship the Doulos. The ships travel around the world and make extended stops at numerous ports. Three examples of receptivity will suffice: in Taiwan in 1988 the Doulos welcomed 23,000 people aboard; in Gydnia, Poland, 92,000 Poles came aboard Logos II in 1990, spurred by TV and radio coverage in the city; in January and February 1993, 123,000 boarded Logos II in Santo Domingo, with 500 making a commitment to Christ. To date over 22,000,000 people have visited operation Mobilizations three ships.

Scripture Translation and Distribution

A very important phase of mission work worldwide is Scripture distribution. The Wycliffe Bible Translators, formally organized in 1942, is dedicated to the task of reducing to writing all the languages of the world and translating at least portions of the Bible into those languages. As of 1992, at least some portion of the Bible has been published in 1,978 languages used by well over 97 percent of the world's people. This compares with portions of the Bible available in only 67 languages at the beginning of the twentieth century. To date, the whole Bible has been produced in 273 languages, the New Testament in 676 languages, and the translation of the New Testament in 1,209 other languages is in progress worldwide.

Wycliffe itself is currently involved in translation and linguistic work on 863 languages in 50 countries. It takes about 15 years of work for two persons to accomplish the Wycliffe goal of reducing a language to writing and translating a portion of Scripture into that language. Wycliffe can vouch for the existence of 6,497 known languages as of December 1991; the number continues to increase. Wycliffe has now completed work in Ecuador and Bolivia and has turned over all further work in those countries to the nationals. As national linguistic societies have come of age, they are able to conduct their own translation work; the mission currently serves as consultants or fraternal workers with 12 national organizations. Wycliffe now has about 6,500 staff members. In addition to translation work abroad, the mission conducts linguistic institutes at several universities in the United States and around the world.

Numerous agencies and individuals are involved in Scripture distribution. The Gideons give out a million Bibles or Testaments every 11 days. During the reporting year ending May 31, 1992, the organization gave away 34,507,000 Bibles or Testaments in 156 countries and 68 languages. This they accomplished with a volunteer staff of 68,000 in the United States and 114,600 worldwide, including the United States. Their target for the former Soviet republics is 400,000 Bibles or Testaments per month. This distribution figure is up from 22,000,000 Bibles and Testaments given away in 135 countries and 60 languages in 1983. The Gideons provide Bibles for such agencies as schools, the armed forces, prisons, hospitals, and hotels.

The American Bible Society distributed its 3 billionth copy of Scripture in 1979; that year was the 164th anniversary of the founding of the Society in 1816. During 1979 the Society distributed 258,939,314 Scriptures worldwide. For that year total distribution of the United Bible Societies (of which ABS is a member) worldwide was almost 500 million Bibles and portions.

The American Bible Society celebrated its 175th anniversary in 1991. In that year the Society distributed 236,902,758 Scriptures worldwide. For 1991 total distribution of the United Bible Societies (of which ABS is a member) worldwide was almost 641 million Bibles and portions. Over these 175 years the ABS had shared a total of 5,609,667,651 Scriptures. By the end of 1992 the total had jumped to 6,105,500,686. During recent years the UBS have been distributing some 640 million Bibles and portions annually worldwide. The International Bible Society, formerly the New York International Bible Society, distributed 30,603,000 Bibles and Scripture portions worldwide during the year ending June 30, 1991. This brought their total distribution of Bibles and Scripture portions since their founding in 1809 to 296,388,000. During recent years the Society's dissemination of Scripture has been confined largely to its translation, the *New International Version*.

Scripture distribution behind the Iron and Bamboo curtains was tightly controlled before the fall of Communism in Eastern Europe, but occasionally Communist governments made gestures toward the local populace or world opinion. For example, in 1980 the Chinese government permitted the printing of 50,000

Chinese New Testaments; and the Bible suddenly became the most sought-after book in the country. In 1981, 20,000 Bibles and 20,000 hymnals arrived in Haiphong harbor aboard a Russian freighter. Printed by the Federation of Protestant churches in East Germany, these were destined for the churches of Vietnam.

In 1982, 195,000 Bibles were printed in Poland; and in addition the Bible Society in Poland arranged the import of 50,000 pocket-sized Bibles. During the same year Soviet authorities gave permission for the annual printing of 10,000 Bibles, 10,000 New Testaments, and 10,000 hymnals. Also during 1982 the American Bible Society sent Bibles and portions to communist Eastern Europe through cooperating agencies in the following numbers: Soviet Union, 10,000 (New Testaments); Yugoslavia, 44,000; Romania, 50,000 (Bibles); Poland, 176,000; East Germany, 402,631; and Hungary, 37,000.

Since the Fall of Communism

Now that Communism has fallen in Eastern Europe, the story of Bible distribution there has changed dramatically. With the coming of Perestroika, the door opened for Bible distribution in the Soviet Union. Between 1988 and 1991 the United Bible Societies supplied the people of the Soviet Union with over 2.5 million Bibles, New Testaments, Children's Bibles, and other Scripture publications in several languages. A four-year project of the UBS (1990-1994) called for $58 million in additional funding to provide a total of 30 million Scriptures for the former Soviet Union and the countries of Central and Eastern Europe. The International Bible Society sent four million New Testaments to the Soviet people in 1990-1991.

A particularly dramatic story of Bible distribution

in Russia occurred on August 20, 1991. As the confrontation built between government forces and the supporters of Boris Yeltsin, members of the Bible Society in the Soviet Union decided to act. Father Alexander Borisov, member of the Moscow City Council and a board member of the Soviet Bible Society, dressed in his clerical robes and took a group of courageous Christians and a mini-bus to distribute 4,500 New Testaments to the troops who had sealed off Red Square. Anatoly Rudenko, director of the Bible Society in the Soviet Union, took another group and 1,500 New Testaments to the troops surrounding the Parliament building of the Russian Federation. They called on the soldiers not to kill their brothers and obey the legitimate authorities. The soldiers received the Scripture with respect and the receipt of Bibles seems to have played a part in the prevention of bloodshed.

Several newly-organized Bible societies have been established across the former USSR, in St. Petersburg, Latvia, Lithuania, Ukraine, and Armenia; and the Bible Society in the Soviet Union itself is establishing branch organizations across the Russian Republic.

In Ukraine, The Bible League, Chicago, and the Master's Foundation, Ontario, joined in 1992 to provide 150,000 copies of the *Ukrainian Children's Bible*, the first Ukrainian translation of the whole Bible for children. Among all the other stories that could be told about Scripture distribution in Eastern Europe, what is being done for school children is especially touching. In 1992 Life Publishers (Assemblies of God) sent 2.3 million copies of its *Book of Life* to all the school children of Czechoslovakia; they also planned to send the *Book of Life* to all 3.5 million in Romania's schools as soon as possible. This publication contains Scripture and a section on making Christ a part of one's life. The Slavic Gospel Association and the Russian Ministry of Education have signed an agreement to provide 62-volume Faith Discovery Libraries for the 65,000 Russian primary and secondary schools, with 25 million students, during the period 1992-1994. In almost all the former Communist countries of Eastern Europe some Bibles are being printed locally

Changes in China

The provision for a regular supply of Bibles in China is very dramatic. During the Cultural Revolution (1966-1969) Red Guards confiscated and destroyed virtually every Bible and Christian book in China. Even after 1979, when the printing of Bibles began again, there was no reliable source of Bibles for the Chinese people. Then permission was granted to the United Bible Societies and the Chinese Amity Foundation to build the Amity Press in Nanjing, China. Ground-breaking took place in November, 1986 and the dedication occurred in July, 1987, a remarkable record of construction even in a capitalist country. The one millionth Bible rolled off the press on September 28, 1989. Almost unbelievably, the troubles connected with the Tiananmen Square massacre of June 4, 1989 and the crackdown following did not hinder production!

The Bible is printed in the new simplified script which about 70 percent of the population can read. The five millionth Bible was produced on the Amity presses in February, 1993, but the need for Bibles remains critical. A wonderful new resource is the *China Study Bible* that went to press in January, 1991. A joint project of the Bible League, Open Doors, and New Life Literature, it is a 2,000-page Bible designed to be a "one-volume biblical library specially designed for itinerant evangelists in Mainland China."

Scripture Distribution in Other Fields

Elsewhere in the Communist world, there has also been a breakthrough for Scripture distribution in Cuba. A million Scripture portions were handed out during the Pan American Games in Havana during August 1991 and Fidel Castro opened the door to allow thousands of Bibles and New Testaments to enter Cuba itself. During 1991 and 1992 the United Bible Societies shipped 51,600 Bibles, 20,000 New Testaments, and 30,000 Gospels. In addition, the Bible Society of Mexico shipped 92,000 Bibles, 45,500 New Testaments, and 20,000 Gospels. The United Bible Societies were also given permission to import 10,000 Bibles to Vietnam during 1991.

Elsewhere, Scripture distribution efforts have also been successful in the last couple of years. A few examples will suffice. "Every Home for Christ" evangelists in India continue their efforts to reach every home in the country. In 1991 they brought their total of hand-delivered gospel booklets to 430 million, with nearly 5 million responses to the message of Christ. In March 1992 the United Nations Security Council committee responsible for enforcing sanctions against Iraq decided to allow a large shipment of Scriptures through. The Bible Society staff and local churches in Jordan sent off a truck with 74,500 Scriptures. This included at least 6,000 Bibles and 21,000 New Testaments. (There are an estimated 1 million Christians in Iraq's population of 18 million.) Also Iraqi refugees in Jordan have received liberal supplies of Scripture portions. Later that year 40,000 Bibles and New Testaments were brought into the country.

Distribution of God's Word in Thailand in 1991 reached almost half of the population. The Malagasy Bible Society of Madagascar shares an average of 1 million copies of the Scriptures annually with the Republic's population of 12 million. The new Malagasy Interconfessional Version of the New Testament was published in 1990. The Bible League of Brazil in cooperation with the churches of the country is engaged in a plan to distribute 25 million New Testaments in schools, homes, and prisons. By mid-1992 a total of 17 million had been distributed. In addition, every day some 25,000 volunteers go out on the streets and into the public places of Brazil to interest people in the Scripture. Conservatively, they reach about 250,000 every day. In 1991 the Bible Society of Brazil distributed more than 136 million Scripture selections, the largest number of selections in the worldwide fellowship of United Bible Societies. In Japan, in March, 1992 the Bible Society realized the sale of its one millionth copy of the new Inter-Confessional Japanese translation, in a country with only about 1 million Christians.

A phenomenon of recent years has been the reception accorded Kenneth Taylor's Living Bible, annually being printed by the millions in dozens of languages. When Living Bibles International (founded 1972) merged with the International Bible Society in April, 1992, Living Bibles had provided easy-to-read Scriptures in 117 languages. In addition, the New American Standard Bible, the Good News Bible, the New International Version, the New English Bible (now the Revised English Bible), the New Revised Standard Version, and the New King James *Version* have sparked new interest in the abiding Word of God.

Christianity Today Worldwide

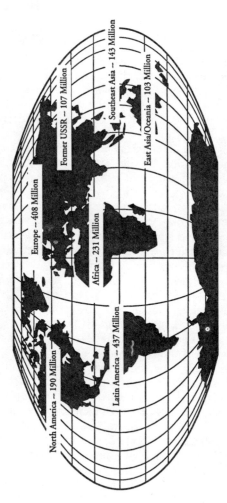

North America — 190 Million

Europe — 408 Million

Former USSR — 107 Million

Southeast Asia — 143 Million

Africa — 231 Million

Latin America — 437 Million

East Asia/Oceania — 103 Million

Source: Barrett and Johnson, *Our Globe*, 1990.

THIRTY-TWO

Response to the Gospel
Europe

IT IS now time to ask what kind of response the gospel is receiving in the world in this supposedly post-Christian era. In comments that follow there is room for only a few tantalizing examples of what God is doing. At this writing it appears there are more Christians in the emerging countries than in Europe and North America. More than one American denomination has been impressed and a little embarrassed watching work it launched in Africa or Latin America outstripping the founding church in size. Numerically at least the future of the church lies with the black and brown peoples of the world. If present trends continue, by the year 2000 only about 40 percent or less of the Christians of the world will be white.

Behind the Iron Curtain

Behind the Iron Curtain before the collapse of Communism, there were real signs of spiritual life, not only in Russia but also in most of the satellite countries of Eastern Europe. In Russia it is estimated that there were some 100 million Christians of all varieties—or about 37 percent of the population. Of these about 70 million were Russian Orthodox; the rest Armenian Orthodox, Roman Catholics, and Protestants. There were two Protestant groups in the country: the All-Union

Council of Evangelical Christians-Baptists (registered with the authorities) and the Council of Churches of Evangelical Christians-Baptist (which refused to register with the government and was persecuted). It is difficult to quantify evangelical strength in the Soviet Union; but responses to evangelical broadcasts beamed into the country, participation in correspondence courses, the desires for Bibles and other Christian literature, and tabulations of reports of overflowing churches and underground house churches indicate the church was experiencing considerable growth despite all efforts to stifle it.

Spiritual Awakening in Eastern Europe

Since before the middle of the 1970s there have been mounting reports of spiritual awakening all over Eastern Europe. If a free flow of information were possible, the Western church probably would have been tremendously impressed by what was going on. In spite of decades of government oppression in East Germany, more than 55 percent of the population was still on the church rolls. This included 8 million claimed by the main Lutheran body (the Federation of Evangelical Churches), 1.3 million Roman Catholics, 35,000 evangelical Methodists, and 21,000 Baptists. A charismatic renewal movement swept the East German Lutheran church in the 1980s; about 10 percent of the clergy, or about 400 pastors, are said to have been involved in it. Some indication of the magnitude of religious stirring in East Germany is provided by the Bible distribution figures noted above.

In Poland government oppression and propaganda also failed to turn the nation to atheism. The vast majority of the people remained staunch Roman Catholics; one report listed 97 percent of the population as at least nominally Roman Catholic. There were reports of considerable spiritual awakening within Polish Catholicism in the 1970s; and Bible distribution reached significant proportions. Throughout the decade of the seventies, reports of revival in Romania were recorded. The Baptists especially benefited. As the revival heightened, the government tightened the screws of persecution.

In Hungary as well, the populace refused to be cowed by atheistic pressures. Over half held Christian beliefs and about one-third of adults attended church regularly. In 1980 the government approved the teaching of the Bible as literature to 80,000 high school students in an agreement worked out with Roman Catholic, Lutheran, and Calvinist churches. This was a unique development in communist East Europe. It is hard to get a clear picture of what was going on in Czechoslovakia, but evidently spiritual revitalization was so extensive there that the government determined to wipe out the multitude of Bible study and prayer groups that seemed to be meeting in secret all over the country.

After the Opening of the Iron Curtain

Then the Berlin Wall was breached on November 9, 1989. Soon thereafter the Communist regimes of Eastern Europe began collapsing one after the other like a house of cards. With equal swiftness Germany achieved reunification on October 3, 1990, and the Union of Soviet Socialist Republics fell apart, with the formal dissolution action on December 26, 1991. These political and social changes quickly brought an end to persecution of Christians in Eastern Europe and opened the door for unlimited church expansion. Perhaps not surprisingly, because persecution purifies the church, the church in Eastern Europe was in relatively better shape than that of the West in 1990.

Europe Report (Greater Europe Mission) for April-June, 1990 listed the following report on evangelicals as a percentage of the population at that time: Eastern Europe: East Germany, 11; Romania, 7.8; Hungary, 3.7; USSR, 2.5; Czechoslovakia, 2.1; Bulgaria, 0.54; Poland, 0.2; Yugoslavia, 0.16; Albania, a handful; Western Europe: Denmark, 5-7; West Germany, 4.3; Netherlands, 2.7; France, 0.63; Ireland, 0.6; Italy, 0.6; Belgium, 0.4; Spain, 0.34; Greece, 0.14.

Europe Report for July-September, 1990 also published very sobering results of a recent survey of German Protestants. Only 29 percent considered the resurrection of Christ to be relevant, 24 percent believed in the virgin birth of Christ, 21 percent believed in the second coming of Christ, and only one in 20 attended church regularly. Such were the results of theological liberalism and materialism.

Now it remains to comment on a few developments in Eastern Europe since the breaching of the wall. Elsewhere the ministry of Billy Graham, Luis Palau, and of the *Jesus Film* have been noted. Special attention focused on distribution of Scripture; nowhere could the new supplies keep up with the demand. Some of the account of Scripture distribution appears in Chapter 31.

New Opportunities for Ministry and Influence

In several countries, especially Hungary and Romania, barriers against religious instruction of public school children have been removed and that effort has gone forward. In Hungary, prison ministries have begun. Word of Life Fellowship has launched work in several countries. For example, in 1990 they began youth camping programs at a 77-acre castle property outside Budapest, and they secured full legal recognition of the government of Poland as a not-for-profit religious organization. This status will permit them to operate camping programs, Bible clubs, and possibly a radio station.

In several countries Christian schools are being established. For example, in East Germany several Christian high schools have been founded—at Leipzig, Magdeburg, Rostock, Potsdam, and Dresden. In Lithuania, the Lithuania Christian College has opened its doors. In Albania, where there is virtually no knowledge of the Christian faith, several groups are engaged in evangelistic and church planting efforts. In recent months at least forty evangelical churches have come into existence. Trans World Radio began broadcasting to all of Eastern Europe from Radio Tirana in the capital of Albania in October, 1992, and Trans World Radio in Monte Carlo continues to beam its broadcasts into Albania.

Romania—A Special Case

Among all the countries of Eastern Europe outside the USSR, the leading evangelical movement is taking place in Romania. This is true in part because of a larger evangelical base there (perhaps 3 million of a total of 23 million or about 13 percent) and in part because the Romanian Missionary Society was planning for the evangelization of the country. First, at their headquarters in Wheaton, Illinois, they began translation of Christian literature several years ago. As soon as Romania opened up, they incorporated their publishing house in the country as a commercial publishing company and now have completed its headquarters building. Second, they have signed a compact with World Christian Radio Fellowship and the Evangelical Alliance of Romania to establish 12 radio stations in Romania and cover it with 24 hours of Christian radio broadcasting. The first station went on the air June 1, 1993. Third, they are establishing Christian high schools in key places across the country; four opened in September 1990. Fourth, they have converted the Oradea Bible Institute into a full-fledged government-approved Christian university. A campus plan has been developed and the land obtained.

Apart from the work of the Romanian Missionary Society, much else is going on in Romania. Congregations that were prohibited construction permits under the oppressive Ceausescu regime are now building churches. Children now have optional religion classes in their school curriculum. Luis Palau conducted a very successful evangelistic campaign in the summer of 1990 when reportedly 39,000 made decisions for Christ. Since then Baptists have started 600 new churches and Pentecostals and Brethren have also been planting congregations. Trans World Radio has been beaming 3½ hours of programs per week into the country from Monte Carlo, including a children's program that helps to make up for the lack of Sunday schools across the country. Finally, late in 1990 four thousand believers gathered for the First General Assembly of the Romanian Evangelical Alliance in the hall of the Palace in Bucharest, where less than a year earlier Nicolae Ceausescu had declared that the reform sweeping other Communist countries would not be tolerated in Romania.

The Soviet Union

The recent story of the church in the Soviet Union

probably should begin with the millennial observance of the official Christianizing of Russia by Vladimir I in 988. The fact that the government decided to participate in the observance and even to mint a gold coin to commemorate the event was significant. Then in December 1989 Mikhail Gorbachev met with Pope John Paul II in the Vatican and pledged to increase religious freedom for all believers in the Soviet Union. Later when talking with a Christian Finnish reporter, Gorbachev said he supported the growth of the church in his country and that he encouraged the reading of the Bible. What began in conversation with the Pope came to fruition on September 26, 1990 when the Supreme Soviet passed a law guaranteeing freedom of religion.

What has been happening in the religious affairs of the Soviet Union has especially involved Bible distribution. In 1988 the Soviet State Council of Religious Affairs permitted Open Doors International to send one million New Testaments to Soviet Christians. In 1991 1.5 million copies of a harmonized version of the life of Christ called the *Book of Life* were placed in Soviet schools. That same year Bibles were given to members of the Russian Parliament. Then when Vladimir Saprykin, vice president of the Ministry of Education in Russia, became a Christian early in 1992, the doors were open to the school system of Russia.

Russian education officials requested that Campus Crusade for Christ provide a video of the *Jesus* film to every school in the country and provide training for Russian teachers in conducting a ten-week course on Christianity. Also, under agreement with the Russian Ministry of Education, the Slavic Gospel Association has begun a two-year program to place Faith Discovery Libraries, which include the life of Christ, in all the

65,000 elementary and secondary schools in the Russian Republic, which has a total student enrollment of 25 million. The Russian Ministry of Education has decided that every child in the Russian Republic should now study the Bible. In another venture, a coalition of 24 churches hand-delivered Gospel booklets provided by Every Home for Christ to 300,000 homes in Moscow. But these examples are only part of the story; millions of Bibles and Bible portions have been distributed all over the former Soviet Union during the last three or four years.

Work Specifically in Russia

Far more than Bible distribution has been going on in the Christianizing of Russia. In 1990 the way was cleared for building a Baptist seminary within walking distance of Red Square in Moscow. The school opened in 1992. St. Petersburg Christian College opened in 1990 and held its first graduation in 1993. Also in 1990 Charles Colson of Prison Fellowship Ministries got permission to launch a Prison Fellowship in the Soviet Union. Two other important developments occurred in 1990. Evangelist John Guest had tremendous reception to his ministry, especially when he spoke at the Army and Naval Academies of the Soviet Union, where reportedly more than two-thirds of the cadets and officers stood up to become Christians. Also, for the first time in the history of the evangelical church in the Soviet Union, the Slavic Gospel Association offered workshops for women, pastors' wives, and other women, who will in turn minister to women and children.

In celebration of the Russian Orthodox Easter season in 1991 Campus Crusade for Christ provided a choir and two other music groups that performed in the Palace of Congress and the Red Army Theater. For one concert the Red Army band provided assistance. One choir performance was aired over Soviet national TV. These performances resulted in several thousand decisions for Christ. That November Strang Communications launched *Khristianskaya Zhism (Christian Life)* magazine to a tremendous response; 254,000 of the first edition sold out. The publisher also held a writers' seminar in Moscow to teach Christians the principles of writing, editing, and publishing. In February 1992 a Swedish building contractor said he had reached a $500 million agreement with the Russian Baptist Union to build 1,000 Baptist churches in Russia.

There are many stories of evangelists and others who have ministered in Russia with great response in recent years. John Robb, director of World Vision's Unreached Peoples' Program, reported, "Tens of thousands have been turning to Christ through public evangelism meetings." These new converts are added to the church that was forced to operate secretly previously. Now as underground churches come out of the shadows, the evangelical movement appears to be much bigger than many in the West ever believed. One evangelical, highly placed in the Russian government, estimates that evangelicals constitute about two percent of the population. Others might put the figure a little higher, but in any case God is at work in Russia. To facilitate evangelization of the former Soviet Union, 60 mission organizations have joined forces under the umbrella of "The CoMission."

Nearby in tightly closed Mongolia, the Mongolian Government issued its first order for the import of New Testaments in 1991. From a tiny handful in 1991, the Mongolian church had grown to a thousand or more in 1993.

THIRTY-THREE

Response to the Gospel
The Far East

Behind the Bamboo Curtain

China

RIPS are beginning to appear in the Bamboo Curtain. In spite of Chinese government attacks on Christianity ever since the Communist takeover in 1949, and in spite of the especially virulent effort of the Cultural Revolution (1966-69) to exterminate Christianity, the church has survived in China. The government officially recognizes both Roman Catholic and Protestant churches, the former known as the Catholic Patriotic Society and the latter as the Three-Self Churches (self-government, self-propagation, self-support). The Northeastern Theological Seminary (Protestant) opened in a suburb of Peking in November 1982 with a first class of 50. Previously a Catholic seminary had opened with 36 students.

Five large churches opened again in Shanghai in 1981, and all have over 2,000 in attendance; in the same year the Chinese government permitted a band of Christians to travel from Peking to the Great Wall to hold an Easter sunrise service. More and more Three-Self churches are being permitted to open, and there are now over 6,000 of them. As the Three-Self movement is allowed to expand, there is increasing persecution of the unofficial house churches that resist registration with the government and governmental interference with their faith. Jonathan Chao, dean of China Graduate School of Theology in Hong Kong, launched a "Seminary of the Air" and beamed it into China to provide a program of instruction for leaders of house churches. In 1980 he believed there might be a million such leaders ministering to perhaps 25 million believers.

Some ten years later, with accumulation of data and an increased conversion rate, Chao upped his estimate to about 50 million. A commonly accepted estimate during the period of 1990-1992 has been 50-60 million believers. In 1991 Gospel for Asia concluded that there were 70 million Chinese Christians. Then on June 28, 1992 the Hong Kong based *South China Morning Post* estimated that there were as many as 90 million Christians in China. The truth is that there are no really accurate figures and the number in the Chinese underground would probably astonish both Christians and Chinese officialdom. More specific are some comments on the Three-Self Church. There are 13 officially sanctioned Protestant seminaries in the country, mostly in the East; and there are 23 officially sanctioned Protestant churches in Shanghai, with a total of about 100,000 members. The China Christian Council became a member of the World Council of Churches in February, 1991.

The lot of believers in China was hard enough before the Tiananmen Square massacre of June 4, 1989. Since that time their situation has dramatically worsened. Although Christians in China are often apolitical, the government has tended to link the increase of Christians with the democracy movement and to paint Christians as enemies of the state. One excuse for doing so was the fact that Christians in Romania and possibly elsewhere in Europe had contributed to the fall of Communism there. The Washington-based Puebla Institute charges that the government crackdown against religious leaders "involves mass arrests, detentions, brainwashing, and torture, as well as church closings and confiscation of Christian literature." It is not meaningful to try to tabulate numbers of arrests or imprisonments because the situation is too fluid. But to give some idea of what is going on, as many as 104 religions leaders were known to be imprisoned or under house arrest late in 1993.

It does appear to be true, however, that the crackdown on the pro-democracy movement so demoralized the students that thousands of them turned to Christ for help. Because Far East Broadcasting Company (FEBC) and Trans World Radio broadcasts have been effective in converting the Chinese, the Beijing government has banned all foreign radio broadcasts and has fined and arrested scores of Chinese believers in at least five provinces, particularly Jiangsu, for listening to such programs.

Estimates of evangelical Christians in China currently range between about 60 and 90 million.

An important means of evangelism in China open to foreigners is teaching. Teachers are needed in science, business, law, and English. An M.A. degree with teaching experience is required for all positions except English. Numbers of American Christian teachers are using this tool, but they must be careful; the Chinese government monitors their activities. Sun

Myung Moon's Unification church has been given permission by the Chinese government to build churches and spread his teachings there in return for his agreement to invest $10 million a year for 25 years in a government-owned auto parts plant in Guangdong Province.

The "Other Chinas"

Christianity is making progress in the "other Chinas" too. The population of Taiwan is now over 7 percent Christian (about two-thirds of which is Protestant). A new opportunity there is a government Department of Education invitation to religious groups to help teach morals to Taiwan's youth and the opening of the public schools to religious activities. Singapore, in the Chinese "dispersion," has increased from about 10 percent to about 19 percent Christian in the last decade. Hong Kong has between 475,000 and 500,000 Christians out of a population of about 5.8 million. The Hong Kong Christian Institute estimates that 20 percent of the state's Christians and 25 percent of its church leaders will leave by 1997 in anticipation of Chinese annexation.

In Vietnam, between 1975, when missionaries had to leave, and 1991 the Evangelical Church of Vietnam (south) has more than doubled in size to over 400,000 members. Some churches report 50 new members a month. The Evangelical Church of Hanoi (northern region) now has 20 congregations and about 10,000 members and the government has given permission to reopen a Bible school and permitted a resumption of shipments of Bibles in 1992, the first major shipments since the closure of the Bible Society in 1981. Substantial numbers of Vietnamese have also been converted in the refugee camps in Cambodia. Ministry to Vietnamese refugees has been conducted in Hong Kong too. There over 50,000 Vietnamese Scriptures were distributed in the refugee camps during 1990 and 1991. As Christianity advances in Vietnam, the government does not stand idly by. Three prominent house church leaders were imprisoned in 1991.

In Cambodia the government officially recognized Protestant churches in the capital city of Phnom Penh in 1990, for the first time in 15 years, and the churches are free to meet for public services. In the spring of 1990, 700 Cambodian Protestants met for the first government-sponsored public evangelistic crusade in more than 15 years; government officials were invited as guests of honor. Also that spring the government permitted delivery of an American shipment of 7,000 pieces of religious literature to the Cambodian Protestant church.

India and Her Neighbors

The government of India has tried to restrict foreign missionary activity in the country in recent years (primarily to service ministries such as nursing and teaching), and the number of missionaries has declined appreciably. For example, the total number of American missionaries there declined from 614 in 1985 to 416 in 1988 and to 279 in 1993. Anti-conversion laws exist in many of the Hindu states, but they are not always enforced. Moreover, there have been numerous accounts of local violence against individual Christians or groups of Christians.

But the number of converts is substantial. Gospel for Asia reports that 6,500 indigenous missionaries were active in the Indian subcontinent (India, Bangladesh, Nepal, Myanmar, Pakistan, Bhutan, Thailand, Tibet) in 1991. In India 4,000 new churches were started through their efforts in 1990, with some 55,000 people making public decisions to follow Christ. Since Christians in India have almost unlimited freedom to go into prisons and share the gospel, Living Bibles and Prison Fellowship International joined forces in 1990 to launch a program to visit every prison in the country. The evangelistic booklet *It's a Great Life* was distributed to 2.3 million households in Calcutta in an outreach that ended in May, 1990. Project director Peter Bose believed that at least 100 house churches had been started by the end of 1992.

Trans World Radio continues to receive up to 50,000 letters per month in response to its Indian broadcasts. The Gospel Association of India holds successful crusades annually in Vijayawada, with a reported 25,000 conversions in 1993. The continuing revival among the Naga people of Nagaland, a state in northeastern India, had resulted in the state's becoming 85 percent Christian by 1993. Over 1,000 young people from Nagaland are currently studying in seminaries and Bible colleges.

After centuries of political authoritarianism and intolerance to Christianity in the Hindu kingdom of Nepal, democracy demonstrations forced King Birenda to grant a new constitution on November 9, 1990. There is now tolerance for a multiparty system and protection against discrimination on the basis of religion. Proselytizing or changing one's religion had long been illegal. Subsequently 500 spiritually hungry Nepalis flocked to the first open gospel meeting in modern history. It is estimated that there are now 100,000 believers in the underground Nepali church. Gospel for Asia supports 79 Nepali missionaries working among their own people. The United Bible Societies reported a distribution of 432,000 Scriptures in this kingdom of 19 million during 1991. Ram Sharon Nepal is a leader in the Nepalese Christian movement and a supervisor of 96 churches.

Korea

South Korea seems to be involved in a continuing revival. The Korean Protestant community approximately doubled its size during each decade from 1940 and 1970 and tripled it during the 1970s. In 1940 there were about 370,000; in 1950, 600,000; in 1960, 1.34 million; in 1970, 2.25 million; and in 1979, 7 million.

Reasons for the Success of the Korean Church

A non-colonialist missionary program that stressed self-support, self-government, and evangelism

Steadfastness of believers under severe persecution

Impact of revival of 1907-1908

Practice of putting all new converts to work at spiritual tasks

---

Since that time the Christian population has continued to grow rapidly and in 1993 South Korea realistically had some twelve million active Christians in a population of 43 million. An estimate that the population is 43 percent Christian seems to be very much on the high side. Korea's army is believed to be 35-40 percent Christian, an even higher percentage than the general population. Korea International Missions, founded in 1968, is a leader in Third World missions and now supports about 2,800 missionaries. The country has over a hundred Protestant colleges and universities, Bible schools and seminaries.

In Korean Christianity the extraordinary becomes almost ordinary, or at least repeatable and capable of being improved on. Billy Graham preached to 1.1 million in the concluding service of his Seoul crusade in 1973. Explo '74, in Seoul, had over a million in attendance at one meeting. In August 1980 the World Evangelization Crusade met in Seoul as part of the total Christianization movement of the country. It was sponsored by 19 denominations. On the final night there was a crowd of 3 million (in a city of 8 million), and 2 million or more attended two of the four evening sessions preceding the final one.

Five all-night prayer meetings continued until 5:00 A.M., with a combined attendance of 600,000. The basic stress of the crusade was on missions, and during the crusade 10,000 university and 3,000 high school students committed themselves to missions. At the last service a declaration was read committing the entire gathering to the use of the Korean church's resources for world evangelization.

In August 1984 the Korean church conducted 5 days of services celebrating 100 years of Protestant Christianity in Korea. At the concluding rally, on Sunday, August 19, Billy Graham addressed over one million people in Yoido Plaza in Seoul.

A truly remarkable feature of Korea's Christian community is Paul Cho's Full Gospel Central Church in Seoul. In 1983 it had 350,000 members and in 1993 membership had risen to about 600,000. Some twenty thousand of his members spend all Friday night in prayer. On Sundays several services are held in the auditorium, which can accommodate twenty thousand; and huge Sunday schools meet simultaneously in other facilities. Cho's church is not the only success story in the capital, however. For example, the Young Nak Presbyterian Church has a membership of over 60,000; the Kwang Lim Methodist Church, over 30,000; and the Choong Hyum Presbyterian Church, 25,000. The new president of South Korea, Young Sam Kim, is an elder in the Choong Hyum church and is the first active Christian to hold the presidency of the nation.

North Korea

Winds of change are blowing in North Korea. In 1991 Kim Il Sung National University agreed to offer religion courses; Dong G. Hong, a refugee from the area and now a professor at William Carey University's Institute of Korean Studies in Pasadena, was engaged to teach the classes on Christianity. Billy Graham preached at the University March 31-April 4, 1992; this was the first time an evangelist from any country has been invited to preach anywhere in North Korea. He also met with President Kim Il Sung.

The current constitution affirms the right to religious belief and the government helped build two churches in the capital of Pyongyang in recent years. There are also some 500 house churches meeting around the country, with a total of 10,000–12,000 Christians now allowed to worship freely. In a further evidence of openness to Christianity, the government has requested that the Christian Federation in North Korea see that a Bible is placed in the library of every school in the nation.

Japan

Japan is the least evangelized of all the leading

industrial nations. Various estimates conclude that only 2-4 percent of her 124 million people are nominally Christian, and far less than that may be classified as evangelical. One report states that 99.8 percent of the population do not attend church. Yet sales of New Age books and paraphernalia are booming and a new religion, Kohungkuno Kagaku (Science of Happiness), reportedly grew from about 25,000 to 1.5 million in 1991-1992. As is true of the New Age Movement, it is a mixture of Western and Oriental beliefs.

> *Japan: 99.8 percent do not attend church, yet sales of New Age books are booming.*

Yet the light of the gospel has not been extinguished in Japan. In 1990 the Japanese evangelical churches had more than 300 missionaries serving outside Japan, according to the Rev. Minoru Okuyama, principal of the Missionary Training Center at Nasu, and the number is increasing. Luis Palau had a successful evangelistic campaign in Osaka in 1990, with some 60,000 in attendance and several thousand decisions for Christ. Then in the summer of 1991 the third Japan Congress on Evangelism was held, with 1,030 people attending from many evangelical denominations. Instituted by the Japanese churches, this congress sought to study evangelistic strategies.

The number of churches in Japan is growing. In 1980 there were 5,875; by 1989 there were 6,789, though many of these churches are small. In 1978 for the first time Japan had a Christian prime minister,

Masayoshi Ohira. When he died in 1980, the cross was prominently displayed at his widely televised funeral.

The Philippines

In 1981 a two-day congress of 488 evangelical leaders representing 81 denominations and parachurch organizations committed themselves to a plan to establish an evangelical church in every ward of the Philippines by the year 2000. This plan to "disciple" would require increasing the existing 10,000 congregations to 50,000.

This concept of having a church within reach of everyone in the country was launched by the 60 Filipino delegates to Lausanne in 1974. Spot checks of 12 denominations in 1978 showed that between 1974 and 1978 there had been an almost six-fold increase in those groups. The dozen denominations surveyed were growing at a rate that would enable them to exceed the goal by the year 2000, and there are 75 denominations in the country. The Christian and Missionary Alliance alone is projecting an annual growth rate of 15 percent during the target period, with an increase from a membership of 60,000 in 900 churches to 2 million in 20,000 churches. If the goal is reached, the present 1 million evangelicals will grow to 4 or 5 million and will equal 6 to 8 percent of an expected population of 80 million by 2000. Perhaps the Philippines will establish

> *The Philippines: by 2000, evangelicals may equal 6 to 8 percent of the population, based on projected growth rates.*

an example that will provide a beacon light for the entire world.

In 1987 evangelical groups in the Philippines set a goal of 2,000 new Filipino missionaries by the year 2000. Half of these will go to unreached groups within the country and half overseas. Then in 1990 Campus Crusade launched "New Life 2000: Manila," a five-month evangelistic effort in the summer and fall. The project involved 5,200 Crusade staff and volunteers from 102 countries and 130 Filipino churches from 27 denominations. Reportedly 500,000 made salvation decisions in the various meetings that involved presentations of Athletes in Action basketball games, showings of the film *Jesus*, and lectures by Josh McDowell.

An action that occurred in 1991 facilitated the spread of the gospel in the Philippines. The Philippines Commission on Human Rights overturned a proposed ordinance banning any form of street evangelism in Manila without a permit. Evangelism of the Philippines took another step forward that same year when Luis Palau preached the "Metro Manila Say Yes! to Christ" crusade November 6-10. Total attendance for the six-day event was 235,000, with 110,000 at the final meeting. Seven thousand reportedly made first-time commitments to Christ. According to a survey conducted by the Philippine Council of Evangelical churches in Manila in 1992, there are 23,000 evangelical churches in the Philippines. About 57 percent of these were planted in the previous 10 years, showing that realizing the goal (noted above) of establishing 50,000 congregations by the year 2000 was just about on schedule.

THIRTY-FOUR

Response to the Gospel
Africa, The Muslim World, and Latin America

Africa

FROM Africa comes a seemingly never-ending tale of spiritual movement. One report estimates that Christians are increasing twice as fast as the continent's total population. Another claims that 1,000 new churches are being organized every Sunday, that 52,000 are being converted every day, and that the continent will be 46 percent evangelical Christian by the year 2000. Of 34 countries in Black Africa, their populations are on average more than 40 percent Christian.

In Marxist-controlled Mozambique, a 1983 report indicated that churches formerly affiliated with the Africa Evangelical Fellowship multiplied tenfold to 44,000 baptized believers in 450 churches during the twenty years of rigid control. The gospel continued to enjoy great receptivity in Marxist-controlled Ethiopia as well. In one church alone in the capital of Addis Ababa, 670 professions of faith were reported in late 1982. In Marxist-led Zimbabwe a revival swept the government schools in 1982 and 1983. At the beginning of 1983, 5,500 professions of faith by children twelve years and older had been reported.

The Ethiopian Evangelical Church grew from

20,000 members in 1951 to 776,000 in 1988, and by the latter date 350 of the churches closed by the government had been reopened under a more liberal governmental policy. But in 1992 and 1993 evangelicals experienced considerable persecution, especially in rural areas, allegedly at the instigation of the Ethiopian Orthodox Church. In 1988 Youth for Christ held gospel meetings in 3,100 South African high schools with a reported 18,000 first-time decisions. In 1991 large numbers of Pygmies in remote Zaire expressed interest in Christianity; 270 are known to have made professions of faith by 1993.

Mali, a predominantly Muslim country, has seen tremendous church growth in recent years. In Uganda, a country where perhaps 50 percent of the population carries the HIV virus, the Bible League Bible Studies program alone reported 8,800 conversions in 1992, with an increase of at least 100,000 church attenders in the latter year. The Bible League (Chicago) placed 99,600 Bibles and 613,000 study courses in Uganda during the period 1986-1992. In Tanzania, the Protestant churches in Dar es Salaam, the capital, joined to promote a united evangelistic campaign in the summer of 1992. Hundreds of meetings took place during a two-week period, under the sponsorship of African Enterprise. Six thousand made public commitments to Christ, including fifty Muslims and ten government

> *In spite of terrible persecution, the expansion of the church in Sudan may be greater than that anywhere else in the world.*

officials. In spite of terrible persecution of Christians in Sudan, reports of genocide, and "one of the worst examples of gross violation of human rights on earth" (according to Africa Watch), the church continues to grow there. In fact, one official on the scene believes that the expansion of the church there is greater than that in any other place in the world.

Which Way Will the Church Go?

As reports pour in of revivals and church growth in Africa, the statistical conclusions may be very confusing. When speaking of the Christianizing of the continent, statisticians commonly lump all kinds of Christians together. That includes large numbers of Roman Catholics who may be merely baptized adherents with little involvement in the church. For example, Lesotho is about 93 percent Christian and Madagascar 51 percent Christian. Zaire is about 94 percent Christian; 48 percent of the total population is Roman Catholic. The Central African Republic is 83 percent Christian; 33 percent of the total is Roman Catholic. Kenya is 73 percent Christian; 26 percent is Roman Catholic. Roman Catholics tend to have a fairly high birth rate and of course have their infants baptized in the church, so increase comes by propagation rather than conversion. Thus some of the Christianizing of the continent does not come through revival and church planting.

As the church grows in Africa, questions constantly arise as to which way the church will go. Will it go the way of Westernization, which tends to too great a degree to equate Western culture and Christian ways? Will it go the route of Africanization or authentication, which tends to conclude that the ancestral is authentic and thus to include some of the old pagan ways in

African Christianity? The proper way will reject both extremes and insist on allegiance to Christ and to the Scripture and will thus distance believers from traditional and/or former culture and religions. Thus African instruments may replace piano and organ in the worship service and worship forms may deviate greatly from Western practices.

Church growth in some places in Africa is so explosive that churches are not able to assimilate the new believers. As one commentator has said, the result is "an exuberant foliage linked to what is widely perceived to be a dangerous and shallow root." Thus churches may not be equipped to conduct their affairs biblically, and untaught persons who have made a profession of faith fall prey to the cults. There is considerable effort to educate the laity all across the continent. To plan effective evangelism and church planting throughout Africa, 13,000 pastors from 45 African nations, representing 2,146 denominations and church groups met in Lagos, Nigeria during the summer of 1992.

Though several Bible institutes have existed in Africa for many years, the maturing of the church there increasingly has required graduate-level seminary training. To meet the need, the Bangui Evangelical School of Theology in the Central African Republic was founded in 1977. This was the first evangelical seminary in Africa under the auspices of the Association of Evangelicals of Africa and Madagascar (AEAM). The school graduated its first class in June 1982. The Evangelical Churches of West Africa launched a seminary at Jos, Nigeria, in 1980 to complement an already existing seminary founded by the SIM International in Igbaja, southern Nigeria.

The Muslim World

Establishing and building the church in a Muslim land is one of the most difficult tasks faced by Christian missionaries today, and some Muslim countries have no organized group of believers. But there are some signs of spiritual life in the Muslim world. There is a report of the moving of the Holy Spirit in Egypt in recent years, especially among Christian Copts; and a significant number of Bible study groups reportedly meet in homes in the Cairo area. The work of God goes on in Lebanon, especially among the Christian minority, in spite of the war. Reports coming out of Iran indicate that the church there continues to function, in spite of all the pressure exerted against it. Though evangelism is forbidden in Iran, radio messages are effective. Trans World Radio reports that more Iranians have become Christians within the last 12 years than in the past century. Many Iranians in the "dispersion" have also been converted; mission work among the 3 million Iranian refugees in Turkey has met with some success.

Construction of the first Protestant church in Islamabad, capital of Pakistan, was completed in the summer of 1992. In Iraq, the 1970 constitution guarantees freedom of religion and worship, but Christian broadcasting and proselytizing are prohibited. There are something less than one million Christians in the country out of a total population of 18 million. Reach out (Boulder, Colorado) reports that the evangelical church of Baghdad has grown from 300 to 900 members since the allied bombings of the Gulf War.

Many Iraqi refugees have received a gospel witness in Jordan. The Christian and Missionary Alliance has been especially active among these nearly 200,000 displaced people and report converts in excess of a couple of hundred. There are now 50 evangelical churches and worship centers in Jordan. Though Bangladesh has now made Islam the state religion, there are reportedly 250,000 Christians in the country.

In Afghanistan there were only 9 known Christians in 1980; that number had grown to 350 by 1990. In 1991 the Evangelical Alliance Mission was teaching about 25,000 young Afghan refugees English as a Second Language (ESL) in Islamabad, Pakistan, to enable them to start a new life in the West. As a result some Afghans are being reached with the gospel.

> *Afghanistan: in 1980, only 9 known Christians, but 350 by 1990.*

The National Evangelical Church of Kuwait has seen its meetings grow from 50 to 500 in attendance in the two years after the Gulf War, apparently primarily because of the church's relief efforts and the resultant favor in the eyes of many. Permission was granted in 1993 for establishment of a Bible society in Morocco. New reception to Christianity has occurred among the Kurds as a result of Western "Christian" protection of these people during and since the Gulf War.

Throughout the Muslim world, radio (especially Trans World Radio) beams the gospel and isolated individuals believe and take correspondence courses. House churches form, sometimes without outside help and sometimes with the help of organizations like Arab World Mission that moves as it can, especially into North Africa.

Of special interest is the revival in Indonesia. After

the 1965 revolution, which became violently anti-Communist, revival broke out on one after the other of the Indonesian islands, notably North Sumatra, Java, and Timor. After 1970 the mass movements of new converts into the churches slowed, but Java experienced another sweeping revival in 1972. On Timor, 200,000 baptisms occurred in 1965 and 1966 alone. Between 1964 and 1971, Protestant church membership doubled from 4 to over 8 million in a nation of 119 million. There have been so many conversions that some areas are predominantly Christian in this Muslim land. Gospel advertisements in Muslim newspapers of Indonesia in 1975 resulted in 21,000 enrolling in Bible correspondence courses and 3,400 making decisions for Christ. World Vision reported a combined attendance of 250,000 in a 1976 crusade in Kupang, Indonesia, with throngs of inquirers responding to the invitation. As of 1991 Indonesia is about 9.6 percent Christian. Thus the Christian community there is strong enough to maintain itself. The new Balinese Bible was dedicated there in 1990 and the Indonesian Bible Society launched a variety of programs. In the last couple of years it has been promoting the use of audio cassettes containing Scripture passages for use in Christian homes where Muslim domestic help is working. The concept has met with some success. Unfortunately the church of Indonesia suffers at the hands of radical Muslims as it does elsewhere. In 1993 Muslims destroyed or damaged 46 churches there, with strong reaction from the government concerning the right of non-Muslims to follow their faith.

Persecution of Christians is also growing more severe in Pakistan, the country with the world's largest Islamic population. There several Christians have been executed in the last year and new religious laws tighten the screws. But Saudi Arabia is the most hostile nation in the world to Christianity. Concerted efforts are currently in process to prevent any Christian church from forming.

Latin America

God is at work in Latin America. Over five thousand new evangelical churches were established in the region in 1974. In that year on December 15, 20,000 people jammed the Jotabeche Pentecostal Methodist Church in Santiago, Chile, for its dedication. The largest evangelical church in the world at that time, it had 80,000 members.

Success Stories in Latin America

About 10% of the total population is now evangelical
Brazil is about 15-20% evangelical
Chile is about 20% evangelical
Guatemala may be 35% evangelical

Members attend the mother church once a month and one of the one hundred branch churches on other Sundays. An important event of 1973 was the preaching of twenty-one-year-old Julio César Ruibal in Colombia and Bolivia. Over 70,000 came to hear him in the soccer stadium in Medellin, Colombia; it was reported to be the largest crowd ever in that city.

In the same year David Wilkerson reported that the Jesus revolution was sweeping the high school and college campuses in Brazil. In 1983 the First Baptist Church of Sao Paulo regularly had about 20,000 in attendance on a Sunday. Child Evangelism and Word of Life staff members are among those teaching required Bible classes in the public schools of the country. The Graham crusade in Rio de Janeiro, Brazil (1974), packed 225,000 into the stadium on the closing day, and television carried Graham's message to the entire nation on that occasion. In 1976 Argentine evangelist Luis Palau had an especially successful crusade in Asuncion, Paraguay. About 10,000 gathered nightly during the twelve-day crusade, and 5,000 made professions of faith. There had been only 3,000 evangelicals in the city before that time.

A revolution is sweeping Latin America. The region is experiencing a great awakening and turning Protestant.

The largest crowd ever to turn out for an evangelical preacher in Central America came to hear Luis Palau in Guatemala City on November 28, 1982; it was variously estimated at between 350,000 and 700,000 persons. Over 3,000 decisions were registered during the eight-day campaign. In October 1990 the Christian Broadcasting Network launched Project Light in Buenos Aires. Fifty thousand trained Argentinian counselors and 3,000 churches were involved in this campaign on prime-time television that blanketed the nation. Some claims of numbers of conversions seem excessive, but probably hundreds of thousands made professions of faith. Following Project Light, Billy Graham conducted a campaign in Buenos Aires in November 1991, when an estimated 259,000 flocked to his meetings. The Univer-

sal Church of the Kingdom of God, an independent
Pentecostal church begun by Edir Macedo de Bezarra
about 1977, now claims 2 million worshipers meeting
in 800 churches throughout Latin America, Portugal,
Angola, and the United States.

Reasons for Success of the Current Gospel Movement in Latin America

It provides a personal, emotional experience of God
It is a movement of the common people
It mobilizes its adherents to fulfill the
Great Commission
It creates community and seeks to meet the social
and economic needs of church members

In the Dominican Republic in 1980 there were
only about 50,000 evangelical Christians. By 1990 the
number had increased to about a half million in the
population of 7 million. A group of Baptist World
Alliance leaders conducted an evangelistic tour of Cuba
in 1992, the first such group allowed to preach openly
in the country in more than 30 years. They reported
every service packed and 900 first-time decisions to
follow Christ. Peru's 1990 election put in office four
evangelical senators, 13 evangelical deputies and an
evangelical second vice president.

In 1991 Costa Rica celebrated the centennial of
the beginning of Protestant missions in the country with
a crusade led by Luis Palau. The three-day evangelistic
campaign included three nationwide telecasts and evening rallies at the National Stadium, with a total attendance of 83,000 and 3,700 decisions for Christ. This

was followed by a day-long celebration when 300,000 marched through downtown San José, the capital, and gathered at a park adjacent to the National Stadium to hear Palau. The list of evangelical activities and triumphs could go on and on and would quickly grow tedious.

What do these and other examples of spiritual movement add up to? A revolution is sweeping Latin America. The region is experiencing a great awakening and turning Protestant. A commonly accepted generalization is that evangelicals in Latin America numbered about 15 million in the late 1960s and that by the end of 1991 had increased to about 40 million, for about 10 percent of the total population. The greatest Protestant advances have been registered in Brazil (now 15-20% evangelical) and Chile (about 20% evangelical) in South America and in Central America generally, where every country is at least 10 percent Protestant. Estimates for Guatemala go as high as 35-38 percent Protestant. There more than 400 groups are presently planting churches, and evangelicals were largely responsible for electing in January, 1991 Jorge Serrano Elias, the first Protestant evangelical president elected in Latin America. There are predictions that within a decade or two Guatemala, Brazil, El Salvador, and Honduras will become predominantly evangelical nations. Reportedly in Brazil over a half million are leaving the Catholic church for evangelical churches each year.

Three Waves of Protestantism

Protestantism has washed onto Latin American shores in three waves. First came ethnic Europeans who brought the Lutheran, Presbyterian, Methodist, and Baptist churches with them as they immigrated to the region especially in the nineteenth century. Early in the twentieth century the faith missions—the Central American Mission, the Christian and Missionary Alliance, the Gospel Missionary Union and the Latin American Mission—for example, invaded Latin America. They were especially active in the middle decades of the century. Because these missions were reluctant to turn over control of their ministries to the nationals and because they could not bring themselves to worship as the Latins wished to worship, they had only moderate success.

The third wave of recent decades has been Latin in personnel and in worship forms and Pentecostal in orientation. In fact, in most countries about 80 percent of the evangelicals are now Pentecostal, and they reproduce rapidly by means of an urgent lay evangelism. The new wave of Protestantism in Latin America is successful because it provides a personal, emotional experience of God to its adherents; because it is a movement of the common people; because it mobilizes its adherents to fulfill the Great Commission; and because it creates community. The poor have a place to belong and others to belong to. The church provides networking to help meet personal, social, and economic needs. It stresses work, providing for one's family, and God-honoring living. Evangelicals are entering public service and government. They are contributing to a growth of family values. In short, they are changing society in many ways. They choose neither to support the left and advance the cause of Liberation Theology or the right but concentrate on the work of God in the lives of people.

Overcoming the Problems

The success of evangelicalism in Latin America must not obscure the problems, however. One major problem is that masses of people are being swept into the churches on an emotional wave, without adequate follow up, discipleship programs, or doctrinal or biblical instruction. The result is that many exit by the back door of the church while others come in the front door. To date there are no adequate studies on the "revolving door" problem. Certainly, however, this element of society is fertile ground for the Jehovah's Witnesses, Mormons, and other cults that, along with the evangelicals, are growing significantly in Latin America. A second problem concerns the danger that as evangelical politicians move into positions of leadership they may not be able to resist effectively the corruption that surrounds them everywhere in society.

Third, evangelicals will have to address the overwhelming social problems of the region effectively. If they do not, they will experience the same repudiation that Liberation Theology, Marxism, and other ideologies confront. Last, there is growing concern among the Catholic hierarchy over the loss of their hold on the region and an angry response of many of the common people to the perception that evangelicals are a disruptive influence in a common Catholic heritage and culture. The result has been Catholic persecution of evangelicals in several countries, especially Mexico, Venezuela, Colombia, and Costa Rica. There is a parallel today to persecution of the early church when popular opposition to evangelicals

> *In most countries about 80 percent of the evangelicals are now Pentecostal, and they reproduce rapidly by means of an urgent lay evangelism.*

was probably even greater than that of the religious establishment or the government.[21]

The new ecumenicity among Latin American Protestants became very visible on April 23, 1982, when the Confraternity of Evangelicals in Latin America (CONELA) was organized in Panama City under the impetus and auspices of the Lausanne Committee for World Evangelization. Ninety-eight Protestant denominations and seventy-four Christian service agencies participated in the event. Designed to facilitate communication among conservative evangelicals rather than to be a decision-making body, the continent-wide alliance will hold the line for conservative, biblical evangelicals. Since its organization CONELA has had wide reception and support across the region. A rider to the constitution declared that CONELA would not join either the World Council of Churches or the International Christian Council. The Confraternity was designed to be an alternative to the Latin American Council of Churches (CLAI), which has ties to the World Council of Churches.

THIRTY-FIVE

Response to the Gospel
Worldwide Ministries

Pentecostal Ministry

AS NOTED above, much of the revival movement in Latin America is led by Pentecostals, who especially appeal to the masses and who have been successful in building large churches all over Latin America. Pentecostals have been active almost everywhere else around the world too. For instance, as of 1976 they had established 200 churches in Thailand with 6,000 members, and they were heavily involved in the Indonesian revival. In the spring of 1991 Russian Pentecostals were able to conduct their first national congress. Pentecostal successes in Africa include the 5-million-member Kimbanguist church of Zaire and the 1.2 million Pentecostals of Kenya. In Bulgaria the Church of God had a membership of 4,000 in 1987; five years later it reported a membership of 20,000.

The charismatic movement has invaded all segments of the American church, but has made a special impact on the Anglican and Roman Catholic churches. In fact, charismatic Roman Catholics may now be found all over the world and are thought to number between 50 and 65 million adherents. In the spring of 1976, 35,000 of them braved a weekend of rain in Notre Dame's football stadium to attend a conference on the

Holy Spirit. In the fall of 1977, 37,000 Roman Catholic charismatics met in Atlantic City. Earlier that year 50,000 charismatics of various faiths met in a week-long conference in Kansas City. And in the spring of 1978, 54,000 charismatics rallied in the Meadowlands Stadium of Rutherford, New Jersey. A tabulation completed in 1978 reported that 8 million American Roman Catholics were Pentecostals. Later the number probably increased to 10 million.

The Catholic charismatic movement began in Pittsburgh, Pennsylvania, in March 1967 and celebrated its 25th anniversary in the same city in June 1992. The movement grew rapidly within the Roman church and in 8 years won the approval of Pope Paul VI, who called it "a chance for the church" as he addressed 10,000 charismatics in Rome in 1975. During its early years ecumenical contact between Catholic and Protestant charismatics was considerable and the Roman church generally held its charismatics within its fold.

> *Brighton '91 chairman Michael Harper claimed that Pentecostals and charismatics number some 391 million worldwide.*

Then during the 1980s ecumenical contact declined and many Catholic charismatics moved into Protestant churches. At the same time some splintering among charismatic Catholics occurred and a decline in their numbers set in. In 1990 and 1991 new controversies rocked some of the charismatic communities and there was decline in membership.

At the same time, there were 3.2 million black

Pentecostals in the United States, and the fastest growing denomination in America is the (multi-racial, but largely white) 2.2 million-member Assemblies of God. Its membership cuts across all social classes. At its annual meeting in 1991 the Assemblies received a report that the church had experienced a new increase of 5 million members worldwide during the previous two years, only 30,000 of whom were from the United States.

The thirteenth Pentecostal World Conference convened in Nairobi, Kenya, in September 1982, with 11,000 participants. The conference met in spite of the uncertainties connected with the attempted coup against Kenyan president Danial Moi, an evangelical Christian. Moi addressed the group, 90 percent of whom were black. More would have attended from abroad if the coup attempt had not taken place. The fifteenth Pentecostal World Conference met in Singapore in the fall of 1989, with an attendance of 40,000.

In July 1991 charismatic leaders from more than 100 countries gathered in Brighton, England to promote world evangelization. Featured on the program was the new Archbishop of Canterbury, George Carey, an Anglican charismatic. The conference chairman, Michael Harper, claimed that there were some 391 million Pentecostals and charismatics in the world. This was a far larger figure than the frequently reported 250 million.

The Pentecostal Resource Center has been completed near the Church of God headquarters in Cleveland, Tennessee. Designed to house an array of data on the Pentecostal movement, the $2.5 million structure is a valuable resource to researchers and writers.

Ministry to Jews

One of the most exciting developments of our time is the inroads of the gospel among the Jews. The leader in the field of Jewish missions today is Jews for Jesus (an outgrowth of the Jesus movement of the sixties), which was founded in 1973. Moishe Rosen is executive director of the organization. Jews for Jesus maintains its headquarters in San Francisco, has nine North American branches, and chapters manned by volunteers in about 50 other cities. It now also has offices in Paris, London, Johannesburg, Buenos Aires, and Odessa, and missionaries in England, France, Ukraine, South Africa, and Argentina, with plans to send missionaries to Brazil and Russia in the near future. Jews for Jesus is especially known for its communications techniques, which may include anything from full-page ads in the *Wall Street Journal* or *New York Times* to preaching on street corners. The ads brought about 280,000 responses during the period 1982-1992. The organization originated Jewish gospel music and has a traveling music group known as the Liberated Wailing Wall. Local music and drama teams minister in several places in the United States.

Jews for Jesus is the largest independent mission to the Jews and currently has over 100 missionaries on the staff. Second in size is Chosen People Ministries (formerly American Board of Missions to the Jews); and third is the Friends of Israel. Among denominational agencies with Jewish missions, the largest is the Assemblies of God, followed by Baptist Mid-Missions, the Conservative Baptists, and the Lutheran Church-Missouri Synod.

Jews for Jesus reports considerable recent success,

especially with its ministry in Odessa and in New York City. In Odessa there were 140 professions of faith during the first nine months of 1992. Street preaching in New York City in the summers of 1991 and 1992 achieved new success with the help of Christian Jews from Ukraine. Chosen People Ministries are seeing greatly increased response to the gospel in Argentina. Reportedly the Jewish community in Israel grew from 3,000 to 4,000 between 1985 and 1992, partly because of the immigration of Hebrew Christians from Russia and conversions among Russian immigrants. There are now over 200 Messianic groups in the United States. *Messianic Times,* published in Toronto, seeks to present the news of the Hebrew Christian movement.

The Ministry of Billy Graham

No account of the contemporary church would be complete without at least a brief word about Billy Graham. He acquired national fame in 1948 with his first Los Angeles crusade, and world fame in 1954 with his first Greater London crusade. After that year, he crusaded with song leader Cliff Barrows and singer George Beverly Shea and others in most parts of the world. In spite of the massive scale of Graham's campaigns, emphasis is on individual conversion. And once individuals are converted, they are followed up and urged to affiliate with a local church.

Through the ministry of the crusade, Graham has preached the gospel to untold millions of persons, with millions responding for conversion and counseling. Since 1950 "The Hour of Decision" radio program has been beamed around the world every Sunday and currently is aired over more than 700 stations in the United

States and abroad. In 1982 a 15-minute broadcast in Spanish was added and is now aired in more than 30 cities where Spanish-speaking people live.

Approximately 1.8 million copies of *Decision* magazine are distributed worldwide; each month the magazine is also produced in braille and on cassette tape for the blind. Graham's best sellers, *Peace with God* (2.5 million copies), *Secret of Happiness* (1.5 million), and *How to Be Born Again* (1.4 million) have been another important part of his impact. The film ministry of the Billy Graham Evangelistic Association, World Wide Pictures, has produced well over 100 films in 23 languages, among the most effective of which have been *The Hiding Place, Caught,* and *Eye of the Storm.* The Association's World Emergency Fund (1973) has assisted many victims of catastrophies, such as the Vietnamese boat people, Cambodian refugees, the starving in Africa, earthquake victims in Guatemala, and Kurds displaced by Desert Storm.

Mission World International is the new Graham program of recent years. It seeks to train counselors, pastors, and others in evangelism and discipleship by satellite, videos, and television in conjunction with major Graham telecasts. The telecasts are beamed over a wide area with music and testimonies geared to local audiences and Graham's message interpreted into the local language. In 1989 the focus was on India. On December 24 on prime time he had an hour that monopolized Indian television, with an estimated audience of 180 million. In 1990 the focus was on Hong Kong. In November he preached to a live audience of 29,000 in the Hong Kong Stadium, with an overflow crowd of 30,000 watching by video in an adjacent athletic field. The meetings, translated into 45 languages, were sent by satellite and video to 30 countries throughout Asia to an audience estimated at 10 million. This was the evangelist's largest single outreach in his 40 years of international ministry. The same technique was followed in Buenos Aires in 1991 and in Essen, Germany in March, 1993. The Essen telecasts were beamed to 55 countries in 40 languages.

Graham has been doing much more than these specials since 1988. In the summer of 1989 he conducted Mission '89 in London. Cumulative attendance for the 13 meetings was 1.2 million, with more than 80,000 reportedly making a commitment to Christ. A total of 73,500 jammed London's Wembly Stadium for the final meeting. Three of Graham's messages were carried via television and satellite to 3 African countries with an estimated audience of 23 million.

Subsequently on July 29, 1989 Graham held a one-night crusade in Budapest where close to 100,000 packed the People's Stadium for the largest public evangelistic preaching service ever held anywhere in eastern Europe. More than 27,000 responded to the invitation to "come to Christ." "An angel came upon the stadium," the front page of a national daily announced afterward. And the entire nation listened on radio and television then and on reruns.

In 1990, on March 10, Billy Graham took advantage of the opening of the Berlin Wall (Nov. 9, 1989) to preach in front of the Reichstag. Eighteen hundred decision response cards were turned in, 1,100 by East Germans. The following year, on July 8-13, he held a Moscow School of Evangelism, the first such event in Russia's history. More than 4,000 Soviet pastors and lay leaders attended. On Sunday, September 22, he spoke to his largest assembled audience in North America on the Great Lawn in Central Park, New York City. That rally brought out 250,000 and was supported by 900 churches representing 40 denominations; 200 Roman Catholic parishes participated as a result of a letter sent by Archbishop John Cardinal O'Connor urging priests and laity to attend.

Then on March 31-April 4, 1992 Graham preached in Sung Il Kim University in North Korea. This was the first time an evangelist from any country had been invited to preach anywhere in North Korea. Graham's Moscow crusade (October 3-25, 1992) for the concluding service drew 50,000 to the Olympic Stadium and 20,000 to an area serviced by an outdoor screen. Reportedly a quarter of the audience responded to the invitation.

The Billy Graham Center at Wheaton College, Wheaton, Illinois, was born out of the desire to make world evangelism the primary concern of Christians today. The Center houses archives, a library of materials on evangelism and missions, and the Wheaton College Graduate School.

To further the cause of evangelism, Graham called an International Conference for Itinerant Evangelists in Amsterdam for ten days beginning on July 11, 1983. Over 3,500 evangelists came from 133 countries—70 percent from the Third World—for instruction and inspiration. Graham[22] called the Second International Conference for Itinerant Evangelists in Amsterdam on July 12-21, 1986, with 10,000 in attendance, a majority of whom came from the Third World. Graham joined 290 other evangelical leaders from 50 countries to "inform, train, encourage, and inspire" those in attendance.

The Ministry of Luis Palau

Luis Palau is sometimes called the Billy Graham of Latin America or a Third World evangelist; but actually he has now become an evangelist to the whole world. Born in Argentina, Palau began his evangelistic crusades in Latin America in 1966. He has been conducting crusades in English for nearly 20 years. Of course most of Palau's campaigns have been in Latin America. Reference has already been made to his 1976 crusade in Asuncion, Paraguay, and his 1982 successes in Guatemala.

Other examples include his 1980 crusade in Guayaquil, Ecuador, and his 1982 effort in Paraguay. The former was a two-week crusade with a nightly attendance of 6,000 and 2,850 making Christian commitments. The latter was conducted in cooperation with four associate evangelists in seven Paraguayan cities, with a cumulative attendance of 155,000. On the final night, with 25,000 in attendance in the capital, 1,700 made decisions for Christ.

Palau's concern for Latins in the United States led him to conduct his first American Spanish-language crusade in the Los Angeles Sports Arena, June 28 to July 6, 1980. Working with a base of about 1 percent evangelicals in a nominally Catholic and largely unchurched Spanish population, he drew an aggregate attendance of 52,000 with about 1,950 making decisions of some sort. Examples of his ministry in Europe have been noted in references to his Helsinki and London crusades. His five-week campaign in Glasgow, Scotland, in 1981 also was significant. At his unprecedented London crusade of 1984, 293,000 attended with 28,000 making professions of faith.

Among his more memorable recent campaigns were those in Romania, Thailand, Japan, Bulgaria, Mexico, Ireland, and Jamaica. In the spring of 1990 he addressed 35,000 Romanians in Oradea, with 6,000 responding to the invitation to receive Christ. Trans World Radio recorded the message, and it was broadcast nationwide. That same year he spoke in Bangkok, Thailand, as part of "Bangkok '90—Answer to Life," where 2,000 dedicated their lives to Christ. Also in 1990 he addressed 60,000 people in Okinawa and Osaka, Japan, with a reported 7,100 decisions for Christ in the several meetings.

In the summer of 1991 he preached to 16,200 people in Sofia, Bulgaria, in the first evangelistic campaign there since 1939. In the three meetings reportedly 5,900 made decisions of conversion. In the spring of 1992 he addressed nine rallies in Mexico City in the soccer stadium and a bullring. Crowds ranged from 7,500 to 20,000 in spite of limited coverage. Proposed changes in the Mexican constitution giving new religious freedom to all churches had not yet been ratified and he had no radio or newspaper coverage.[23] In Palau's May, 1992 crusade in Dublin he had a combined weekend audience of 17,400 with 1,367 public commitments to Christ. Crusade chairman Declan Flanagan said, "This is the first time this century that such a broad spectrum of Christians has united in our city." During his February, 1993 crusade in Jamaica, Palau spoke to 245,000 in eleven cities with a reported 17,500 professions of faith.

Ministry through Christian Literature

Another facet of the work and success of the Christian church today is Christian literature. Whether one considers the books of Billy Graham, James Dobson, Charles Swindoll, Francis Schaeffer, Hal Lindsey, Elisabeth Elliot, or scores and scores of others, he sees that both popular and more scholarly Christian literature from secular houses and the growing number of evangelical publishers has made a profound impact in most parts of the world. And of course Christian magazines such as *Christianity Today, Moody Monthly, Campus Life,* and others all play their parts.

Campus Ministries

The old veteran in the field of campus ministries is InterVarsity Christian Fellowship. It had its beginnings in Britain in the 1860s and 1870s. From there it spread to Canada and from Canada came to the United States in 1937. InterVarsity was organized in the United States in 1941, and in 1948 C. Stacey Woods (who had been responsible for its establishment in the United States) was instrumental in organizing the International Fellowship of Evangelical Students (IFES), of which the United States' InterVarsity is a member. There are now IFES affiliates in over 130 countries, and the coordinating office is in London.

In the United States more than 480 full-time staff members serve 634 college and university chapters with a membership of over 26,000. Recently IVCF has started to organize graduate school chapters. They have also begun Marketplace Ministries, which seeks to help college graduates apply Christian principles as they serve God in the business world. Nurses Christian Fellowship (with 86 campus chapters) is another InterVarsity ministry, and as previously noted, IVCF organizes triennial missions conferences at Urbana, Illinois. In addition, it has campgrounds and centers for summer training and weekend retreats and a rapidly expanding book publishing division.

New Generation Ministries in 1992 marked its tenth anniversary of reaching black college students with the gospel. Nine hundred attended the NGM annual conference in Norfolk, Virginia.

One of the most dynamic and most effective agencies in the outreach of the church today is Campus Crusade for Christ. Founded in 1951 by Bill Bright, it sought first to reach American campuses through use of the "four spiritual laws." In connection with that ministry, it has worked effectively on the beaches of Florida to evangelize students there and has branched out to include ministries to athletes, military personnel, high school students and others. In 1992 Campus Crusade had about 30,000 staff members working in 164 countries around the world. The 1,517 field staff in the United States conducted evangelism and discipleship ministry on 250 college campuses.

Campus Crusade's film Jesus *is available in 231 languages and is viewed by some 500,000 per day.*

The film *Jesus* is Crusade's greatest single evangelism tool. Based on the gospel of Luke, it is now available in 234 languages (projected to 271) and is viewed by some 500,000 per day. Some 500 million people have seen it in 197 countries, with a reported 35 million professions of faith. The Crusade lost no time in showing the film in Hungary, Bulgaria, Russia, Mongolia, and elsewhere in the East Bloc when the area began to open up. It has now been translated into 26 Eastern

European languages. The film has also been shown in prisons in most of the 50 states.

Campus Crusade has launched "Here's Life" campaigns in various American cities and foreign countries in saturation evangelism programs. A good example of the latter was the 1982 effort in the Netherlands. In March a 48-page magazine entitled *There Is Hope (Er Is Hoop)* was distributed to each of the 5.2 million households in the Netherlands, marking the beginning of the nationwide "Here's Life" campaign. Trained church members committed themselves to contacting every home in the country during the next two years. In "New Life Manila" (1990), delegates from 102 countries presented the gospel to 3 million Filipinos.

A major American effort of Campus Crusade during 1983 was KC'83, a post-Christmas conference in Kansas City designed to stimulate college students to revolutionize their campuses for Christ. A total of 19,000 attended., "Explo '85" was the largest worldwide Christian satellite conference that linked 97 countries on five continents for evangelism and discipleship. During that same year "Youth Congress '85" trained 17,000 high school students in evangelism and discipleship.

Athletes in Action is a sports ministry conducted by Christian athletes under the sponsorship of the Crusade. The program has been functioning for 15 years, and it had a staff of 278 in 1992. Student Venture is the Crusade ministry to high school students. As part of that program the Crusade sponsors "Something's Happening USA" conferences. The third conference convened on December 30, 1992 and brought together 2,500 students, youth leaders, parents, and others from across the nation and abroad. The focus was to mobilize prayer and pursue spiritual awakening nationwide.

THIRTY-SIX

Doctrinal Developments

The Fundamentalists

AN ANSWER to what is going on in the church must concern more than growth or decline or the success of its mission in the world. It must also deal with the question of what has happened to beliefs and attitudes within the church during this century? To begin with, the departure from conservative theology became increasingly pronounced during the early years of the century. One effort to combat this tendency was the publication of a twelve-volume paperback set produced under the successive editorship of A. C. Dixon, Louis Meyer, and R. A. Torrey (1910-1912). Called *The Fundamentals*, these books especially upheld the virgin birth of Christ, His physical resurrection, the inerrancy of Scripture, the substitutionary atonement, and the imminent, physical second coming of Christ. Millions of copies were distributed free, and those who subscribed to the doctrines set forth in them came to be known as "fundamentalists."

With increasing intensity a controversy raged between fundamentalists and liberals, or modernists, in almost all religious bodies of the land, but it was especially divisive in Baptist and Presbyterian circles. Several splits resulted within those denominations, launching such denominations or movements as the Orthodox Presbyterians, the Bible Presbyterians, the Presbyterian

Church in America, the General Association of Regular Baptists, the Conservative Baptist Association, the North American Baptist Association, and the Independent Fundamental Churches of America. And a host of churches all over the land went independent as community churches, Bible churches, or independent Baptist churches.

For a long time fundamentalists were known as negative or combative and anti-intellectual, but a great many of them have developed more positive attitudes in recent years and have built hundreds of Bible colleges, liberal arts colleges, and theological seminaries all over the world. Early in the century they tended to neglect social ministries, somewhat in reaction to the Social Gospel. But that observation has been considerably overdrawn, because they have always supported rescue missions, children's homes, and many other home missions projects, in addition to an incalculable number of hospitals, clinics, schools, and other philanthropic works all over the world. Educational systems in many areas of developing countries owe their existence to these conservative Christian groups.

Second, there has come a basic change in outlook in the Christianity of recent decades. During the latter part of the nineteenth century and the early part of the twentieth, optimism pervaded Christianity. In liberal circles this was expressed in terms of the perfectability of human nature and the idea that mankind was improving. Ultimately a utopian state would be reached. The Darwinian concept of evolution and the striking number of new inventions that promised a better future for mankind gave credence to that view. In more conservative circles this optimism was expressed in terms of postmillennialism, according to which it was thought that the gospel would pervade all of society and bring in a reign of righteousness on earth.

But two world wars, a devastating depression, German inhumanity toward the Jews, widespread purges of dissenters by the Communists in lands they took over, and a world divided between two powers engaged in a nuclear arms race have virtually annihilated the old utopian or millennial dreams and the concept of perfectability of human nature. Increasingly, mankind is viewed as being incurably bad. Pessimism has become the creed of the day in many circles. Oswald Spengler's *Decline of the West*, written in 1918, expresses this pessimism.

With the change from optimism to pessimism or realism has come a change in attitude toward the Bible. As a result of archaeological and historical study, it has become increasingly clear to scholars and laypersons that the Bible is an essentially accurate historical document. The views of such higher critical schools as Wellhausen and Tübingen moderated greatly. In fact, liberalism in general has become more moderate in attitude toward the Scripture.

Neo-orthodoxy

As the old optimism died and as the old liberalism moderated, it also became clear that the antisupernaturalism of previous generations was inadequate for a day when the very foundations of society seemed to be quivering. Some churchmen said, "We have removed the supernatural from the Bible; we have humanized the person of Christ; we have emptied the churches—now what?" The answer for many seemed to be neo-orthodoxy.

Led by Karl Barth and Emil Brunner, neo-orthodoxy provided a via media between the old conservatism and the old liberalism. While holding on to some of the higher critical views of Scripture on the one hand, it stressed on the other hand a supernaturalism, the virgin birth, and a sinful humanity who needed salvation; and many of them spoke of the substitutionary death of Christ. God was viewed as the transcendent one, the wholly other, who breaks in on human beings in a crisis experience. The Bible while fallible, *contained* the word of God and *became* the word of God whenever it spoke to the reader. In other words, neo-orthodoxy confused revelation with illumination, which is the Spirit's ministry in teaching through the Word. Because neo-orthodox theologians tended to use the same vocabulary as conservatives but poured new meaning into common terms, often it was not clear exactly what they did believe.

Karl Barth

Karl Barth[24] (1886-1968) was the leading spokesman of the movement. Born in Basel, he studied in Switzerland and Germany and became a pastor in Switzerland. He found that his liberal theology offered little hope for people gripped in the horrors of war, and in 1919 he broke with liberalism in the publication of his commentary on Romans. Thereafter, he taught in German universities until expelled by the Nazis in 1930. Then he returned to Basel to teach. Though he wrote over five hundred books and articles, his commentary on Romans and his four-volume *Church Dogmatics*, produced late in life, are among his most important works.

His views changed over the years, but Barth's teaching of a sovereign God who spoke to people through the written word did not. Barth viewed mankind as sinful and spoke of Christ's dying and suffering rejection for all so all might be redeemed in Him. At times this teaching seemed to border on universalism, but Barth denied that he taught universalism. Eventually Barth found that he satisfied neither conservatives nor liberals, but his influence was, nevertheless, very great indeed. He seems to have been closer to the conservative position on the virgin birth, the resurrection of Christ, and other cardinal doctrines than were Brunner and the Niebuhrs.

Emil Brunner, Reinhold Niebuhr, and H. Richard Niebuhr

Emil Brunner (1889-1966) was also a Swiss Theologian; he eventually broke with Barth because he put more stock in natural theology than Barth did. Independently of Barth he reevaluated his liberal views during World War I. Ultimately he came to view revelation as personal encounter with God, who communicates Himself. Many of his views were similar to those of Barth; but he differed with Barth in holding that God may be known partially through nature, and he held that the image of God in man is not completely lost.

The leading American exponent of neo-orthodoxy was Reinhold Niebuhr (1893-1971). While a pastor in Detroit, he developed an interest in social and economic problems and carried this interest with him in his long professorship at Union Theological Seminary in New York. He wrote seventeen major books, among which were *Moral Man and Immoral Society* and *Faith and History*. Like Barth, he saw God as the "wholly other" and believed that society needed drastic changes; but he differed with Barth's lack of social concern. He believed that God's encounter with man would enable man to overcome his sin of pride and selfishness and to achieve good in a sinful society. Niebuhr helped to found Americans for Democratic Action and the National Council of Churches.

Another major representative of American neo-orthodoxy was H. Richard Niebuhr (1894-1962), Reinhold's younger brother and the more scholarly of the two. Among his several books produced during his professorship at Yale was *The Kingdom of God in America,* in which he moved away from his earlier liberalism and looked for a restoration of Reformation roots in American society.

Rudolf Bultmann and Paul Tillich

Neo-orthodoxy nearly conquered Protestant Europe in the 1930s and 1940s and made a determined bid for control of American theological schools. Gradually, Bultmann and Tillich took over some of the territory Barth had controlled.

Rudolf Bultmann made a tremendous impact on the theological scene in the late 1940s and 1950s. He spoke of the need to "demythologize" the concepts of the New Testament and showed himself skeptical of the historical content of the gospels. Yet he did not abandon a need for some kind of decision for Jesus Christ, even though he was not at all clear on what one should base the decision.

Paul Tillich's[25] theological influence was especially great in the 1950s and 1960s. His beliefs are difficult to put into simple language, because his views were based on Platonism, mysticism, and existentialism. He understood God as the "Ground of Being"; man derives his own being by participation existentially in the "Ground of Being." Many accused him of holding to a kind of pantheism and an impersonal deity. He also taught that it was only through the myths or symbols of Scripture that human beings could grasp or understand God, the "Ground of Being." Tillich (1886-1965) sought to mediate between Christian theology and secular thought, between religion and culture, and in so doing often did not satisfy either the secularists or the theologians. He held that no theology could portray the reality of God, therefore theology must always be in process. Barth, Bultmann, and Tillich were all in one way or another products of existentialism: they tended to split religious experience from objective, scientific knowledge.

During the 1960s, as a kind of fallout of Tillich and a reaction to Barth, the "God is dead" movement developed. In a sense its adherents were saying, "We have lost special revelation entirely if we don't have the Barthian experience with God." That is to say, if the Bible only becomes the Word of God when He speaks through it, if there is a word of God only when God speaks in the existential moment or in the crisis experience, then when God does not speak there is no word of God. Therefore, it is impossible to know God. So they became intellectual agnostics and a few of them atheists. The most important men in the American movement were Thomas J. J. Altizer, William Hamilton, Paul Van Buren, and Harvey Cox.

Trends in the Seventies and Eighties

In the later 1960s and 1970s, the influence of neo-orthodoxy waned, and there was a shift to both the right and the left. On the right, there was a new worldwide acceptance of a literal approach to Scripture. Certainly this is the position of evangelicalism in general in the United States, of the worldwide Pentecostal movement, of the great revival and missionary movements of Latin America and Africa and the Far East, of the great following of Billy Graham, and of many others in the world.

Though neo-orthodoxy is no longer the dominant force it was at seminaries and universities, it influences many who follow a kind of middle way in their view of Christianity and the Scripture. On the left is process theology. This is a kind of neoliberalism with an emphasis on the immanence of God. In it, there is no absolute authority. The Bible has value along with other religious texts. This system is a kind of synthesis of everything theological that has been going on during the 1950s and 1960s. God Himself as well as the universe is in the process of "becoming." Absoluteness of being is denied. Becoming is the ultimate category.

Process theology[26] was developed on the basis of the philosophy of Alfred North Whitehead and Charles Hartshorne, by such American theologians as John Cobb, David Griffin, and Schubert Ogden. Process theology identifies God and the universe but sees God as more than the universe or existing beyond it. In some process theologians God is the cosmic process, growing and changing. Christ is commonly viewed as one who lived in complete obedience to God, who most perfectly followed the attraction of God's way in the world. So he provided an example of a whole new way of living. Thus a new kind of community is born, consisting of people who live like that, the church. Now mankind can be radically different, can be evolving for the better. The Holy Spirit is considered to be God's contribution of higher aims; thus the view of God is unitarian. Commonly they envision a time in human evolution, the human process, when God's aims will overcome evil and bring about a true community of love and peace.

So, many in Christendom are traveling the paths of a threadbare liberalism today. They will find no more vitality in their pursuits than their forebears who trod the same lanes when they had different names. Disillusioned, some of them will leave the church, others will continue to go through the motions of playing at church, and yet others will return to the authority of the Bible and its life-giving message.

Liberation Theology

A current theological movement that has arisen primarily in Latin America but has numerous North American exponents is liberation theology.[27] It originated in 1965, the year that Vatican II finished its work. At that time fifteen Roman Catholic bishops, speaking on behalf of Third World nations, affirmed that the church should unite with all the exploited in those peoples' efforts to recover their rights; that property should have a collective destiny; and that the church should not be "attached to financial imperialisms." Liberation theology endeavored to erect a system of theology based on such presuppositions.

The Peruvian theologian Gustavo Gutierrez wrote the most systematic account of the movement in his *A Theology of Liberation* (1973). As the movement has developed, it has especially attracted Roman Catholics (and some Protestants) with widely varying viewpoints on how the needs of humanity are to be met and how Scripture is to be used. Therefore it is difficult to generalize with any degree of accuracy as to what the *theologies* of liberation teach. What follows should be taken as a broad approximation of some facets of the movement; in each case there are nearly as many nuances of opinion as there are spokesmen involved.

Generally speaking, liberation theologians start with historical reality rather than with propositional truth as revealed in the Bible; and they have a tendency to find in the social sciences the tools for a construction of theology. For them the most important reality of life, especially as it is viewed in Latin America, is that humanity is oppressed and in need of liberation. The oppression is analyzed in Marxist terms, as resulting from the vested interests of capitalist power structures. At least most of the leading spokesmen believe existing structures must be destroyed in order to free humanity. A primary duty of the church must be to promote social and economic justice.

Liberation theology's view of human nature normally is rather optimistic; human beings are thought of as capable of improving society and are not considered to be as sinful as the Bible says they are. The attention to salvation from political, social, and economic oppression causes these thinkers to ignore the need for spiritual salvation and release from bondage of sin. Frequently salvation is viewed as a collective matter, concerning the whole of society instead of the individual. Liberation theologians place heavy emphasis on the Bible's teaching concerning the poor, which they commonly conclude refers to the economically poor. And they tend to ignore the religiously or spiritually poor, which includes all mankind. The positive uses of suffering and suffering as judgment are largely overlooked in the rush to eliminate all suffering.

The supernatural gets short shrift in liberation theology. The ministry of the Holy Spirit, prayer, and pietistic concerns generally are incidental. In the hands of most liberation theologians the Bible no longer is a fixed absolute from which flow the truths concerning salvation and Christian conduct. The place of the church in the life of the believer is ignored or marginalized. Jesus as teacher and messiah (small *m*) often is presented as a violent reactor to all forms of social and political oppression, and appears more in the role of a Judas Maccabeus than the ruler of a new spiritual kingdom.

Liberation theology has an anti-American bias and almost seems to conclude that the United States cannot do anything right, even though Americans help feed two-thirds of the world and are still considered by many of the world's oppressed and poor as the greatest hope for relief. Most of the world's oppressed would favorably entertain the thought of moving to the United States if that were possible.

Liberation theology tends to be blind to bondage and oppression anywhere except in Central and South America; it needs to be more ecumenical in its humanistic sympathy. It has commonly ignored victims of Soviet and Eastern European oppression, Cuban exiles, and black victims of black dictators in Africa because by definition socialist countries cannot oppress. Moreover, the selective thinking of liberation theologians leads many of them to adopt an idealized vision of Marxism that ignores the weaknesses or failures of Marxist economic systems.

Liberation theologians generally see poverty as produced by exploitation, which comes from local and international capitalism. Multinational corporations often bear the brunt of the attack. The solution to the problem commonly is thought to be overthrow of the economic system. Normally there is no patience with technocrats who argue that the real problem is lack of education or managerial skill, the lack of productivity, or the lack of capital. Without a knowledge of history, liberation theologians blame capitalism for a situation created by Spanish and Portuguese feudal economic and social systems erected at the time of colonization—long before the impact of capitalism.

Evangelicals worry that liberation theology tends to desupernaturalize the Bible, to politicize Christ, to ignore the need for personal and spiritual salvation, to present a slightly spiritualized Marxism, and merely to recast the old social gospel in a new form. They observe that if all the social and economic ills of Latin America were solved without proper attention to spiritual needs, the region would be no better off spiritually than it is now; life involves more than social and political freedom and two cars in every garage. Moreover, patriotic Americans find its anti-American bias distasteful.

In short, liberation theology has endorsed four basic positions:

- a Marxian class struggle analysis
- a condemnation of private property
- an endorsement of violent revolution
- the ability of the "new man" to redeem himself

Marxism has fallen into disfavor in Europe and almost everywhere else except in China and neighboring states. A democratic spirit has swept across Latin America and numerous democratically elected governments have been installed. At the same time, an evangelical movement has pulled masses of people out of the Roman Catholic churches and established them in a variety of Protestant fellowships, reducing the power base of the

Roman Catholic liberation theologians. There does seem to be a way of modifying the economy and government of Latin America short of the violent revolution that Marxism and liberation theology have advocated. Liberation theology appears to be at a crossroads today. A democratic evangelical alternative that is moving among the masses provides a powerful antidote to liberation theology.

As implied in the earlier discussion of Pentecostal advances in Latin America, there is a tendency for evangelicals in Latin America to ignore the debates and appeals of Liberation Theologinas (largely in the Catholic churches). They emphasize the need for conversion, the need to evangelize, and the need for the brothers and sisters to look out for one another in the churches. Thus churches may provide what amounts to employment offices, food pantries, or clothes rooms where the needs of members may be met. In their affort to meet social concerns they tend to sidestep the debate over economics and social philosophy.

Black Theology

Like Latin American liberation theologians, many black theologians believe that Christianity demands engaging in the struggle for political, economic, and racial equality. But the Black Theology movement had its roots especially in the response of North American black church leaders to the civil rights movement in the 1960s. Black Theology got its earliest definition from James H. Cone in *Black Theology and Black Power* (1969). To him Black Theology was the religious counterpart of the secular term *Black Power*. Proponents of Black Theology accept the traditional Christian belief in Jesus as the

Redeemer but believe that His message to His followers today is one of freedom from oppression. They also believe that blacks by pressing their claims for equality can redeem white Christianity from its sins of racial prejudice and economic exploitation. Black Theology rejects the notion that Christianity is the white man's religion, as held by Malcolm X and black nationalists, but holds that Black Power "*is* the Gospel of Jesus Christ" (Cone).

Black theology involves a black reading of Scripture and a black view of Christ as the liberator of black people. Black people read the Scripture different from their white oppressors and therefore did not as slaves reject Christ and the gospel. They find in the Jesus of the Black Gospel the liberator denied them by white Christians. A voice in the Black Theology movement more moderate or more cautious than that of Cone is J. Deotis Roberts of Eastern Baptist Seminary in Philadelphia, author of *Liberation and Reconciliation: A Black Theology* (1971).[28]

Black theologians have recently been reaching out to black women and South Africans and to the people in the pews. To too large a degree in earlier years theirs was a theology of the classroom. Currently, there is some tension in the Black Theology movement; some in black Pentecostalism criticize Black Theology for playing down the role of the Holy Spirit in the world. A conference on Black Theology met at Riverside Church in New York in October 1989, with 300 theologians and pastors in attendance. One concern of the conference was to bring the Black theology of the classroom to the pews of the black churches.

THIRTY-SEVEN

The Challenge Before the Church

NOW we return to the question raised at the beginning of chapter 28. How does the church stand on the threshold of the twenty-first century? It depends on whether one wants to look at the glass as half full or half empty—as an optimist or a pessimist. Much discussed in Part VII should encourage us:

- Christianity is on the march in Latin America, Africa, Korea, and elsewhere.
- A host of ministries report phenomenal success.
- Eastern Europe, not privileged to benefit from the Reformation, is seeing new life.
- Christian global broadcasting effort reaches into most of the unreached parts of the world.
- The Christian population of the world is the largest it has ever been; in fact, someone has calculated that there are as many Christians alive in the world today as in all the other periods of church history put together.
- And the total number of Christians is not only larger but is a growing percentage of the world population. The world population is estimated to have been 34.4 percent Christian in 1900. That percentage slowly declined to 32.8 percent in 1980, rose to about 33.3 percent in 1991, and is expected to top 34 percent in the year 2000.

Moreover, the unevangelized population of the world is constantly dropping in numbers and is expected to fall to about one billion in the year 2000.

But what about the glass half empty? The task before the church is herculean.

- Only 33 percent of the population of the globe can be called Christian in any sense of the term, and only part of that is evangelical.
- Over half of the population of the world lives in countries where normal missionary work cannot be conducted. Areas that are open to missions are in dire straits spiritually. For example, Greater Europe Mission estimates that there are 250,000 towns, cities, and villages in Europe that do not have a gospel preaching church. Western Europe generally has little interest in the gospel.

And other challenges call for renewed evangelical commitment:

Biblical Illiteracy

In the United States, all across the land, there is mounting concern over biblical illiteracy. Even the evangelical churches stress little teaching of biblical factual or doctrinal content. Publishers complain that it is increasingly hard to sell commentaries or most other books of an instructional nature. People want inspirational or self-help or problem-solving types of literature. Most of the Christian colleges have cut their Bible or religion requirements drastically, often requiring only some kind of introduction to Christianity or comparative religion course. The Christian public is not getting enough exposure to biblical content or doctrinal understanding or ethical principles to stand on their own two feet when faced with questions of how to live or how to deal with cults or non-Christian religions. An example of how bad things are comes from a Gallup poll in 1988 when three in ten teens did not know why Easter is celebrated—even among those who attend religious services regularly.

Breakdown of Values

Moreover, there is a breakdown of moral and ethical values across the nation. Our school systems generally no longer teach values. Churches are not working hard enough at the task. Even evangelical Christians increasingly do not live lifestyles consistent with the doctrinal positions they profess. Periodically corporate leaders hold meetings in which they report a rapid erosion of moral and ethical values in American businesses. Because of a widespread lack of honesty, fairness, reliability, and responsibility within their corporations, they worry about lawsuits, instability, and erosion of respect for business as a profession.

The Problem of Suffering

Finally, if the church expects to be heard in the present and the future, it will have to come to grips with human suffering even more than it has in recent years. More than half of the world's population lives in countries where the per capita income is less than 500 American dollars per year. Most people in the former Soviet Union, China, and India live on less than a dollar a day. Most of Sub-Saharan Africa has a per capita income of 300 dollars per year or less. Bread for the World (Washington, D.C.) in 1992 said that fully one billion people, 20 percent of the world's population, live in households too poor to obtain an adequate diet for an active work life. This of course saps the energy from church members and evangelists alike. Armed conflict in many places around the world, recurrent droughts, and largely non-existent educational opportunities in many places compound the human misery index.

Then there is the worldwide problem of the cities with untold millions living/existing in incredibly squalid conditions in shanty towns around their perimeters, in garbage dumps, and even cemeteries. Worse is the plight of the homeless, and worse yet the indescribable plight of the children. World Vision estimates that 100 million children are now living, working, and dying on the streets of the world's cities, and their number is expected to double by the year 2000. In New York about 16,000 children are living on the streets. A 1990 survey conducted by the Welfare Department of the West Bengal State Government and the UN Children's Fund determined that Calcutta now has 70,000 street children. World Vision reports that there are 700,000 street children in Sao Paulo, Brazil. One estimate puts the total number of street children in Brazil at 7,000,000. And the reports go on and on. Homeless children learn to scavenge through trash, beg, steal, sell drugs, and prostitute for food. And among them AIDS is beginning to spread.

The staggering figures of people in need often numb us and lead us to conclude that we can do nothing. But we can do something. Nurses, doctors, public health personnel, and teachers can make a difference in the Third World. Craftsmen of all kinds can teach trades to Third World people. Agricultural missionaries can help the farmers of the world produce more and better food-stuffs. Business people could help nationals set up small businesses that would provide employment for church members and an economic base to help support missionary and social agencies. Business people or others could also try to develop inexpensive means of processing soybeans and thus provide a protein supply for the vast tsetse-infested regions of Africa where cattle cannot be raised. These are only a few examples of what Christians of the more developed world might do for the Third World.

As we look out on our world with its physical, material, and spiritual need, many in the American evangelical camp must realize that they have become too insulated by a comfortable orthodoxy. The growing respectability of evangelical Christianity and the effects of materialism have lulled a host of them into a lethargic state. A large percentage of evangelicals have too little spiritual power and too little impact for good on the society around them. In the midst of moral and social decay, they provide too little salt with its preservative quality or too little of the light of the gospel. And in a land surfeited with biblical literature of all kinds, ignorance of the Word of God is abysmal. There seems to be far too little evidence of the power of the gospel to affect life-style. Alcoholism, an increasing divorce rate, and other social evils plague the church as they do society in general. There is little individual concern for living a holy life. Thus the church utters a muffled or uncertain sound, instead of a clear and prophetic voice to a confused and dying world. It is time for an agonizing reappraisal. It is time for the church of Jesus Christ to be up and doing.

Endnotes

PART I

1. Helpful discussion on the resurrection appears in William Milligan, *The Resurrection of our Lord* (London: Macmillan, 1890); Grant R. Osborne, *The Resurrection Narratives* (Grand Rapids: Baker, 1984); and Terry L. Miethe, ed., *Did Jesus Rise from the Dead?* (New York: Harper & Row, 1987).

2. Admittedly not all agree that the church originated at Pentecost. But note that individuals become members of the church by means of the baptism of the Holy Spirit, which joins them to the mystical Body of Christ (1 Cor. 12:13 ff.). The baptism of the Holy Spirit was future in the gospels (Matt. 3:11; Mark 1:8; Luke 3:16; John 1:33; cf. Matt. 16:18) and in Acts 1:5, which states that the event would occur "not many days from now." It is past in Acts 11:15-16. Where else could one logically begin the baptism than at Pentecost? If the beginning of the baptism of the Holy Spirit, by which one becomes a member of the church, occurred at Pentecost, the church must have begun there.

3. An especially useful book among the more recent publications on the earliest days of the church is Everett F. Harrison, *The Apostolic Church* (Grand Rapids: Eerdmans, 1985); an older excellent work is F. F. Bruce, *The Spreading Flame* (Grand Rapids: Eerdmans, 1953).

4. If India was evangelized during the first century, it is entirely reasonable to suppose that believers also reached China with the Christian message. Contacts between China and India were extensive at that time. Furthermore, Roman subjects traded directly with India and through middlemen with China during the first and second centuries after Christ. Since ideas flow along the arteries of trade, it is possible that the gospel reached the Far East in this way.

There is also evidence that the Christian message appeared in Britain in the first century. On the general question of the spread of the gospel over the Roman Empire, remember that many lands were represented at Pentecost: Parthia, Media,

Elam, Mesopotamia, Judea, Cappadocia, Pontus, Asia, Phrygia, Pamphylia, Egypt, Libya, Rome, Crete, and Arabia (Acts 2:9-11). Certainly these converts would witness of Christ upon return to their homelands. Also, Paul and others ministered in cities having a large percentage of transient people, e.g., Corinth, Ephesus, and Antioch.

5.   William Hendriksen, *Colossians and Philemon* (Grand Rapids: Baker, 1964), 51.

PART II

1.   Some have thought he may have been the Clement referred to in Philippians 4:3 (evidently written from Rome), others that he may have been an ex-slave of the family of Titus Flavius Clemens, cousin of the Emperor Domitian. One tradition claims that he was the second bishop of Rome, immediately after the apostle Peter; another tradition indicates that two bishops served between Peter and Clement. He is an important witness to the canon of the New Testament, alluding to 1 Corinthians, Matthew, Mark, Luke, Acts, Romans, Galatians, Ephesians, Philippians, 1 Timothy, Titus, Hebrews, and 1 Peter.

2.   *Apology* in its basic meaning signifies "defense"; it is so used by the Apologists. The fact that the word has taken on the connotation of "making excuse" should not confuse the reader.

3.   See chap. 7. An important new book on Gnosticism is Giovanni Filoramo, *A History of Gnosticism* (Oxford: Basil Blackwell, 1990).

4.   Jacques Le Goff, *The Birth of Purgatory* (Chicago: University of Chicago Press, 1984), 52.

5.   Henri Crouzel is acknowledged as the foremost contemporary Origen scholar. He has written eleven books on Origen, including his *Origen*, translated by A. S. Worrall (New York: Harper & Row, 1989).

   To check out the influence of Philo, see *The Works of Philo Complete and Unabridged*, Trans. by C.D. Young (Peabody, MA; Hendrickson, 1993)

6.   Le Goff lists Origen with Clement of Alexandria as co-"inventors" of Purgatory, *Loc. cit.*

7. See Crouzel, 54-55.

8. Eusebius of Caesarea lived about 260-341 and composed a church history that serves as a mine of information about the early church. Although it is not a great literary work or a well-balanced work (the writer's meager knowledge of Latin prevented him from knowing much about the Western church), the *Ecclesiastical History* does provide a great deal of information that otherwise would be lost. His testimony concerning the canon is particularly valuable.

9. E. E. Ryden, *The Story of Christian Hymnody* (Rock Island, IL: Augustana Press, 1961), 19.

10. *Confessions,* Book IX, Chap.6

11. Some of Ambrose's hymns appear in F. Forrester Church and Terrance J. Mulry, *The Macmillan Book of Earliest Christian Hymns* (New York: Macmillan, 1988). As the title implies, the book includes even earlier hymns, such as those by Ignatius, Hippolytus, and Clement of Alexandria.

12. Vernon J. Bourke, *The Essential Augustine* (Indianapolis: Hackett Publishing Co., 1974), is still in print. Two good biographical studies of St. Augustine are Peter Brown, *Augustine of Hippo* (New York: Dorset, 1967); and Frederic Van der Meer, *Augustine the Bishop* (London: Sheed & Ward, 1961).

13. For documentation, see Tacitus, *Annales,* xv. 44.

14. Pliny the Younger, *Epistles,* 10:96, 97.

15. Justin Martyr, *Second Apology,* 68.

16. The Nag Hammadi texts are available in *The Nag Hammadi Library in English,* ed. James M. Robinson, Rev. Ed. (San Francisco: Harper, 1988; paperback ed., 1990).

17. At first readings were taken from the Old Testament only. Later they were chosen from the "Memoirs of the Apostles." The fact that Judaism had formed an Old Testament canon was important for establishing the principle of canonicity that would lead eventually to a New Testament canon.

18. Marcion was a native of Asia Minor; there his own father, a bishop, condemned him as a heretic. Thereafter, he went to Rome and established separatist congregations with views vaguely similar to those of the Gnostics.

19. The trend is to increasingly earlier dates for composi-

tion of New Testament books, even in liberal circles. As an example of what is happening, the Anglican bishop John A. T. Robinson of Trinity College, Cambridge, has radically altered his previous position and has gone so far as to insist that all New Testament books were written between A.D. 47 and 70 (*Can We Trust the New Testament?* [Grand Rapids: Eerdmans, 1977], 63). Archaeological evidence for the dating of New Testament books comes especially from the Egyptian papyri, which show that the vocabulary and grammar of the New Testament date from the first century A.D. See, e.g., Millar Burrows, *What Mean These Stones?* (New York: Meridian, 1957), 53-54.

20. For a discussion of New Testament canonicity, see especially F. F. Bruce, *The Canon of Scripture* (Downers Grove, IL: InterVarsity Press, 1988); Everett F. Harrison, *Introduction to the New Testament*, Rev. Ed. (Grand Rapids: Eerdmans, 1971), Part IV; Henry C. Thiessen, *Introduction to the New Testament* (Grand Rapids: Eerdmans, 1948), Chap. 1.

21. For a useful discussion of Pelagian and Augustinian views, see Otto W. Heick, *A History of Christian Thought* (Philadelphia: Fortress Press, 1965), I, 196-206.

PART III

1. See, e.g., *Epistle to the Smyrnaeans*, viii.

2. J. Stevenson, ed., *Creeds, Councils, and Controversies* (London: S.P.C.K., 1972), 148.

3. That is, they followed the teachings of Arius, condemned at the Council of Nicea in 325 (see chap. 9).

4. The Third Council of Toledo in 589 declared Roman Catholicism to be the official religion of his kingdom.

5. One of the finest studies on Gregory is Carole Straw's *Gregory the Great* (Berkeley: University of California Press, 1988).

6. Monasticism, with its ascetic approach to life, arose very early in the East, where its adherents generally lived a hermitic existence. Basil of Caesarea developed the movement on more of a community or communal basis during the fourth century, and about the same time the great Athanasius introduced it to the West. But it was St. Benedict of Nursia or

Norcia in central Italy (c. 500), who was responsible for the general monastic rule of poverty, chastity, and obedience and the type of monasticism that grew up in western Europe—a type that was more productive and practical than that of the East.

7.   R. P. C. Hanson, *The Life and Writings of the Historical Saint Patrick* (New York: The Seabury Press, 1983), 19-25. Hanson deals effectively with numerous questions concerning the life and ministry of St. Patrick. See also E. A. Thompson, *Who Was Saint Patrick* (New York: St. Martin's Press, 1985).

8.   At Clonard, about thirty miles northwest of Dublin, the monastery grew to a large community, numbering its members, scholars and students in the thousands (Máire and Liam de Paor, *Early Christian Ireland* [New York: Frederick A. Praeger, 1958], 52).

9.   For some useful books on Islam, see bibliography at the end of this book.

10.   Name applied to the eastern part of the Roman Empire, which became essentially Greek after the fall of the West to the barbarians.

11.   For an up-to-date evaluation of the Bede, see Benedicta Ward, *The Venerable Bede* (London: Cassell Publishers Limited, 1990). See also, D. H. Farmer, ed., *The Age of Bede*, rev. ed. (London: Penguin Books, 1988).

12.   For a study on the early history of the Papal State, see Thomas F. X. Noble, *The Republic of St. Peter; The Birth of the Papal State, 680-825* (Philadelphia: University of Pennsylvania Press, 1984).

13.   It is significant to note that King John's humiliation at the hands of Innocent, as well as his military defeats in France, put him in such a weakened position at home that he was unable to stand against his rebellious barons, and he was forced to sign the Magna Carta in 1215. The great charter granted certain rights and liberties to all freemen of England.

14.   A sect with doctrines akin to Gnosticism and Manicheism of the early church. The Roman church launched a crusade against the Albigensians in southern France and virtually exterminated them in a terrible blood bath. See Jacques Madaule, *The Albigensian Crusade* (London: Burns & Oates,

1967); Zoé Oldenbourg, *Massacre at Montségur* (New York: Dorset Press, 1961); and especially Joseph R. Strayer, *The Albigensian Crusades*, revised edition (Ann Arbor: University of Michigan Press, 1993).

15.   Especially the philosophy of Aristotle and the theology of St. Augustine. Very useful is Etienne Gilson, trans., *The Philosophy of St. Thomas Aquinas* (New York: Dorset Press, n.d.). A modern translation and condensation of Thomas Aquinas's theology is now available in paperback: Timothy McDermott, ed., *Summa Theologiae, A Concise Translation* (Westminster, MD: Christian Classics, 1991).

16.   A useful introduction to the thought of Bernard is Gillian R. Evans, trans., *Bernard of Clairvaux: Selected Works* (New York: Paulist Press, 1987).

17.   Rome was not always the tranquil place some have envisioned it. During the two centuries prior to 1305 the popes had spent more than half of their time outside the city because of internal unrest or outside interference. In fact, it was Cardinal Albornoz's pacification of the Papal States that led Gregory XI to conclude that Rome was safe enough to return in 1377 and end the Babylonian Captivity.

18.   An interesting portrayal of the period appears in Marzieh Gail, *Avignon in Flower* (London: Victor Gollancz, 1966).

19.   The paganization of the papacy also involved such unreligious activities as the raising of armies and military action. Julius was part of the effort to turn back the armies of Louis XII of France, who sought to expand into Italy. While no effort has been made to catalog the seamy side of the lives of the popes, Julius was also a very sensual man, having fathered three daughters while a cardinal. A significant and insightful book on humanism in Rome between about 1420 and 1527 is John F. D'Amico, *Renaissance Humanism in Papal Rome*.

PART IV

1.   See Matthew Spinka, *John Hus' Concept of the Church* (Princeton: Princeton University Press, 1966).

2.   What apparently happened is this. Hus entered Con-

stance early in November 1414, alone and defenseless. The emperor Sigismund arrived on Christmas night. By that time Pope John XXIII had ordered Hus's arrest and had imprisoned him. After several stormy sessions with the pope over the treatment of Hus, without success, the emperor finally capitulated to the seemingly inevitable (Matthew Spinka, *John Hus* (Princeton: Princeton University Press, 1968), 230-37.

3. A book that helps to recreate effectively the activities of Savonarola in the context of his times is Rachel Erlanger, *The Unarmed Prophet: Savonarola in Florence* (New York: McGraw-Hill, 1988).

4. Two especially useful books on this new piety are John Van Engen, trans, *Devotio Moderna* (New York: Paulist Press, 1988), and Oliver Davies, *God Within: The Mystical Tradition in Northern Europe* (New York: Paulist Press, 1988).

5. When Constantinople fell to the Muslim Turks, the center of power of the old Eastern Orthodox church was destroyed. Thereafter, the Orthodox church eventually broke up into national churches: Russian Orthodox, Hellenic Orthodox, Serbian Orthodox, Syrian Orthodox, etc. These national churches do not differ appreciably in theology and liturgy.

6. The development of printing with movable type occurred in Mainz (now Germany) about 1450. Several individuals had a part in the process but paramount among them was Johann Gutenberg. Other important contributors include Johann Fust and Peter Schöffer.

7. Two of the best newer biographies of Luther are James M. Kittelson, *Luther the Reformer* (Minneapolis: Augsburg Publishing House, 1986); and Heiko A. Oberman, *Luther: Man between God and the Devil* (New Haven: Yale, 1989). A good biography by an East German scholar is Gerhard Brendler, *Martin Luther* (New York: Oxford, 1991). Three good older biographies are James Atkinson, *Martin Luther and the Birth of Protestantism* (Baltimore: Penguin Books, 1968); H. G. Haile, *Luther, An Experiment in Biography* (Garden City, NY: Doubleday and Company, 1980); and Gerhard Ritter, *Luther* (New York: Harper & Row, 1963). A record of his struggle with the papacy appears in Scott H. Hendrix, *Luther and the Papacy* (Philadelphia: Fortress, 1981). Paul Althaus has

provided a definitive statement of his theology in *The Theology of Martin Luther* (Philadelphia: Fortress, 1966). While Luther was a prolific writer, Timothy F. Lull has edited a very useful paperback collection of his theological writings (755 pages), *Martin Luther's Basic Theological Writings* (Minneapolis: Fortress, 1989).

8. The probable date was 1483, on November 10, but Luther himself once gave the year as 1484.

9. The first German university, founded 1379.

10. An evangelical, Staupitz almost became a Reformer but died as a faithful son of the Roman church in 1524. If he had lived longer, he might have made the break later, when Saxony became more strongly Lutheran.

11. Scholars have been unable to date this event precisely. Probably it came during 1515 when he was lecturing on the early chapters of Romans.

12. Evidently Luther intended that the theses should be debated by the theological community at Wittenberg; they were posted in Latin, not German. Moreover, the door of Castle Church served as something of a bulletin board for the university.

13. Luther used Erasmus's Greek Testament of 1516, the first printed Greek Testament, for his New Testament translation work. Later, with the help of others, he translated the Old Testament. Luther's German Bible, because if its widespread use, was very significant in standardizing the German language, which at the time was spoken and written in many local dialects. Luther became to German what Dante was to Italian and what, to a degree, Wycliffe and Calvin were to English and French respectively.

14. See Jean Rilliet, *Zwingli: Third Man of the Reformation* (Philadelphia: Westminster, 1964); Ulrich Gäbler, *Huldrych Zwingli*, trans. by Ruth C. L. Gritsch (Philadelphia: Fortress Press, 1986); W. P. Stephens, *The Theology of Huldrych Zwingli* (Oxford: Clarendon Press, 1986); S. M. Jackson, ed., *Ulrich Zwingli, Selected Works* (Philadelphia: University of Pennsylvania Press, 1972); Charles Garside, *Zwingli and the Arts* (New Haven: Yale, 1966). Zwingli had a restricted view of the arts, essentially denying validity of whatever the Scripture did not

specifically sanction, while Luther admitted whatever Scripture did not specifically deny.

15. See J. Wayne Baker, *Heinrich Bullinger and the Covenant* (Athens, Ohio: Ohio University Press, 1980).

16. Especially useful books on the Anabaptists include George H. Williams and A. M. Mergal, ed., *Spiritual and Anabaptist Writers* (Philadelphia: Westminster, 1957); George H. Williams, *The Radical Reformation* (Philadelphia: Westminster, 1962); Cornelius Krahn, *Dutch Anabaptism* (The Hague: Martinus Nijhoff, 1968); A. L. E. Verheyden, *Anabaptism in Flanders 1530-1650* (Scottdale, Pa.: Herald Press, 1961), and J. K. Zeman, *The Anabaptists and the Czech Brethren in Moravia 1526-1628* (The Hague: Mouton, 1969).

17. Two new biographies of Calvin are William J. Bouwsma, *John Calvin* (New York: Oxford University Press, 1988) and Ronald S. Wallace, *Calvin, Geneva and the Reformation* (Grand Rapids: Baker, 1988). An older useful biography is Emanuel Stickelberger, *John Calvin* (Cambridge: James Clarke & Co., 1959). An important book on Calvinism as a movement is John T. McNeill, *The History and Character of Calvinism* (Oxford: Oxford University Press, 1954). Calvin's influence is well described in W. Stanford Reid, ed., *John Calvin: His Influence in the Western World* (Grand Rapids: Zondervan, 1982). A useful book on his years in Geneva is E. William Monter, *Calvin's Geneva* (New York: John Wiley & Sons, 1967).

18. Lewis W. Spitz, *The Protestant Reformation* (New York: Harper & Row, 1985), 213.

19. For a study of the Reformation in Strasbourg, see Miriam U. Chrisman, *Strasbourg and the Reform* (New Haven: Yale University Press, 1967); Lorna Jane Abray, *The People's Reformation* (Ithaca, New York: Cornell University Press, 1985).

20. Puritanism in America adopted the Congregational form of church government, but retained Calvinistic theology.

21. J. E. Neale, *The Age of Catherine de Medici* (New York: Harper & Row, 1962) is especially helpful in unscrambling the extremely complicated story of French affairs at the height of the Reformation there.

22. Although the French Reformation became essentially Calvinistic in character, evidently that is not the way it began, because the Protestant movement had a good start at the time of Calvin's conversion. Lutheran writings had been widely distributed in the country, and there is growing evidence of indigenous aspects of the movement, in part rising out of humanist seed-plots.

23. Richard S. Dunn, *The Age of Religious Wars, 1559-1715*, 2nd ed. (New York: W. W. Norton & Co., 1970), 33.

24. Though "Roman Catholic versus Protestant" is a convenient way of describing the so-called religious wars of the last half of the sixteenth century, it is evidently not strictly accurate. Commonly the battle raged for political or social reasons, as indicated above. More than once a Protestant group and a Roman Catholic group joined hands against another Roman Catholic group. And Protestant Henry of Navarre (later Henry IV) rose to power in part through the efforts of Politiques, liberal Roman Catholics who served loyally in his army. It must be recognized that people have economic, social, political, and cultural interests as well as religious interests. Rarely does one set of concerns motivate to the exclusion of all others.

25. See Patrick Collinson, *The Elizabethan Puritan Movement* (Oxford: Clarendon Press, 1967); paperback edition, 1990); D. Martyn Lloyd-Jones, *The Puritans: Their Origins and Successors* (Edinburgh: Banner of Truth Trust, 1987).

26. For a useful sketch of Baptist origins, see H. Leon McBeth, *The Baptist Heritage* (Nashville: Broadman Press, 1987), Chap. 1.

27. James VI of Scotland was the son of Mary Stuart (Mary Queen of Scots), who was the daughter of James V. James V was the son of James IV and Margaret Tudor, sister of Henry VIII and daughter of Henry VII. When the Tudor line in England came to an end with the death of Elizabeth, James VI of Scotland was now heir to the throne of England as well as that of Scotland. Because his mother was a Stuart, the Stuart line now came to rule England.

28. The English civil war was not merely a religious squabble between Puritans and Anglicans, but a struggle between

social, political, and economic groupings in which religion played a part.

29.   See Ian B. Cowan, *The Scottish Reformation* (London: Weidenfeld and Nicolson, 1982); A. M. Renwick, *The Story of the Scottish Reformation* (Grand Rapids: Eerdmans, 1960); Jasper Ridley, *John Knox* (New York: Oxford University Press, 1968); J. D. Mackie, *A History of Scotland*, 2nd ed. (New York: Dorset Press, 1978).

30.   The fuller title is *History of the Reformation of Religion Within the Realm of Scotland.* In a polemical era characterized by very partisan literature that often distorted the truth, Knox's work stands out as a good piece of historical writing and a valuable source of information about the times.

31.   See Peter Geyl, *The Revolt of the Netherlands, 1555-1609*, 2nd ed. (New York: Barnes & Noble Imports, 1980); Noel G. Parker, *The Dutch Revolt* (Ithaca, NY: Cornell, University Press, 1977).

32.   Marvin R. O'Connell, *The Counter Reformation* (New York: Harper & Row, 1974; Anthony D. Wright, *The Counter-Reformation* (New York: St. Martin's Press, 1982).

33.   An authoritative history of the Jesuits is J. C. H. Aveling, *The Jesuits* (New York: Dorset Press, 1981). A recent biography of Loyola is Philip Caraman, *Ignatius Loyola* (San Francisco: Harper & Row, 1990). George E. Ganss has edited an important compendium of Ignatius' works and provided a brief biography in *Ignatius of Loyola: Spiritual Exercises and Selected Works* (Mahwah, N.J.: Paulist Press, 1991).

34.   This development was also part of pre-Reformation stirrings in the Roman Church, as noted earlier.

35.   Among the more useful books on the Thirty Years War are C. V. Wedgewood, *The Thirty Years War* (Baltimore: Penguin, 1938); Georges Pagès, *The Thirty Years War* (New York: Harper & Row, 1970); Theodore K. Rabb, *The Thirty Years War* (Lanham, Md: University Press of America, 1981); Geoffrey Parker, *The Thirty Years War*, 2nd ed. (London: Routledge & Kegan Paul, 1987); and Henrik Tikkamen, *The Thirty Years War* (Lincoln: University of Nebraska Press, 1987).

36.   While the destruction and loss of life were terrible,

recent research has revised casualty figures downward. Though it is true that some German towns at the end of the war were only a fraction of their pre-war size, it is now clear that disease, starvation and war casualties were not always the reason. Sometimes large numbers of people simply fled a battle area and did not return years later when it was possible to do so.

PART V

1.　E. E. Ryden, *The Story of Christian Hymnody* (Rock Island, IL: Augustana Press, 1959), 140.

2.　A new biography of John Wesley is Henry D. Rack, *Reasonable Enthusiast: John Wesley and the Rise of Methodism* (Philadelphia: Trinity Press International, 1989). A useful collection of John Wesley's writings that reveal his person and his theology is Albert C. Outler, ed., *John Wesley* (New York: Oxford University Press, 1964). A perceptive selection of the writings of John Wesley and his translation of some German hymns, and a collection of Charles Wesley's hymns, may be found in Frank Whaling, *John and Charles Wesley* (New York: Paulist Press, 1981). A recent biography of Charles Wesley is Arnold A. Dallimore, *A Heart Set Fire* (Westchester, IL: Crossway Books, 1988). Older biographies include Frederick C. Gill, *Charles Wesley, The First Methodist* (New York: Abingdon Press, 1964); and Charles Wesley Flint, *Charles Wesley and His Colleagues* (Washington: Public Affairs Press, 1957).

3.　Arnold A. Dallimore is one of the more recent biographers of Whitefield. In 1980 he published his two volume *George Whitefield* (London: Banner of Truth) and in 1990, George Whitefield: *God's Anointed Servant in the Great Revival of the Eighteenth Century* (Wheaton, Il: Good News). A few years earlier John Pollock wrote *George Whitefield and the Great Awakening* (London: Hodder & Stoughton, 1973). An older definitive work is Luke Tyerman, *The Life of the Reverend George Whitefield*, 2 vols. (London: Hodder & Stoughton, 1876). A primary source on Whitefield is *George Whitefield's Journals* (London: Banner of Truth, 1960).

4.　Figures vary on the number of hymns that Charles Wesley wrote. The figure of 7,270 hymns is accepted in some circles; others use a total of 6,500. Another compilation gives him credit for about 9,000 poems, not all of which were hymns. Perhaps his three best known or most highly rated hymns are "Hark! The Herald Angels Sing," "Love Divine, All Loves Excelling," and "Jesus, Lover of My Soul." John Wesley also wrote a few hymns but is better known for his translations of some of the outstanding German hymns. The preaching of John Wesley could not have been so successful without the hymns of his brother Charles, which sung the gospel into the hearts of the masses. Contemporary with Charles Wesley was another great hymn writer, Isaac Watts (1674-1748), who is often called the "Father of English Hymnody." He is credited with about 600 hymns. John Newton (1725-1807) began his hymn-writing ministry as Wesley was passing off the scene.

Other great composers of church music of the century include Johann Sebastian Bach (1687-1750), George Frideric Handel (1685-1759) and Franz Joseph Haydn (1732-1809). Bach stands apart as the greatest composer of church music of the century. The list of his organ and choral works composed in Leipzig is long indeed. Handel, born in the Pietistic center of Halle, migrated to England, where he made his greatest contribution, including his magnificent oratorios, of which *The Messiah* is the best known. He was a friend of the Wesleys. To be sure, Haydn wrote many symphonies, but he composed at least a dozen Masses, a setting of *The Seven Last Words*, and is especially known for his oratorio *The Creation*.

5.   The significance of Methodism for English social and political development is detailed in J. Wesley Bready's *This Freedom Whence?* and *England Before and After Wesley*. Bready believed that the Wesleyan revival helped spare England from going through the upheaval that France suffered during the French Revolution. Though these books have been attacked, much of what they say about the contribution of Methodism is valid. The latter is especially useful.

6.   This evangelical party is known as the Low Church party. There is in the Anglican church also a High Church party, Anglo-Catholic in sentiment, and the Broad Church party, which seeks to take the middle way of compromise and make Anglicanism the church of the nation. For a study of the

impact of this revival, see Earle E. Cairns, *Saints and Society* (Chicago: Moody Press, 1960).

7.   Robert Raikes (1735-1811) is commonly given credit for launching the Sunday school, which taught neglected children reading and writing and provided Bible instruction. Actually Thomas Stock (1749-1803) started a Sunday school in Ashbury, Berkshire, England, which influenced Raikes to start one in Gloucester in 1780. The movement then expanded rapidly; a London society for establishing Sunday schools was founded in 1785, and the movement took off from there. Raikes never claimed to be the movement's founder. When the Sunday School Union was established in 1803, hundreds of thousands of children were enrolled in schools all over Great Britain.

8.   This view seems to be rather pro-British, however. The Movavians were very missionary minded from the beginning. They founded their missionary society in 1732 and had 165 missionaries in non-Christian lands when Carey went to India (Ryden, *op. cit.*, 140).

9.   Important to the success of Moody's ministry was the gospel song, especially the ones composed by Fanny Crosby. This blind poetess is credited with about 9,000 gospel songs, which have been sung all over the world. The list of favorites is long, including "Rescue the Perishing," "Draw Me Nearer," "Safe in the Arms of Jesus," "Saved by Grace," and "To God Be the Glory." A useful survey of Fanny Crosby's life and impact is Bernard Ruffin, *Fanny Crosby* (Philadelphia: United Church Press, 1976).

PART VI

1.   See, for example, Robert H. Fuson, trans., *The Log of Christopher Columbus* (Camden, ME: International Marine Publishing Company, 1987). In an entry for Wednesday, December 26, 1492 (157), written in the New World, Columbus referred to using the profits from this venture to conquer Jerusalem and indicated that Ferdinand and Isabella were favorable to the idea.

2.   The literature on the Puritans is extensive, but five books should be especially useful. Perry Miller's *New England*

Mind From Colony to Province (Boston: Beacon Press, 1961) provides a more intellectualized view of the Puritans. Norman Pettit in *The Heart Prepared: Grace and Conversion in Puritan Spiritual Life*, 2nd ed., (Middletown, CT: Wesleyan University Press, 1989) gives something of a corrective to Perry Miller's intellectualized approach to the Puritans. J. I. Packer, *A Quest for Godliness: The Puritan View of the Christian Life* (Wheaton, IL: Crossway, 1990) sets forth their concern for holy living. Leland Ryken, *Worldly Saints: The Puritans as They Really Were* (Grand Rapids: Zondervan, 1986), presents them as real people. An excellent new survey of Puritanism is Allen Carden's *Puritan Christianity in America: Religion and Life in Seventeenth Century Massachusetts* (Grand Rapids: Baker, 1990). Carden's excellent bibliography provides ample information for anyone who wishes to study the Puritan movement further.

3. A useful discussion of the responses of various church groups in America to the Revolution, their place in the formulation of revolutionary ideology, and the place of the Revolution in the religious history of the United States appears in Mark A. Noll, *Christians in the American Revolution* (Grand Rapids: Eerdmans, 1977).

4. Whether or not one agrees that Jonathan Edwards was "America's greatest theologian," he has tremendous stature and has given rise to an extensive body of literature. Six books will help introduce one to the great revivalist and theologian: Perry Miller, *Jonathan Edwards* (New York: Meridian, 1959); Harold P. Simonson, *Jonathan Edwards, Theologian of the Heart* (Grand Rapids: Eerdmans, 1974); John H. Gerstner, *Jonathan Edwards: A Mini-Theology* (Wheaton, IL: Tyndale House, 1987); Iain H. Murray, *Jonathan Edwards: A New Biography* (Edinburgh: Banner of Truth Trust, 1987); Robert W. Jenson, *America's Theologian: A Recommendation of Jonathan Edwards* (New York: Oxford, 1988); Nathan O. Hatch, ed., *Jonathan Edwards and the American Experience* (New York: Oxford, 1989).

5. J. Edwin Orr, *The Eager Feet* (Chicago: Moody, 1975), 8.

6. Ibid., 7.

7. The outstanding recent biography of Finney is Keith J. Hardman, *Charles Grandison Finney* (Grand Rapids: Baker, 1987).

8. James F. Findlay, Jr., *Dwight L. Moody: American Evangelist, 1837-1899* (Chicago: University of Chicago, 1969) is the definitive scholarly biography of Moody. An emphasis on his evangelistic efforts appears in J. C. Pollock, *Moody: A Biographical Portrait of the Pacesetter in Modern Mass Evangelism* (New York: Macmillan, 1963). Stanley N. Gundry, *Love Them In: The Life and Theology of D. L. Moody* (Grand Rapids: Baker, 1976) overcomes some of the weaknesses of earlier biographies of Moody in dealing with Moody's theology, and provides a masterful bibliography for any wishing to study Moody further.

9. As noted in the last chapter, much of the success of Moody's campaigns must be attributed to the impact of Fanny Crosby's gospel songs.

10. The Presbyterian church underwent a schism in 1837, and the New School formed its own organization the following year. The New School (composing 4/9 of the church) was the more liberal element in doctrine and in organizational approach. After the Old and New Schools had split along sectional lines, the two southern groups united as the Presbyterian Church in the Confederate States (later Presbyterian Church in the United States) in 1864.

11. For a useful introduction to Phoebe Palmer, see Thomas C. Oden, ed., *Phoebe Palmer: Selected Writings* (New York: Paulist Press, 1988).

12. A good survey of Rauschenbusch appears in Winthrop S. Hudson, ed., *Walter Rauschenbusch: Selected Writings* (New York: Paulist Press, 1984).

13. For some of the important writings of Channing, see David Robinson, ed., *William Ellery Channing: Selected Writings* (New York: Paulist Press, 1985).

14. Bushnell is sometimes called the "Father of American Liberalism," and he is known for his reinterpretation of Reformed theology in light of the Romanticism of the early part of the nineteenth century. Conrad Cherry, ed., *Horace Bushnell:*

Sermons (New York: Paulist Press, 1985) shows in a collection of Bushnell's sermons the major tenets of his thought.

15.   Seventh-Day Adventists are now operating in over 180 countries with a total membership if 6,661,000. Membership in the United States and Canada stands at 733,000. The name "Seventh-Day Adventist" was chosen in 1860, and in 1863 the General Conference of the church was organized. Today the denomination supports in North America ten liberal arts colleges, two universities, a theological seminary and numerous other schools. Comments on Mormons and Jehovah's Witnesses appear in the next chapter. The Christian Science movement does not publish membership figures, but it is known to have declined in popularity in recent years.

PART VII

1.   The account presented in this section on The Church in The Contemporary World is based on endless contacts with church leaders all over the United States and in England, where leaders from the Continent were interviewed. Many of the statistics and other details about various ministries (e.g., Campus Crusade, Inter-Varsity, Jews for Jesus, Prison Fellowship, Evangelical Missions Information Service, and Bible distribution organizations) were obtained in oral and written statements made directly to me by the directors or other officers or statisticians of the organizations discussed. I appreciate the kind responses to many telephone calls to organizational headquarters. Denominational membership statistics, attendance records, and other pertinent facts are published annually in the *Yearbook of American and Canadian Churches, The World Almanac,* and in less detail in the Encyclopedia Britannica Book of the Year. Missions statistics appear in *Mission Handbook,* published by MARC (World Vision); the fifteenth edition came out in 1993.

2.   The total population of the earth is now set at about 5.4 billion. The Muslim population has risen to about 1 billion and the Hindu population to about 730 million. "Christian" as used in this chapter refers to all varieties of Christians, unless it is specifically used in a more restrictive sense.

3.   J. Gordon Melton, ed., *Encyclopedia of American Relig-*

ions (Detroit: Gale Research, 1989), XLIV. One should not conclude from what is said here or from popular assumptions that people coming from non-Christian lands are likely to be non-Christian. Interestingly, a City University of New York Graduate Center religious poll taken in 1991-92 revealed that of the 100,000 Asian immigrants interviewed, 50 percent were Christian.

4. Joseph does not espouse the view; he only provides an objective overview and definition of it.

5. For a more comprehensive view of the New Age Movement, see J. Gordon Melton and others, *New Age Encyclopedia* (1990). Though efforts to deal with the New Age Movement proliferate, Douglas Groothius' *Confronting the New Age* (1988) and *Revealing the New Age* (1990), and Walter Martin's *The New Age Cult* (1989) are among the more useful books on the subject.

6. *New York Times,* June 7, 1991, 18.

7. *Gallup Study on America's Youth 1977-1988* (Princeton: The Gallup Organization, 1988), 168.

8. Elizabeth F. Brown and William R. Hendee, "Adolescents and Their Music," *Journal of the American Medical Association,* September 22, 1989, 1659. This is an especially perceptive and fair article that does not claim more than the research currently demonstrates.

9. The Edinburgh Missionary Conference of 1910 led some to think of a united church, and in that year Faith and Order was organized. This society concerned itself with differences in belief among the churches. Subsequently the Life and Work Movement was founded to deal with social and political responsibilities of the churches. These organizations were involved with conferences at Lausanne in 1927 and Edinburgh in 1937; at the latter a decision was reached to form a World Council of Churches. A provisional constitution was drawn up at Utrecht in 1938, but the war prevented formal organization until the Amsterdam meeting in 1948.

10. See A. P. Flannery, ed., *Documents of Vatican II* (Grand Rapids: Eerdmans, 1975).

11. See Avery Dulles, Vatican II and the Extraordinary Synod (Collegeville, MN: The Liturgical Press, 1986). An-

other book that helps to bring the contemporary reader up to date on the Roman Catholic church is Adrian Hastings, ed., *Modern Catholicism, Vatican II and After* (New York: Oxford University Press, 1991).

12. The Congregational Church and the Christian Church merged in 1931, were joined by the Evangelical and Reformed Church in 1957, and completed their union with the adoption of a constitution for the United Church in 1961. Reported membership in 1991 was 1,583,000.

13. See also "They'd Rather Fight Than Switch," *Christianity Today,* March 5, 1990.

14. Lyle E. Schaller, "Megachurch," *Christianity Today,* March 5, 1990, 22. Schaller lists the top ten churches in terms of weekly attendance.

15. George Gallup, Jr. and Jim Castelli, *The People's Religion* (New York: Macmillan, 1989), 93.

16. Young Life, founded by Jim Rayburn in 1940, celebrated its fiftieth anniversary in San Diego in January, 1990. Currently it has an international ministry in 38 countries, with a career overseas staff of over 60. In addition it has a United States ministry staffed by 12,000 volunteers. About 50,000 young people attend Young Life meetings weekly, with another 60,000 attending camps.

17. Operation Mobilization, founded in 1957, is engaged in evangelism, church planting, literature distribution and support of national workers. Currently it has an overseas staff of 219 working in 22 countries and a home staff of 58.

18. Youth With A Mission, founded in 1960, is engaged in evangelism, relief aid, and training. One of the largest missions agencies, it has over 7,200 permanent staff members in 110 countries and almost 20,000 involved in short-term projects worldwide.

19. Pulse, Evangelical Missions Information Service, Feb. 7, 1992, 5.

20. Mission Aviation Fellowship began as Christian Airmen's Missionary Fellowship in New York, in part as an outgrowth of Jack Wyrtzen's Word of Life ministry. The following year it joined with newly-formed aviation missionary societies of the United Kingdom, Australia, and New

Zealand in a consortium called Missionary Aviation Fellowship. In 1972 MAF Canada and in 1977 MAF Finland joined the coalition. The organization changed its name to Mission Aviation Fellowship in 1971. Headquarters currently are in Redlands, California. Betty Greene was the first pilot, serving in Mexico, Peru, Nigeria, East Africa, and Irian Jaya.

21.   Two important books on the Latin American scene by careful researchers and "outsiders" are *Tongues of Fire: The Explosion of Protestantism in Latin America* (Basil Blackwell) by British sociologist David Martin and *Is Latin America Becoming Protestant?* (University of California Press) by author David Stoll. Several articles on the phenomenon appear in *Christianity Today* for April 6, 1992.

22.   The authorized biography of Billy Graham is *Billy Graham* by John Pollock (1966); the newer highly-rated treatment of the evangelist is *A Prophet with Honor* by William Martin (1991).

23.   Mexico's new law on Religious Associations and Public Worship took effect on July 16, 1992. It makes all religious groups equal under the law and prohibits discrimination or coercion because of religious beliefs. It also permits religious groups to organize and sponsor nonprofit institutions to provide assistance, education, and health services.

24.   See Karl Barth, *The Epistle to the Romans* (London: Oxford, 1933); *Dogmatics in Outline* (New York: Harper, 1959); *Credo* (New York: Scribner's, 1962); Eberhard Jüngel, *Karl Barth, A Theological Legacy*, trans. by Garrett E. Paul (Philadelphia: Westminster, 1986); Cornelius Van Til, *Christianity and Barthianism* (Philadelphia: Presbyterian and Reformed, 1962); Gregory Bolich, *Karl Barth and Evangelicalism* (Downers Grove, IL: InterVarsity, 1980).

25.   His main theological work was *Systematic Theology*, 3 vols. (Chicago: University of Chicago, 1951, 1957, 1963). His important early work was *The Courage to Be* (New Haven, CT: Yale, 1953). Later he wrote *Theology of Culture* (New York: Oxford, 1959) and numerous other works. See also Wilhelm and Marion Pauck, *Paul Tillich, His Life and Thought* (New York: Harper & Row, 1989 ed.).

26.   An evangelical appraisal of process theology appears

in Ronald Nash, ed., Process Theology (Grand Rapids: Baker, 1987) and a response to the Nash volume by an outstanding process theologian is Lewis S. Ford, "Evangelical Appraisals of Process Theism," Christian Scholars Review, December, 1990, 149-63.

27.   Especially useful books on liberation theology include Robert McAfee Brown, *Theology in a New Key* (Philadelphia: Westminster, 1978); Orlando E. Costas, *Christ Outside the Gate* (Maryknoll, New York: Orbis, 1982); Rosino Gibellini, ed., *Frontiers of Theology in Latin America* (Maryknoll, New York: Orbis, 1975); J. Andrew Kirk, *Liberation Theology* (Atlanta: John Knox, 1979) and *Theology Encounters Revolution* (Downers Grove, Ill: InterVarsity, 1980); Gerald H. Anderson and Thomas F. Stransky, eds., *Mission Trends No. 4: Liberation Theologies in North America and Europe* (Grand Rapids: Eerdmans, 1979); Emilio A. Nunez, *Liberation Theology* (Chicago: Moody, 1985); Christian Smith, *The Emergence of Liberation Theology* (Chicago: University of Chicago, 1991); Ronald H. Nash, ed., *Liberation Theology* (Milford, MI: Mott Media, 1984); Gerard Begnhoef and Lester DeKoster, *Liberation Theology* (Grand Rapids: Christian's Library Press, 1984); Paul E. Sigmund, *Liberation Theology at the Crossroads* (New York: Oxford, 1990); Justo L. González, *Mañana: Christian Theology from a Hispanic Perspective* (Nashville: Abingdon, 1990).

28.   An especially important book on the Black Theology movement is Gayraud S. Wilmore and James H. Cone, eds., *Black Theology: A Documentary History 1966-1979* (New York: Orbis Books, 1979), which contains an annotated bibliography.

Books for Further Study

A select list of works widely available in libraries and book stores probably will be more valuable to the reader than an extensive bibliography or a number of primary source works. Because many readers have special interest in the American scene (including revivalism) or the Reformation, the bibliography has separate sections for each of these areas, as well as a general section. Also, because Muslims now number about one-fifth of the world's population and constitute a growing threat to the church in the West, a section on Islam is included. Some more specialized books appear in the end-notes.

General

Bainton, Roland H. *The Medieval Church*. New York: Van Nostrand, 1926.

Barrett, David. *World Christian Encyclopedia*. Oxford University Press, 1982.

Bedell, Kenneth B., ed. *Yearbook of American and Canadian Churches, 1993*. Nashville: Abingdon Press, 1993.

Bettenson, Henry, ed. *Documents of the Christian Church*. 2nd ed. New York: Oxford, 1963.

Cairns, Earle E. *Christianity Through the Centuries*. Rev. ed. Grand Rapids: Zondervan, 1981.

Chadwick, Henry. *The Early Church*. London: Penguin, 1967.

Chadwick, Henry and Evans, G. R., eds. *Atlas of the Christian Church*. New York: Facts on File, 1987.

Cheetham, Nicolas. *Keepers of the Keys* (a history of the popes). New York: Scribner's, 1983.

Cross, F. L. and Livingstone, E. A., eds. *The Oxford Dictionary of the Christian Church*. 2nd ed. New York: Oxford University Press, 1983.

Detzler, Wayne A. *The Changing Church in Europe*. Grand Rapids: Zondervan, 1979.

Douglas, J. D., ed. *The New International Dictionary of the Christian Church*. Grand Rapids: Zondervan, 1974.

_____. *New 20th-Century Encyclopedia of Religious Knowledge*. Grand Rapids: Baker, 1991.

Dowley, Tim. *Eerdman's Handbook to the History of Christianity*. Grand Rapids: Eerdmans, 1977.

Elwell, Walter A., ed. *Evangelical Dictionary of Theology*. Grand Rapids: Baker, 1984.

Falk, Peter. *The Growth of the Church in Africa*. Grand Rapids: Zondervan, 1978.

Ferguson, Everett, ed. *Encyclopedia of Early Christianity*. New York: Garland, 1990.

Ferguson, Sinclair, ed. *New Dictionary of Theology*. Downers Grove, IL: InterVarsity, 1988.

Gail, Marzieh. *Avignon in Flower*. London: Victor Gollancz, 1966.

Grousset, René. *The Epic of the Crusades*. New York: Orion, 1970.

Hastings, Adrian, ed. *Modern Catholicism, Vatican II and After*. New York: Oxford, 1991.

Heick, Otto W. *A History of Christian Thought*. 2 vols. Philadelphia: Fortress, 1965.

Hill, Bennett D., ed. *Church and State in the Middle Ages*. New York: Wiley, 1970.

Hillgarth, J. N., ed. *Christianity and Paganism, 350-750*. Philadelphia: University of Pennsylvania, 1986.

Hoke, Donald E., ed. *The Church in Asia*. Chicago: Moody, 1975.

Jedin, Hubert, and Dolan, John, ed. *History of the Church*. 10 vols. New York: Crossroad/Continuum.

Kelley, J. N. D. *The Oxford Dictionary of the Popes*. New York: Oxford, 1986.

Latourette, Kenneth Scott. *Christianity Through the Ages*. New York: Harper, 1965.

_____. *A History of Christianity*. Rev. ed. 2 vols. New York: Harper, 1975.

McManners, John, ed. *The Oxford Illustrated History of Christianity*. New York: Oxford, 1990.

Margoulias, Harry J. *Byzantine Christianity*. Detroit: Wayne State University Press, 1982.

Markus, Robert. *The End of Ancient Christianity*. Cambridge: Cambridge University Press, 1990.

Marty, Martin E. *A Short History of Christianity*. Cleveland: Collins World, 1959.

Neill, Stephen. *A History of Christian Missions*. Rev. ed. New York: Penguin, 1986.

O'Brien, John M. *The Medieval Church*. Totowa, NJ: Littlefield, Adams, 1968.

Pelikan, Jaroslav. *The Christian Tradition: A History of the Development of Doctrine*. 5 vols. Chicago: University of Chicago Press. Vol. 1, 1971; 2, 1974; 3, 1978; 4, 1984; 5, 1989.

Renwick, A. M. *The Story of the Church*. Grand Rapids: Eerdmans, 1958.

Roberts, W. Dayton, and Siewert, John A. *Mission Handbook*. 15th ed. Monrovia, CA: MARC, 1993.

Schaff, Philip. *The Creeds of Christendom*. 3 vols. 6th ed. Grand Rapids: Baker, 1985.

——————. *History of the Christian Church*. 8 vols. New York: Scribner's, 1910. Reprint. Grand Rapids: Eerdmans, 1960.

Southern, R. W. *Western Society and the Church in the Middle Ages*. Grand Rapids: Eerdmans, 1970.

Stevenson, J. *Creeds, Councils, and Controversies*. London: SPCK, 1966.

Tucker, Ruth A. *Daughters of the Church*. Grand Rapids: Zondervan, 1987.

——————. *From Jerusalem to Irian Jaya*. Grand Rapids: Zondervan, 1983.

Urban, Linwood. *A Short History of Christian Thought*. New York: Oxford, 1986.

VanElderen, Marlin. *Introducing the World Council of Churches*. Grand Rapids: Eerdmans, 1991.

Walker, Williston. *A History of the Christian Church*. 3d ed. New York: Scribner's, 1970.

Ware, Timothy. *The Orthodox Church*. New York: Penguin, 1984.

Welch, Claude. *Protestant Thought in the Nineteenth Century.* 2 vols. New Haven: Yale University Press; vol. 1, 1972; vol. 2, 1985.

Woodbridge, John D. *Great Leaders of the Christian Church.* Chicago: Moody, 1988.

Wuthnow, Robert. *Christianity in the 21st Century.* New York: Oxford University Press, 1993.

The Reformation

Bainton, Roland. *Here I Stand.* New York: New American Library, 1950.

_____. *The Reformation of the Sixteenth Century.* Boston: Beacon Hill, 1952.

_____. *Women of the Reformation.* Minneapolis: Augsburg, 1971.

Brigden, Susan. *London and the Reformation.* Oxford: Clarendon Press, 1989.

Cameron, Euan. *The European Reformation.* Oxford: Clarendon Press, 1991.

Chadwick, Owen. *The Reformation.* New York: Penguin, 1972.

Chaunu, Pierre, ed. *The Reformation.* New York: St. Martin's, 1986.

Daniel-Rops, H. *The Catholic Reformation.* New York: Dutton, 1962.

Dickens, A. G. *The English Reformation.* New York: Schocken, 1964.

George, Timothy. *Theology of the Reformers.* Nashville: Broadman, 1988.

Grimm, Harold J. *The Reformation Era.* Rev. ed. New York: Macmillan, 1965.

Holl, Karl. *The Cultural Significance of the Reformation.* Cleveland: World, 1959.

Jones, R. Tudur. *The Great Reformation.* Downers Grove, IL: InterVarsity, 1985.

LeHuray, Peter. *Music and the Reformation in England.* New York: Oxford, 1967.

McNeill, John T. *The History and Character of Calvinism.* New York: Oxford, 1954.

Meeter, H. Henry. *The Basic Ideas of Calvinism*. 6th ed. Rev. by Paul A. Marshall. Grand Rapids: Baker, 1990.

Moss, George L. *The Reformation*. 3d ed. New York: Holt, Rinehart, 1963.

Ozment, Steven E. *Protestants: The Birth of a Revolution*. New York: Doubleday, 1992.

_____. *The Reformation in the Cities*. New Haven: Yale University Press, 1975.

Parker, Geoffrey. *The Thirty Years War*. London: Routledge Chapman, 1985.

Parker, Noel Geoffrey. *The Dutch Revolt*. Ithaca, NY: Cornell University Press, 1977.

Powicke, Maurice. *The Reformation in England*. London: Oxford, 1941.

Rabb, Theodore. *The Thirty Years War*. 2d ed. Lanham, MD: University Press of America, 1981.

Reid, W. Stanford, ed. *The Reformation—Revival or Revolution?* New York: Holt, Rinehart, 1968.

Reardon, Bernard M. G. *Religious Thought in the Reformation*. New York: Longman, 1981.

Spitz, Lewis W. *The Protestant Reformation*. New York: Harper & Row, 1985.

Tikkamen, Henrik. *The Thirty Years War*. Lincoln, Nebraska: University of Nebraska Press, 1987.

Wedgewood, C. V. *The Thirty Years War*. New York: Penguin, 1957.

Williams, George H. *The Radical Reformation*. Philadelphia: Westminster, 1962.

Wright, A. D. *The Counter-Reformation*. New York: St. Martin's, 1982.

The American Church

Ahlstrom, Sydney. *A Religious History of the American People*. Garden City, NY: Doubleday, 1975.

Banks, William. *The Black Church in the United States*. Chicago: Moody, 1972.

Bedell, George, et. al. *Religion in America*. New York: Macmillan, 1972.

Bedell, Kenneth B. & Jones, Alice M. *Yearbook of American and*

Canadian Churches. Nashville: Abingdon, published annually.

Bonomi, Patricia U. *Under the Cope of Heaven.* New York: Oxford, 1986.

Brauer, Jerald. *Protestantism in America.* Philadelphia: Westminster, 1972.

Bushman, Richard. *The Great Awakening.* New York: Norton, 1972.

Cairns, Earle E. *Christianity in the United States.* Chicago: Moody, 1964.

_____. *Christianity Through the Centuries.* Rev. ed. Grand Rapids: Zondervan, 1981.

Carden, Allen. *Puritan Christianity in America.* Grand Rapids: Baker, 1990.

Curry, Thomas J. *The First Freedoms.* New York: Oxford Universityi Press, 1986.

Gaustad, Edwin S. *Faith of our Fathers.* New York: Harper, 1987.

_____. *The Great Awakening in New England.* Gloucester, MA: Peter Smith, 1965.

_____. *A Religious History of America.* New York: Harper & Row, 1966.

Gewehr, Wesley. *The Great Awakening in Virginia.* Gloucester, MA: Peter Smith, 1930.

Handy, Robert T. *A History of the Churches in the United States and Canada.* New York: Oxford, 1976.

Hardman, Keith J. *Charles Grandison Finney.* Grand Rapids: Baker, 1987.

Hatch, Nathan O. and Stout, Harry S., eds. *Jonathan Edwards and the American Experience.* New York: Oxford, 1988.

Heimert, Alan. *Religion and the American Mind.* Cambridge, MA: Harvard, 1966.

Jenson, Robert W. *America's Theologian.* New York: Oxford, 1988.

Lloyd-Jones, D. Martyn. *The Puritans.* Edinburgh: Banner of Truth, 1987.

McGiffert, Michael, ed. *Puritanism and the American Experience.* Reading, MA: Addison-Wesley, 1969.

Marty, Martin E. *Modern American Religion.* 2 vols. Chicago: University of Chicago, 1986.

_____. *Pilgrims in Their Own Land.* New York: Penguin, 1984.

Maxson, Charles. *The Great Awakening in the Middle Colonies.* Gloucester, MA: Peter Smith, 1920.

Mead, Frank S. *Handbook of Denominations in the United States.* 9th ed. Rev. by Samuel S. Hill. Nashville: Abingdon, 1990.

Murray, Iain H. *Jonathan Edwards.* Edinburgh: Banner of Truth, 1987.

Noll, Mark A. *A History of Christianity in the United States and Canada.* Grand Rapids: Wm. B. Eerdmans, 1992.

Noll, Mark A. and others, eds. *Eerdman's Handbook to Christianity in America.* Grand Rapids: Eerdmans, 1983.

Olmstead, Clifton E. *History of Religion in the United States.* Rev. ed. Englewood Cliffs, NJ: Prentice-Hall, 1960.

Orr, J. Edwin. *Campus Aflame.* Glendale, CA: Regal, 1972.

_____. *Eager Feet.* Chicago: Moody, 1975.

_____. *Fervent Prayer.* Chicago: Moody, 1974.

_____. *Flaming Tongue.* 2d ed. Chicago: Moody, 1975.

Pollock, John. *George Whitefield and the Great Awakening.* London: Hodder and Stoughton, 1973.

Reid, Daniel G. and others, eds. *Dictionary of Christianity in America.* Downers Grove, IL: InterVarsity, 1990.

Riss, Richard M. *A Survey of 20th-Century Revival Movements in North America.* Peabody, MA: Hendrickson, 1988.

Smith, Timothy L. *Revivalism and Social Reform.* Magnolia, MA: Peter Smith, n.d.

Stout, Harry S. *The New England Soul.* New York: Oxford, 1986.

Sweet, William W. *Religion in Colonial America.* New York: Cooper Square, 1942.

_____. *The Story of Religion in America.* Rev. ed. New York: Harper, 1950. Reprint. Grand Rapids: Baker, 1973.

Islam

Andrae, Tor. *Mohammed.* Salem, NH: Ayer Co, 1936.

Brockelmann, Carl. *History of the Islamic Peoples*. London: Routledge Chapman & Hall, 1980.

Denny, Frederick M. *Islam*. New York: Harper & Row, 1987.

Glassé, Cyril. *The Concise Encyclopedia of Islam*. New York: Harper & Row, 1989.

Glubb, John. *A Short History of the Arab Peoples*. New York: Dorset, 1969.

Hodgson, Marshall G. S. *The Venture of Islam*. 3 Vols. Chicago: University of Chicago Press, 1961.

Hourani, Albert. *A History of the Arab Peoples*. Cambridge, MA: Harvard, 1991.

Jansen, G. H. *Militant Islam*. New York: Harper & Row, 1979.

Mahmud, S. F. *A Short History of Islam*. 2nd ed. New York: Oxford, 1988.

Mortimer, Edward. *Faith and Power: The Politics of Islam*. New York: Random House, 1982.

Payne, Robert. *The History of Islam*. New York: Dorset, 1959.

Pickthall, Mohammed M., trans. *The Meaning of the Glorious Koran*. New York: New American Library, 1953.

Shorrosh, Anis A. *Islam Revealed*. Nashville: Thomas Nelson, 1988.

Von Grunebaum, Gustav E. *Muhammadan Festivals*. New York: Olive Branch, 1988.

General Index